Guide
to
Natural
Health

Using the Horoscope as a Key to
Ancient Healing Practices

About the Author

Jonathan Keyes graduated from Evergreen State College with a bachelor's degree in science, where he studied herbalism and health sciences. He went on to study with various shamans in Ecuador, Mexico, and the Pacific Northwest, and learned to practice Plant Spirit Medicine, a blend of shamanism, herbalism, and Chinese medicine. Jon now lives in Portland, Oregon, where he works as an astrologer, herbalist, and healer.

Jon is a regular contributor to the online astrology website StarIQ.com, where he writes a lunar health column. His writings have also appeared in *The Mountain Astrologer*, *Essences* magazine, and numerous Llewellyn almanacs and calendars. Jon has just finished writing a book on traditional European herbalism and is actively interested in the intersection of astrology, herbalism, pagan wisdom, and shamanism.

To Write to the Author

If you wish to contact the author or would like more information about this book, please write to the author in care of Llewellyn Worldwide and we will forward your request. Both the author and publisher appreciate hearing from you and learning of your enjoyment of this book and how it has helped you. Llewellyn Worldwide cannot guarantee that every letter written to the author can be answered, but all will be forwarded. Please write to:

Jonathan Keyes
℅ Llewellyn Worldwide
P.O. Box 64383, Dept. 0-7387-0224-2
St. Paul, MN 55164-0383, U.S.A.
Please enclose a self-addressed stamped envelope for reply,
or $1.00 to cover costs. If outside U.S.A., enclose
international postal reply coupon.

Many of Llewellyn's authors have websites with additional information and resources. For more information, please visit our website at:
http://www.llewellyn.com.

Guide
to
Natural
Health

*Using the Horoscope as a Key to
Ancient Healing Practices*

Jonathan Keyes

2002
Llewellyn Publications
St. Paul, Minnesota 55164-0383, U.S.A.

First Edition
First Printing, 2002

Cover images © 2002 by Digital Vision, Eyewire, Digital Stock, Photo Disc
Cover design by Lisa Novak

Special thanks to Melissa Mierva for the herb precautions

Library of Congress Cataloging-in-Publication Data

Keyes, Jonathan, 1971–
      Guide to natural health : using the horoscope as a key to ancient healing practices /
  Jonathan Keyes.— 1st ed.
        p.   cm
      Includes bibliographical references and index.
      ISBN 0-7387-0224-2
        1. Astrology—Therapeutic use. 2. Medical astrology. I. Title

    RZ999 .K49 2002
    133.5'861—dc21   2002072905

Disclaimer: The remedies and recipes in this book are not meant to substitute for consultation with a licensed healthcare professional. Please use herbs within the guidelines given and heed the cautionary notes regarding potentially dangerous herbs. The publisher assumes no responsibility for injuries occurring as a result of herbal usages found in this book.

Llewellyn Worldwide does not participate in, endorse, or have any authority or responsibility concerning private business transactions between our authors and the public.
    All mail addressed to the author is forwarded but the publisher cannot, unless specifically instructed by the author, give out an address or phone number.
    Any Internet references contained in this work are current at publication time, but the publisher cannot guarantee that a specific location will continue to be maintained. Please refer to the publisher's website for links to authors' websites and other sources.

Llewellyn Publications
A Division of Llewellyn Worldwide, Ltd.
P.O. Box 64383, Dept. 0-7387-0224-2
St. Paul, MN 55164-0383, U.S.A.
www.llewellyn.com

 Printed in the United States of America on recycled paper

Acknowledgments

Thank you to Nick Keyes, Jennifer Shafer, and especially my mom, for their support and their help proofreading my manuscript. Thanks to Kate for her heartfelt love and support. Thanks to all my teachers for the wisdom they have shared with me. And thanks finally to Spirit—all of the rivers flow back to you.

Dedication

To Brigid, for lighting my path.

Contents

Introduction

Everything we have been talking about comes down to this, that our spirit, when it is correctly prepared and cleansed through the things of nature, can receive from the spirit of worldly life a great deal through the rays of the stars. Since the life of the world is based in everything, it is propagated plainly in herbs and trees, as if they were hair on its body. It is propagated in stones and metals, as if they were its teeth and bones. It is produced in living shells, adhering to rocks and earth.[1]

Over 500 years ago, Italian scholar and physician Marsilio Ficino wrote these words to describe the relationship of humankind, nature, and the stars. Ficino believed that by studying the stars through the use of astrology, and through the use of healing agents found in nature, people could harmonize their health and constitution. Ficino based his beliefs on ancient Egyptian and Greek philosophies that integrated medicine and astrology.

The idea that humankind, nature, and the stars are part of the same fabric, interconnected into one whole, has been largely lost to the Western, scientific mind. But in earlier times, the practices of astrology, medicine, and philosophy were intertwined and not divided into separate branches of thought and learning. For 2,000 years in the Western world, people looked to the planets to find clues about human health and disease. The heavens were seen as a macrocosmos and the earth was seen as a microcosmos. Astrology infused the planets and the zodiac with meaning, and by understanding the movements in the skies, people could understand their own nature, health, and purpose in life.

Through the study of astrology, the Western world saw life as being made up of four elements: fire, water, air, and earth. In this system, each element relates to a season, certain emotions, organs of the body, and things found in nature. For ex-ample, the fire element relates to the warmth of summer, feelings of anger, the pulsing heart, and the rays of the sun. The air element relates to the spring season, a cheerful expression, the lungs, and the currents of the wind.[2]

In this Western tradition, the astrological chart could describe our internal bal-ance of elements and show which ones were strong and which ones were lacking. A strongly fiery person may be passionate and expressive, but may also have illnesses of excessive heat and heart problems. A strongly watery person may be artistic and compassionate, but may also have problems with dampness, allergies, and frequent colds. In earlier times, one could work with tools from nature to strengthen weak elements and balance strong elements, and thus harmonize and heal illness. This ancient practice is what I call four element medicine.

Medicine in earlier times was not confined to prescribing drugs, but could be practiced by wearing a talisman, performing a ritual, or wearing a particular fra-grance that helped balance extremes of temperament. Balancing the elements did not just mean taking medicine to cure oneself physically. It could mean choosing to live near water to balance out a fiery temperament, or it could mean being near lively and joyous people if one were too earthy and melancholic. In the four ele-ment medicine tradition, a more energetic relationship to healing was forwarded. A particular herb could cure a person physically, and perhaps emotionally as well. By seeing and smelling an herb like calendula in a garden, one's spirit could be en-livened and depression could be abated. By wearing a particular talisman, the po-tent spiritual effects of the amulet could protect, heal, or bring prosperity.

Most of these concepts are lost to us now, but this vast reservoir of knowledge and wisdom sits untouched beneath our fingertips. In modern times, we have grown to appreciate the rich lore of Indian and Chinese medicine that has come to the West in the last few decades. Yoga, pulse reading, herbs, and acupuncture have all been accepted as valid methods for healing and curing illness. On the other hand, the ancient practice of traditional Western medicine sits largely unused and is often-times scorned and derided. This is unfortunate, because this medicine has much to offer us in the way of healing ourselves not only physically, but spiritually as well.

In this book, I am not looking to reconstitute traditional Western medicine, but to draw forth the ancient wisdom and basic philosophical practice of the Western healers from our past. Fundamentally, four element medicine is the study of astrology to understand our own constitutional strengths and weaknesses and the use of nature to restore balance to our health. When we treat the Earth with respect, the natural world offers us healing through its animals, birds, stones, metals, foods, and herbs. Four element medicine points to working with nature on a number of different levels to heal us physically, emotionally, and spiritually.

On another level, four element medicine offers a way of not only healing ourselves, but healing our relationship with nature. By showing respect to the natural world, we can gain an understanding of its true value. Trees can no longer just be seen as a source of timber, a hill can no longer be seen as a depository of mineral wealth, and an Arctic refuge cannot simply be seen as a holding ground for petroleum fuel.

Modern society has become fixated on growth and progress as a means to happiness and fulfillment. In our quest for dominion, we have damaged or destroyed huge tracts of forested land, strip-mined hills and mountains, and used up and polluted many of our natural resources. In short order, we have gone to battle with the natural world and have seen an immense denigration of the earth in our lifetimes. This is truly sad, for the natural world provides an immense depository for healing us physically, emotionally, and spiritually. The practice of four element medicine is the integration of humans with nature in order to harmonize our health and well-being. If we destroy much of the natural world, we destroy our chances of coming into harmony and balance.

In the four element medicine tradition, nature is seen as alive and luminous. Everything from a perched eagle to a seemingly inert boulder has life and vitality. The earth carries spirit and is alive, an *anima mundi*. When we drink water from a river, we are not just taking in water, we are drinking in the river itself, the mountain it came from, and the snow that fell before. When we eat an animal, we take in the spirit of where it came from, and how it was born, grew, and died. When we see a bird, we not only see a flying creature, but an expression of part of our own soul, an archetypal representation made manifest in the outside world.

The four element tradition arose in Egypt and Babylon, but has similarities with traditions throughout the world. Most indigenous peoples see the world and their surroundings as alive and full of spirit. Many cultures have natural systems of healing that see the world energetically and elementally. It is only in the last few hundred years that the Western world has adopted a vision of life that is more mechanistic and has divorced meaning from the natural world. Many of our modern illnesses are related to this split of humans from nature. Processed foods and an unhealthy diet, antibiotics, stimulants, chemicals, and pollutants in the earth and the atmosphere have led to an increase in numerous diseases such as cancer, heart disease, diabetes, schizophrenia, and depression. I believe that though we have been able to extend the quantity of life in the industrialized world, we have lessened the quality of life dramatically in modern times.

Though modern allopathic medicine is quite adept at analyzing and assessing illness and helping in the case of acute illnesses such as heart attacks, wounds, and broken bones, it has proved very poor at curing more chronic, long-term diseases. Much of the reason for this is that chronic illnesses are most often caused by one's lifestyle choices, dietary habits, and emotional underpinnings. On a deeper level, I believe chronic illnesses stem from human society being out of balance with the natural world. Very often, modern medical doctors emphasize the importance of taking drug medication instead of choosing holistic therapies and making lifestyle changes. Though many of these drugs can be life-saving in certain cases, they often cause numerous side effects as well.

Holistic and energetic therapies have proved to be much more effective in healing chronic health problems because they see the larger patterns of one's life, one's habits, and one's environment. Dietary changes, stress-reducing techniques such as yoga and meditation, herbs, and nonintrusive therapies such as acupuncture and massage are often very helpful for healing chronic debilitating ailments. They also are much less likely to cause adverse side effects that only worsen the problem. In essence, holistic therapies emphasize prevention and healing the whole person instead of treating the symptoms. The Western world has a rich and beautiful tradition of this type of holistic care that has been neglected and lost in the past few hundred years. It is my hope that the four element tradition can be revived in the years ahead.

---

1. Marsilio Ficino, *The Book of Life*, trans. Charles Boer (1489; reprint, Irving, TX: Spring Publications, Inc., 1980) 115.

2. Graeme Tobyn, *Culpeper's Medicine: A Practice of Western Holistic Medicine* (Rockport, MA: Element Books, Inc., 1997) 51.

1

The History and Practice of Four Element Medicine

This fall a few friends and I drove out along the Columbia River gorge in Oregon to go stargazing about thirty miles east of Portland. The wind was strong and the night was bitterly cold, but that didn't stop a number of us amateur astronomers from setting up a base camp near the side of the river. With telescopes, I was able to make out the moons of Jupiter and the rings of Saturn. A few meteors shot overhead as I watched the panorama of stars stretch out through the night sky. I had never seen the moons of Jupiter before, and this event thrilled me with a sense of discovery and joy. Almost 400 years ago, the famous Italian scientist Galileo looked up in the night sky to spot these same moons. In his texts, he wrote:

> *"Accordingly, on the seventh day of January of the present year 1610, at the first hour of the night, when I inspected the celestial constellations through a spyglass, Jupiter presented himself. And since I had prepared for myself a superlative instrument, I saw that three little stars were positioned near him—small but very bright. Although I believed them to be among the number of fixed stars, they nevertheless intrigued me because they appeared to be arranged along a straight line . . . but when, on the eighth, I returned to the same observation, guided by I know not what fate, I found a very different arrangement. For all three little stars were to the west of Jupiter and closer to each other than the previous night, and separated by equal intervals."*[1]

Galileo used a new, little-known piece of technology known as the telescope, a tool that would revolutionize the field of astronomy and would herald the demise of astrology over the next 100 years. Prior to the discovery of the telescope, people had used the naked eye to view the stars and planets and infuse the heavens with meaning, mythology, and spiritual reverence. By the end of the 1600s, a new view of the cosmos had emerged, one based on rational principles and mathematics and without the traditional astrological and religious associations that had been integrated with astronomy since antiquity. In his book *Conversing with the Planets*, astronomer and anthropologist Anthony Aveni writes:

> *"Within a generation of Galileo, Sir Francis Bacon would produce the* Great Instauration, *a manifesto that called for human action in nothing less than an all-out assault on nature . . . Bacon's program reads almost like a set of traffic rules telling what each discipline should contain, what data should be acquired, what ought to be diminished as foolish. The greatest promise of all, he argues, lay in technology, for only by extending the senses could we unmask nature's deeper and darker submerged secrets. The new philosophy, framed in a mechanistic way of thinking, would be driven by an aggressive optimism that everything from music to morals could be cast under the umbrella of natural law. The new science would be spread about the literate and educable public via demonstrations, popular lectures, magazines, and libraries. It was the beginning of the Age of Enlightenment and of the demise of planetary astrology."* [2]

This radical change in perception, thought, and philosophy affects us to this day, and although there has been a reemergence of astrology, the scientific community by and large vehemently abhors the practice. This differs markedly from the community of scientists and astronomers in the Renaissance period who often integrated occult concepts such as astrology and alchemy into their scientific practice. Scientists such as Newton, Copernicus, and Kepler saw the importance of linking facts and figures with myth and meaning. This practice predated them by thousands of years through Greek scholars such as Plato and Pythagoras. It was only after the Age of Enlightenment that spiritual meaning was divorced from the natural world.

Before this massive change in perception, medicine was also integrated into the study of the stars, and physicians often consulted the horoscope to help understand health, the etiology of illness, and the proper curative measures. Many learned men followed the edict of "As above, so below," and determined that man's physical constitution was related to the planetary configurations as the microcosm is related to the macrocosm. This notion that all of creation was related and integrated came under sharp attack during the Enlightenment, as a slow shift toward a mechanical and reductionist model of health emerged.

In this new scientific model, each human could be viewed as a separate, distinct entity composed of component parts and certain physiological processes. By applying chemicals and drugs, any necrotic tissue, disease, or malformation could be battled and conquered, and returned to normalcy. This new vision of health replaced earlier healing philosophies that posited natural cures, and balancing and harmonizing one's nature with the environment and the cosmos to achieve strength and vitality. Astrological medicine came to be viewed as superstition, unscientific and irrational. The four elements that made up the ancient practice of medicine were discarded for the new mechanistic models that arose. In China and India, the early models of medicine formulated thousands of years ago continue to thrive to this day. It is only in the West that we have ignored and disregarded our ancient medical traditions. To understand how these traditions arose and how they evolved, we need to look to the past into the world of our ancestors.

A Brief History of Four Element Medicine

The Early Days

In our most ancient records of early man, researchers discovered notches left on reindeer bones and mammoth ivory that dated back to the last Ice Age. It is believed that these marks signify the recording of lunar cycles.[3] It is likely that these early carvings had to do with understanding time and making the rudiments of a calendar. We know little of these early people, but these early artifacts point toward humankind's eventual journey toward understanding the skies.

These early nomadic people were keenly aware of changes in the seasons, the best times to hunt and gather food from the land, and when to gather herbs for healing ailments and maladies. By looking to the skies and observing the phases of the moon and where the sun rose and set each day, early tribes gained an understanding of the relationship of the heavens to their life on earth. The stars above them became more than just twinkles of light; they became entwined in their myths and fables, intimate partners in the fabric of their lives and vital elements of their cosmologies.

As these tribes coalesced, some of them developed permanent communities, and as early as 6000 B.C., the Sumerians built the first-known structures designed to observe and mark the sky.[4] In Mesopotamia around 3000 B.C., tall towers known as ziggurats were constructed as high as 270 feet from which to watch the stars. A cast of priests and astrologers developed in these communities to mark the procession in the skies. The planets became associated with gods and goddesses as a divine pantheon that traveled through the heavens. In Babylon, Mars was known as Nergal, the powerful, warlike god of the underworld. In Persia, they called Venus Anahita, a sweet, seductive, and voluptuous goddess. In Greece, Mercury was known as Hermes, the winged messenger-god of thieves and of communication.

Anthony Aveni has noted:

"Designating the planets by name and imbuing them with omens lay at the foundation of the astrally based religions practiced by nearly all our cultural predecessors. For them, what happened in real life was mirrored by what took place in the sky."[5]

Because of this relationship of the stars to religious belief, these early people celebrated and worshiped the gods/planets through elaborate rituals and ceremonies. These rites cemented a proper relationship between the earth and the skies and were believed to bring about good fortune and prosperity. Ritual played an essential role in these cultures, and the astrologer-priests were vital in ascertaining the right times to hold these events. This relationship of humans with the stars exists to this day in many cultures. In India, Vedic astrologers pick appropriate times to perform certain rituals that mitigate the negative effects and augment the positive effects of the planets.

The Four Elements and Medicine

Around 500 B.C., the Sicilian philosopher Empedocles introduced the idea of the four elements. In his theory, the four elements—fire, water, earth, and air—constitute the root of all of creation. Empedocles' theories were taken up by the leading physician of his time, Hippocrates. Hippocrates was born about 460 B.C. on the island of Cos in the Aegean Sea. In his school on Cos, he formulated the concept of *Vis Medicatix naturae*—the idea of the healing power of nature and the tendency for life to heal itself. Hippocrates advocated gentle remedies in the form of herbs, diet, and exercise to naturally assist ill people back to health.

Hippocrates believed that the four elements made up the human constitution, and when they were in balance, human beings would be in perfect health. Hippocrates also illustrated the concept of the four temperaments, or constitutional types, in the human body: choleric for fire, melancholic for earth, sanguine for air, and phlegmatic for water. Each temperament was associated with a humor and quality as well. Humors did not just refer to a body fluid, but described essences that flowed throughout the body and helped in the balance of health and well-being. Each temperament and humor had a quality attached to it that described its temperature and condition as well. If one of the humors dominated, then disease and ill health would arise. Early Greek medicine became based on the concept of balancing the humors.

The Elements	Fire	Water	Air	Earth
Temperaments	Choleric	Phlegmatic	Sanguine	Melancholic
Humors	Yellow bile	Phlegm	Blood	Black bile
Qualities	Hot and dry	Cold and moist	Hot and dry	Cold and moist

Hippocrates promoted the use of the four element system of curing illness, and in a treatise called *Affections*, he writes:

"In men, all diseases are caused by bile and phlegm. Bile and phlegm give rise to diseases when they become too dry or too wet or too hot or too cold in the body." [6]

Hippocrates also wrote that these diseases are caused by imbalances in food, drink, and exercise, as well as by injuries, sexual excesses, and environmental conditions. On Hippocratic medicine, the noted astrological historian Zolar writes:

"The patient was the reality; the disease was not an entity like the savage's demon but a fluctuating condition of the patient's body, a battle between the morbid humors and the natural self-healing tendency of the body. Treatment centered upon assisting the patient, through his particular nature, to react in his individual way against the disease that was an imbalance of the four humors." [7]

Hermetic Thought

Along with the four element theory, firmly rooted in Hippocrates' school of medicine on Cos, there was also a great influx of ideas from Egypt around the fourth and third centuries B.C. that linked parts of the body to the signs of the zodiac. The linking of herbs, animals, and stones with the planets and the signs probably occurred a little later, between the second century B.C. and the first century A.D. [8] Much of this wisdom and lore comes from texts attributed to Hermes Trismegistos, an Egyptian philosopher, astrologer, and physician. In all likelihood, these texts were probably written by a number of learned Egyptians.

This Hermetic literature included many works on alchemy, magic, physics, astronomy, natural history, and astrological medicine. One of the most profound philosophical statements to be found in this body of thought is the Emerald Table of Hermes, a series of pronouncements inscribed on an emerald stone. It says, "What is below is like that which is above, and that which is above is like that which is below." This linking of the microcosm with the macrocosm is at the root of all medical astrological thought. The idea that one could look to the stars and determine patterns that would help elucidate the nature of health and illness profoundly influenced physicians for the next 1,500 years.

In Hermetic thought, all of creation can be ordered according to basic principles and can be linked to the planets, the elements, and the zodiac. The smallest pebble in some way relates to, and is in sympathy with, other stones, animals, plants, and planets. This relationship implies that there is a web, a framework, within nature that humans are part of as well. The paths of astrology and medicine were wedded by these hermetic concepts. Astrological medicine postulates that by understanding our own makeup of elements and planetary strengths and weaknesses, we can use the manifestations of nature to help balance us and assist us back to health. Though Hippocrates helped establish the integration of astrology and medicine, many years passed before this wedding was firmly set as part of medical practice. It took a famous Roman physician named Galen to cement this relationship through his writings and discourses.

Galen

Galen was born around A.D. 130 in the Greek city of Pergamum in modern-day Turkey. He started his medical career as a doctor for wounded gladiators in Pergamum and later in Rome. Eventually he became the court physician for the emperor, Marcus Aurelius. Galen's form of medicine was based primarily on Hippocrates' four element system and his use of simple and natural medicines such as herbs and diet to effect a cure. Galen's books became the basis for the practice of medicine throughout the Middle Ages and into the Renaissance. In the course of his illustrious career, Galen wrote numerous books, including *Prognostication of Disease by Astrology* and *Critical Days*, both of which advanced the practice of astrological medicine.

In his books, Galen describes the influence of the Moon in each sign of the zodiac and in its relation to other planets. Through the use of astrology, he describes what diseases a person may incur, how to treat them medically, and what the prognosis of each illness is. Galen specifically focused on the phases of the Moon and their importance in illness and healing. Galen wrote about avoiding surgery on parts of the body when the Moon was transiting a sign that ruled that body part. In Galen's writings, we see that astrology formed a vital aspect of medical practice.

The Arabic World

After the fall of the Roman Empire, the centers for the study of astrology and medicine moved to Arab lands. In the ninth century, a famous foundation was formed in Baghdad known as the House of Wisdom, a place devoted to translating scientific texts. The head of this institution was named Ibn Masawayh, who helped translate practical handbooks for practicing medicine. His most famous pupil, Hunayn ibn Ishaq, also authored a number of influential medical texts, including one with the Latin title *Isagoge*, a book that encapsulated the concepts of the four elements, humors, and temperaments.

Two of the most famous physicians of these times included Ibn Razi (known as Rhazes in Europe), author of the *Comprehensive Book of Medicine*, in the ninth century, and Ibn Sina (also known as Avicena), the tenth-century author of *The Canon of Medicine*. Both of these books borrowed from Hippocratic and Galenic ideas and forwarded medical knowledge through writings on diseases, therapeutic principles, and medicines.

In Loudon's *A History of Medicine*, the author writes:

"Yet Islamic culture did not simply provide custodial care for classical medicine, serving as a mere transmitter of ancient Greek medicine and learning to medieval Europe. Islamic physicians produced a vast medical literature of their own, in which they imposed a logical and coherent structure on the earlier Greek medicine. They also added an extended pharmacology, more elaborate notions of medical pathology, a knowledge of new diseases (for example, smallpox and certain eye diseases), new therapies, and new surgical techniques and instrumentation."[9]

Astrological wisdom also flourished in Arabian lands in the 800s. Al-Kindi and his pupil Abu Ma'shar wrote influential texts concerning astronomy, astrology, the metaphysical basis of magic, and the cosmic sympathy between planets and human activity. Abu Ma'shar writes in his book *Introductorium:*

"The doctor studies the changes in the elements; the astrologus follows the movements of the stars to arrive at the causes of elementary changes."[10]

Through the writings of these ancient Arab scholars, the practice of astrology and medicine continued to thrive. Eventually this wisdom found its way to the European world. The practice of traditional four element medicine continues to this day in Islamic countries such as Syria, Iran, and Pakistan. Known as Unani-Tibb, this medicine is based on Hippocratic and Galenic sources as well as the work of the Arabic scholars from the Middle Ages.

Medieval Europe

Much of the wisdom encapsulated in the Arabic tradition, along with the original Greek texts, was translated into Latin in the eleventh and twelfth centuries and became the basis for a rebirth in medicine and astrology in Europe. In the town of Salerno in southern Italy around the year 1100, a school of medical study developed that focused on the old Greco-Arabic texts. By the thirteenth century, universities in Paris and Montpellier had become centers for medical study. Through the universities a new group of men who received academic training in medicine began to develop, and a division emerged between those with professional credentials and those who were "folk-trained" and uneducated. Often these university-trained physicians scorned the local healers with their use of folk remedies and charms. Since the universities only accepted men into their programs, women were left out of this elite training and could no longer act as professional healers. In Elizabeth Brooke's book *An Astrological Herbal for Women*, she writes:

> *"For example, Jacoba Felice, born in 1280, who was charged with illegally practicing medicine, was found guilty and prohibited from working under pain of excommunication. There was no evidence of medical malpractice produced at her trial in 1322; her crime was simply to have been a woman physician."*[11]

In the Middle Ages in hamlets and towns throughout Europe, medicine and healing were often practiced by this "lower caste" of herbalists, midwives, and witches. Though limited in book knowledge, many of these folk healers had a profound knowledge of the land, its herbs, and natural medicines, and were adept at curing maladies and illnesses. Such practices continue in many corners of the world today, where modern medicine has not yet been introduced and where villagers are content with the herbal medicines and folk cures found in their environment.

Many of these local healers used astrological wisdom in performing treatments. The moon was believed to provide the greatest aid to healing, and often herbs would be gathered under the light of the Full Moon and medicinal plants would be grown and harvested only during certain lunar phases. The use of charms, amulets, and sorcery was widespread, and magic was often deemed essential for ridding oneself of evil spirits, protecting one's health from harm, and ensuring soundness of mind and body.

Folk healing, magic, witchcraft, and pagan rites and rituals all stemmed from the ancient tribal practices that had originated in different parts of Europe thousands of years earlier. The celebration of solstices, equinoxes, and the cross-quarter points such as Beltane and Samhain were practices that were firmly rooted in ancient custom. These pagan rites celebrated the turning of the seasons, the cycles of birth, growth, decline, and death, and the importance of the natural world.[12] Throughout Europe, such practices continued to exist alongside the Christian church, with folk healers keeping alive the tradition of linking humankind's health, nature, and the stars.

The Renaissance: Ficino and Paracelsus

In the late 1400s, an Italian writer, astrologer, philosopher, and physician named Marcilio Ficino was contracted to translate ancient Greek and Egyptian texts. Among them were texts attributed to Hermes Trismegistos known as the *Corpus Hermeticum*. Ficino's translations had the effect of reintroducing hermetic philosophy into Renaissance Europe. In these texts, it is written that "nothing happens in man that is not connected with cosmic sympathy." This idea of resonance between different aspects of creation became popularized and made its way into the philosophy, art, science, and literature of the time. Astrology was seen as a natural part of systems of correspondences and helped relate humankind to the divine. In his book *A History of Western Astrology*, historian Jim Tester writes:

> *"The acceptance of astrology as a learned and scientific study was a common, if not normal, attitude down to the eighteenth century, and it is impossible to understand men like Kepler and Newton unless astrology is seen for what the Greeks made it, a rational attempt to map the heavens and to interpret that map in the context of that "cosmic sympathy" which makes man an integral part of the universe."*[13]

Ficino believed that the stars foretold our health, but that we have the free will to augment and nourish ourselves and to fend against our vulnerabilities with natural remedies. Writing about this famous philosopher, noted astrologers Ariel Guttman and Kenneth Johnson write:

> *"Ficino also developed a doctrine of inner planets which held that the astrological planets were, in fact, internal psycho-spiritual entities, and that by means of meditation, talismans, and other sympathetic magical practices, one could enhance or harmo-*

nize the influence of those inner planets so as to produce beneficial effects in one's life."[14]

The hermetic translations and Ficino's writings helped set the stage for herbalists and healers interested in integrating magic and astrology into their practice. One of the most famous physicians was the Swiss-born rebel Paracelsus. Though he studied medicine formally in Italy, Paracelsus gained much wisdom from folk healers throughout his travels after completing his schooling. Known as the father of chemistry, Paracelsus helped elucidate many of the ideas on its arcane predecessor, alchemy. Alchemy not only involved the transmutations of base metals into gold, it also involved the spiritual and psychic transformation of man from a lesser being toward reaching his divine core. Paracelsus also fiercely battled the established medical world of his time and tried to reform outdated concepts and superstitions.

Paracelsus believed in the use of astrology for determining health, illness, and curative measures. In one essay, he wrote:

> *"The sympathy between planet and planet, so easy of observation, is a proof of the diffusion of collateral elements throughout the various channels of expression and of a constant stream of influences for ever interacting between those that stand thus related to each other. Every metal and every plant possesses certain qualities that may attract corresponding planetary influences, and if we know the influences of the stars, the conjunctions of the planets and the qualities of the drugs, we shall know what remedies to give to attract such influence as may act beneficially upon the patient."*[15]

Like Ficino, he also believed in free will and argued against the planets determining one's destiny. He believed that if one took the proper curative measures, one could avoid the ill effects and the "fate" of certain planets, like Saturn causing early death or Mars acting malefically on the constitution. In one of his books, Paracelsus outlines the effect of the planets on the body:

> *"The Sun is dry, hot, and sanguine and acts chiefly on the heart.*
> *The Moon is wet, cold, and phlegmatic and acts chiefly on the stomach.*
> *Venus is wet, hot and choleric and acts chiefly on the bladder and kidneys.*
> *Mars is dry and hot and acts chiefly on the head and brain.*

Saturn is dry and cold and acts chiefly on the legs to cause dropsy and gall.
Jupiter is wet and hot and acts chiefly on the shoulders and lungs.
Mercury is wet and hot and acts chiefly on the shoulders and lungs."[16]

Culpeper

Another famous adherent of medical astrology was the famous English physician Nicholas Culpeper. Culpeper lived from 1616 to 1654 and published numerous books on herbs, healing, and astrology, including *Culpeper's Complete Herbal*, which describes an immense compendium of plants, trees, and shrubs along with their planetary rulers and their medicinal values. Of garlic, for example, Culpeper writes:

"Mars owns this herb. This was anciently accounted the poor man's treacle, it being a remedy for all diseases and hurts (except those which itself breeds.)"[17]

Though immensely popular among his countrymen (to this day), Culpeper incurred the wrath of the Royal College of Physicians, who viewed him with anger for publishing books that popularized medical knowledge they deemed sacrosanct. With this knowledge in the hands of laypeople, these physicians were scared that they would lose some financial gain as well as personal power. Founded in 1518 by King Henry VIII, these physicians had grown in political power and sought to fine and imprison unlicensed practitioners for practicing medicine.

Though Culpeper had difficulty with his adversaries, he nonetheless popularized the relationship of astrology to herbalism and medicine. He also subscribed to another hermetic concept known as the Doctrine of Signatures, which related the color, taste, and smell of herbs to their healing properties. Writing about the herb pilewort, he noted:

"Behold here another verification of that learning of the ancients, viz that the virtue of a herb may be known by its signature, as plainly appears in this; for if you dig up the root of it, you shall perceive the perfect image of that disease which they commonly call the piles."[18]

Culpeper also employed the concept of using the right astrological moment for treating illness. Known as astrological election, Culpeper made special note of the Moon sign for administering medicines.

> *"Each of the four administering virtues is best strengthened by giving medicines for the purpose when the Moon occupies a zodiac sign of the same qualities. For example, when a person subject to continual vomiting is made weak by the inability to keep anything down, there is a need to strengthen the retentive faculty. The appropriate medicines should be given when the Moon is in an Earth sign which corresponds to the retentive faculty."*[19]

Culpeper and other astrologers of the Middle Ages, such as William Lilly, used a system of astrology known as decumbiture to understand the etiology of disease, the treatment plan, and the prognosis. This complex system of ascertaining health and illness is too broad a subject for me to tackle in this book, but it played an important role in understanding health. By looking at the placement of the planets at the onset of a disease, one could determine which vital organs could be affected and what types of herbs and dietary remedies would prove most effective.

The End of Traditional Western Medicine and the Formation of Modern Allopathy

Although Culpeper's form of humoral and astrological medicine was very popular in his time in the mid-seventeenth century, a tremendous shift was taking place in the intellectual and medical communities of his time. Scientific discoveries were radically changing Renaissance views of health, and healing and astrology were falling out of favor because of their links to magic, paganism, and superstition. The modern rationalistic approach viewed life mechanistically and reductionistically, and holistic, hermetic concepts began to be viewed with suspicion if not outright scorn by the new cognoscenti of the late seventeenth century. The Age of Enlightenment heralded the end of Galen's medical beliefs, with their link between the stars and our health.

Eventually, new mechanistic medical concepts formed the basis of the modern practice of allopathic medicine. Allopathy focuses primarily on the nature of disease and illness in terms of aberrations and pathologies of the physical body. Remedial measures are usually taken in the form of chemicals, drugs, and surgery to repair illness. Advancements in the creation of drugs have led to cures for polio, help for diabetes, and antibiotics that fight off bacterial-born illnesses. Therapies focus primarily on combating symptoms and suppressing the illness. Though many of these therapies have proved to be potent and successful, many also cause countless dangerous side effects and often are ineffective against chronic problems as diverse as arthritis, back pain, or anxiety. On modern allopathy, the Ayurvedic physician Hans Rhyner writes:

> *"Only in the last few centuries, with the emergence of natural sciences, such as physics, chemistry, and biology, has medicine been separated from philosophy. Modern medicine has become primarily a somatological science, resting on an experimental basis. Every healing method is subjected to clinical trials and rejected if proved ineffective. This leads to an exaggerated emphasis on somatological and physiological processes, which have become the criteria by which pathological manifestations of an illness or its symptoms are evaluated."* [20]

Paradigms of Holistic Healthcare

As the new medicine took hold in Europe, the humoral and astrological methods of viewing health waned from public consciousness. Now, several hundred years later, there is a reemergence of interest in the concepts that underlay the traditional practice of medicine in Europe for 2,000 years. In the East, traditional holistic medicine has enjoyed an unbroken lineage. Ayurvedic and Chinese medicine are still widely practiced in Asia and are now becoming quite popular in the West. Ayurveda (literally meaning "science of life") is the Indian form of natural healthcare with roots in Vedic texts written thousands of years ago. Ayurveda is intimately intertwined with the philosophy and spiritual traditions of India. Ayurvedic health practitioners regularly use Indian (Jyotish) astrology and often prescribe mantras, rituals, yoga, and amulets, along with herbs, diet, and massage in their practice. In Chinese medicine, practitioners study the pulses and use acupuncture, herbs, massage, and diet to help restore balance to clients.

Both of these traditional systems view the person as a system and framework of energy. By understanding the meridians and flow of chi (Chinese term for energy), or the chakras and the movement of prana (Sanskrit term for energy), health practitioners work to strengthen and nourish optimal health. Naturopathic healthcare has also grown in the West, with its emphasis on providing dietary, emotional, and lifestyle advice as well as prescribing herbal supplements and hydrotherapies to strengthen clients' health. Naturopathic healthcare has a fundamentally scientific viewpoint in assessing illness, but uses holistic methods to assist a return to health. These systems are becoming highly regarded in the West as comparably inexpensive and effective ways to bring good health to a client in a way that is noninvasive and usually lacking in deleterious side effects.

Jung and the Four Types

The resurgence of interest in traditional humoral concepts of health may have begun in the twentieth century with the eminent psychologist Carl Jung. Jung formulated a number of influential ideas, including the notion of archetypes—the idea that human experience can be encapsulated in certain images, myths, and metaphors. The notion of the anima and animus are two of the fundamental archetypes Jung forwarded. The anima is the female aspect present in the collective unconscious of men, and the animus is the male aspect present in the collective unconscious of women. Jung also postulated a theory of four dominant personality types that closely resemble the four temperaments of ancient Western medicine. In his theory, the four types include the Intuitive, Feeling, Thinking, and Sensing types.[21] In terms of four element medicine, Intuitive relates to the fire element, Feeling to water, Thinking to air, and Sensing to earth.

Jung also studied astrology and alchemy in-depth and wrote numerous texts on the relationship of humans to psychology and to the occult arts. In his book *Synchronicity*,[22] Jung described how two events that are not linked causally could be meaningfully related. He recounted how a client was discussing a dream involving a scarab and a beetle, when at that very instant, a beetle flew through the window. Or we may think about a loved one, and a couple minutes later, that person calls.

Jung believed that instances like these are indications of how we are connected not only with our fellow humans, but with nature in general.'

Jung used astrology in his practice as a way to better understand his patients. Through his interest in astrology and alchemy, Jung helped move the field of astrology closer toward a psychological framework. He also helped resurrect the ashes of a system that had died during the Age of the Enlightenment. Through his belief that stars could be synchronistically related to human health and behavior, he kept alive the ancient practice of four element medicine.

Modern Western Astrology

Much of modern-day Western astrology merges twentieth-century psychological concepts with Eastern philosophy and ancient astrological ideas. In 1936, Dane Rudhyar published *Astrology of Personality* and forwarded a more psychologically driven model of astrology. Many concepts used in modern-day astrological readings, such as archetypes, parental complexes, neuroses, the Shadow, actualizing potential, and releasing emotional wounds, have their basis in works written by psychologists such as Jung, Freud, and Maslow. This modern-day merger has led to profound and in-depth analyses of character through the astrological chart. Authors such as Liz Greene and Stephen Arroyo have written powerful books relating the planets to cycles of growth and developmental stages in life. Linking the planets and their mythologies to human understanding is at the forefront of modern Western astrology. Dane Rudhyar writes in his book *The Pulse of Life*:

> *"It is because astrology can be seen as a most remarkable technique for the understanding of the life-process of change in so many realms—and theoretically in every field—that its renaissance during the last two decades in the Western world is particularly important as a sign of the times. But this importance is conditioned upon a grasp of astrology which is truly modern. Nineteenth century approaches and classical or medieval biases should be discarded in the light of the new twentieth century understanding of physics and above all else psychology, in astrology as in every realm of thought. The emphasis should once more be placed on human experience, and away from the transcendent categories and the mythological entities belonging to an ideology which today is, in the main, obsolete."*[23]

Along with psychological innovations, Western astrology has also incorporated a wide variety of Eastern philosophy and wisdom that became especially popular in the 1960s. Indian gurus like Maharishi Mahesh Yogi, Sri Chimnoy, and Yogi Bhajan helped popularize concepts and practices such as reincarnation, karma, and yoga. Western philosophers including Alan Watts and Ram Das helped further elucidate oriental philosophy and introduce practices such as meditation and vegetarianism to the public. Eastern philosophy began to be integrated into astrological practices in the West, and we now have authors such as Jeff Green who posit that astrology teaches us who we are, our potentials and limitations, through the progression of our past lives and in terms of the evolution of our soul.

A modern-day Western astrologer is often quite adept at discussing character, likes and dislikes, and strengths and weaknesses, and can willingly act as a counselor to discuss aspects of family background, career ambitions, and one's love life. Astrologers can outline basic traits and archetypes and match the client's personal experience within a planetary and mythological framework. Thus, someone whose Neptune is prominent in the natal chart can express a range of traits, including being a martyr, a spiritual adept, a drug addict, a visionary, or a liar. Working within this framework, an astrologer may recommend avoiding the negative possibilities and embracing a more empowered, "actualized" self that takes the best from the archetypal potentials found in the astrological chart.

Alternative Therapeutic Models for Western Astrology

Though Western astrologers are often adept at analyzing character and personality, there is often a smaller range of therapeutic tools to work with a client. The primary approach is a kind of psychological and spiritual advice akin to how counselors work in their practice. Many of the tools and concepts forwarded by Renaissance astrologers like Marsilio Ficino or by Vedic astrologers, such as the use of gems, herbs, talismans, and rituals for balancing and harmonizing one's nature with the planetary forces, are seldom used by modern Western astrologers. This is unfortunate because these therapeutic models offer a doorway into immense growth and healing for clients. They link our mundane lives with the natural world around us. Nature acts as an intermediary force between humans, the microcosmos, and the stars, the macrocosmos. We can find an unending depository of healing agents in the environment that help us transform physical and emotional illnesses and also bring us a deeper reverence for the natural world, which is sorely needed in these times.

Modern Four Element Medicine

The modern practices of four element medicine and Western medical astrology have survived only minimally in European countries. In Arabic countries, four element medicine, known as Unani, continues to be practiced by local healers. In the West, there are only a handful of practitioners and no colleges or major educational centers that teach this ancient art. Because traditional humoral methods of understanding health and illness have been largely lost, modern medical astrologers use a wide variety of alternative holistic therapies to balance the constitution as determined by the astrological chart. These therapies include acupuncture, herbs, natural diet, flower essences, the use of gems and metals, yoga, and meditation, as well as many other practices. Though medical astrologers base their work on the philosophy of traditional Western medicine, the practice of this art often differs tremendously from Renaissance or medieval astrological medicine. Perhaps, in time, we will regain much of the wisdom and lore of this ancient practice and learn to integrate it into a modern, holistic health practice.

A Holistic Approach to Astrology: Four Element Medicine

When we take a holistic approach to astrology, we can see the patterns and mythologies of the stars not only in ourselves but in the natural world around us. The four elements present themselves to us every day when we walk outside. The elements come to life as fire from the sun, air from the wind, water from the rain, rivers, and lakes, and earth from the ground, trees, plants, and rocks. The natural world is a living, breathing depository for elemental energy. When we are depleted, in need of balance and nourishment, nature provides healing at a basic level.

Not only are the elements represented, but the modalities, the planets, and the signs are represented in nature as well. Think of the gentle and graceful movements of a whale. Its serenity and oceanic habitat link this creature with the planet Neptune. The beautiful chirping and bold-red breast of a robin link it with the Sun. The pungent and stimulating qualities of garlic link this herb with the planet Mars.

When we take a close look at the natural world, we see that everything expresses an energy, a set of characteristics, or a personality that defines each individual strand of grass, pebble, and tall tree. This is also true in the world of people. Imagine going to a party and interacting with a number of guests. One person is bright and expressive with a lot of zest and energy. Another is quiet, but seems to have some wise and interesting things to say. Another is impressionable and artistic and seems to be able to read your mind. All of these people have characteristics that express themselves in certain ways that have an effect on the outside world. The high-energy person may be fun and stimulating, but may also be exhausting at times. The quiet, interesting one may be a great person with whom to have a deep talk, but may not be that great on the dance floor.

Energy is all around us, in the form of people at a party, or in the form of plants and flowers in our garden, birds in our backyard, or in our pet dog or cat. By observing, listening, and paying attention, most of us can see the basic characteristics and personality of anything with which we come into contact. These things impact us at an emotional level. We may feel repelled or attracted, excited or frustrated, depending on what we are feeling and what we need at the moment. A huge crush of people drinking and yelling may be just what we need on New Year's Eve, but may be awful on many other nights of the year.

We pick our partners, friends, careers, and homes because of their personality or energy. Sometimes we choose people and jobs to balance out parts of ourselves that are lacking. For example, we may need a loud, boisterous person as a friend if we are quiet and timid. We also pick experiences that mimic our own energetic lifestyle. If we are fun loving and like to socialize, oftentimes we will choose people and experiences that will bring out and nourish this part of ourselves.

When we look to the natural world for healing, we can use many of the same techniques when choosing what to work with. The gentle and graceful flight of a great blue heron, the twittering nervousness of a chickadee, or the grand stillness of an alpine lake all have a relationship to our own consciousness. These sympathies are also found in the plant, mineral, and rock worlds, and we soon see that we can find sustenance and tremendous healing from the world around us. All of these be-ings can act as agents of transformation and growth. We can wear cedar bark as a talisman to shift us energetically toward the state of a cedar, toward more stillness, beauty, and grace. We may want to watch a gathering of elk to understand and in-corporate their nobility, strength, and serene power. We may want to wear an ob-sidian stone on our chest to help ground and protect our heart energy.

These are all natural expressions of a living world, an anima mundi, and as a liv-ing and interconnected world, we can access many of its forms to help us shift and grow. Astrology gives us powerful insight into what we may need in the natural world, and much of this book is dedicated to illuminating just that. When we take this natural approach to astrology, we see that psychological awareness and advice is only one piece of the puzzle. There are kinesthetic and natural approaches to working with our horoscope as well. Four element astrology points us in a new di-rection, one with deeper contact with our environment, one with deeper contact with our energetic and spiritual selves.

If we start to view our lives in this way, as a powerful interplay of energetic rela-tionships, then we start to get to the core of what this natural approach to astrology is about. Four element medicine describes our energetics and then points to how this is related to the natural world around us. The "medicine" in four element medicine does not just refer to physical medicine; it expresses a medicine for the soul, a natural medicine to help balance and heal us emotionally and spiritually. In the practice of four element medicine, we see ourselves as instruments that can be tuned and brought into perfect harmony with the universe.

Time and Technology

Unfortunately, the modern world is not geared toward attuning ourselves with the natural world and cosmos. We can be easily distracted by our computers, televi-sions, news sources, telephones, pagers, and other gadgets. These can be tremen-dously useful, but in many ways we have not learned to have a balanced relation-ship with this technology. Gadgets can easily drain us and take our energy away in the form of time.

The functioning of our modern world is fundamentally based on our sense of time. Time is a peculiar and flexible notion and one that has different meanings and principles according to one's culture and heritage. How we view time is integrally important to how we live and shape our lives. Since the advent of the clock, we have divided the days and nights into hours, minutes, and now seconds. Work schedules, dates, appointments, vacations, time alone, and entertainment are all planned around the clock. It has become such a daily part of our lives that it is difficult to think about life without it.

But it has been only hundreds of years since the clock was invented. Before then, and even now in some indigenous societies, life was more readily measured by the placement of the sun and moon, by the positions of the stars. Daily activity was more in sync with environmental rhythms. Nowadays we can shop twenty-four hours a day and work graveyard shifts due to the existence of electric light, but in older times, natural sunlight often determined our daily work and activity schedules. Life was slowed down because it had to be. There was little other choice, as it would be very difficult to accomplish tasks at night. A rest period fell that was adhered to naturally. This is no longer necessary, as it is not necessary to pay attention to any of the normal environmental cues. We no longer need to decrease our activities in the winter or allow for more activity in the summer. We can be indifferent to seasonal and daily rhythms.

Linear and Cyclical Models of Time

In the modern world, we have chosen to view time as a continuum, a line that starts from one point and goes toward another. This linear model is married to our cultural belief in growth and development that will lead to success and happiness. In this linear growth model, we start at one point and, through hard work and determination, progress toward great achievement over a specific amount of time. This linear model of time has resulted in incredible wealth for industrialized countries as well as tremendous technological and scientific achievements. On a darker level, millions of indigenous people have been conquered and killed in the name of progress and civilized advancement. The industrialized world lives at the pinnacle of wealth and scientific achievement, but only at the expense of much of the rest of the world.

The linear growth model has also brought us to the brink of environmental catastrophe. We are a world in crisis on many levels. Whole species of animals, birds, and fish are rapidly becoming extinct, our atmosphere has dangerous ozone holes, and our waters and lands are polluted with industrial pollution, including nuclear waste that will not decay for thousands of years. We live in schizophrenic times; on the one hand, we are at the pinnacle of achievement, and on the other hand, we are quickly moving toward ecological devastation. It is difficult to imagine that this model can continue successfully for many more hundreds of years. Much of the habitable world has been conquered and subdued, populated and used. With nowhere left to go, we look to space as our final frontier.

A cyclical approach to life long outdates the linear, scientific mentality. In fact, it is tens of thousands of years old and is in tune with the natural rhythms and cycles of the earth and the solar system. A cyclical sense of time involves a repetition of themes and patterns in a never-ending circle of experience. Cycles are at the basis of all perception, the cycles of the planets and the moon around the earth, the cycles of the seasons, and the cycles of the stages of life. Cycles teach that everything is connected to the same framework and is immeshed in the same patterning. The Greek mythologies that describe human nature are still relevant to this day. The archetypes of human growth and development hold true cross-culturally. These patterns are repeated again and again in human experience.

At a core level, pre-industrial societies based their beliefs on the unending series of cycles and the fundamental spiritual importance of their environment. For ancient Egyptians, that meant a reverence for the sun and the regular flooding of the Nile River, which allowed for crops to grow. For some Native Americans, this means a deep connection to the spirit of buffalo, elk, and deer, and patterns of hunting and feasting. For indigenous European peoples, solstices and equinoxes have been times for celebration and gratitude.

Astrology is akin to indigenous views of life not only because it sees the interlinking of humankind, nature, and the stars in one vast web of creation, but also because it views life as a never-ending series of cycles. The wheel of the zodiac is intimately entwined with the turn of the seasons and the processes of birth, growth, and death. When we study astrology, we see that there are natural times for development and progress, and natural times for reserve and stillness.

Astrology teaches us how to link ourselves back to the natural cycles of the year and the cycles of our lives. Fundamentally, the linear-growth model of life is a defense against the inevitable decay in life. Because we need to constantly grow and progress, there is little respect for the process of slowing down, the processes of aging, death, and dying. An astrological viewpoint can teach us to embrace the natural cycles in life and to honor and respect the different phases of life as deeply meaningful and important. Instead of hurtling along at breakneck speed, we can slow down and view ourselves as part of a vast web of cycles and honor our own process in this web as valuable and sacred.

Four Elements and the Anima Mundi

When we study astrology and four element medicine, we begin to incorporate a worldview that is different from society's norm. In astrology, we honor the four elements: fire, earth, air, and water. These elements are the core, the spine of the practice. We see people as having different blends of these elements in their personal makeup. These elements can be interpreted metaphorically or realistically. Four element astrology is the linking of the two into our everyday lives. We can see someone as having a fiery temperament (i.e., creative, dynamic, angry), and also see fire in our hearths, in the fierceness of a bear, and in the radiance of the sun. The elements take on deep and spiritual significance when viewed from this level. They become essential ingredients in our appreciation and perception of the universe.

When the metaphors of the constellations, planets, modalities, and elements are incorporated into our worldview, we start to see everything as a complex web of interactions that are linked at energetic levels. We see that we are fundamentally of the same material as the rocks, trees, and stars. We start to see the universe as infused with meaning and spirit. How we move, breathe, act, and think affects this web, and who and what we choose to interact with and incorporate into our lives becomes deeply meaningful.

The Chinese Philosophy of Chi

When we look at ourselves as energetic beings, capable of affecting the web of creation, it becomes essential to learn ways of nourishing ourselves for optimal resonance. Just like a well-tuned guitar, a person can be more expressive, soulful, and happy if he or she is resonating well. Nourishing ourselves means discovering the optimal sources for positive and harmonious energy that will enliven and strengthen us. The natural world is one of the best places to discover this optimal energy because it has not been adulterated, processed, or changed from its original form at all. Pure expressions of elemental energy are the best sources for balancing and healing ourselves.

In Chinese philosophy, the pure expression of energy moving through life is known as chi. Chi is seen as the basic energetic hum that underlies all of the elements. Chi moves and flows through the body in vessels called meridians. Chi is also found in nature, in the rustling of leaves, the blowing of the wind, and the swift-moving river. It is the basic current of all life. Chi can become blocked, muddied, and stuck in certain places if not allowed to flow smoothly. This is the etiology of disease in Chinese medicine. When chi becomes blocked or stagnated, abnormalities and disease develop. Acupuncture, moxibustion, massage, and herbs can be given to help the chi flow freely again. This alleviates the pain and ultimately cures the disease.

When I go out to dinner, I look at the quality of the food served in terms of chi. If the meal is prepared well, then the food looks like it is truly glowing. The vegetables look alive and fresh, almost dancing on my plate. This is what I call a high chi meal. When the food looks limp or soggy, dull and lifeless, this is what I call a low chi meal. No matter how good the ingredients are, or how healthy the meal should be, if the food is low chi then it will not nourish the body and its energetic currents well. Food that is lifeless or low chi is often found in prepared and packaged foods and processed and frozen meals.

With food, the freshest, cleanest, and closest to handpicked is the best; but the way it is chopped, cooked, and prepared is also vital. If we place a great deal of mindfulness into preparation, if the onions are lovingly cut, the broccoli is cooked on not too high a flame, and the ingredients are gently sautéed, then a very high level of chi remains. With our home, if we take the time to lovingly clean it, open the windows to allow fresh air circulation, and burn sage or incense to sweeten the smell, then the chi level of the home increases. This in turn nourishes the chi of the inhabitants and makes them stronger. In industrialized countries, we like to cover up odors with perfume, get facelifts to make us look younger, and eat radical diets to slim our bodies. These things do nothing to improve our overall chi levels, our energetic equilibrium; in fact, they can even damage it.

This lack of vitality and inner glow is fundamental to many of the psychological and physical health problems we have in industrialized countries. Pollution, excessive noise, chemicals, pesticides, drugs, and even electricity act to lower our chi levels, help give us wrinkles and neuroses, and damage our sense of inner contentment and joy. Though we believe we gain much by living in a modern world, we actually create a tremendous amount of self-inflicted damage. If we appreciated life on this level, energetically, instead of viewing life in terms of quantities, superficial looks, and appearances, then we would radically shift our relationship to the world. We would no longer be satisfied with simply attaining material wealth. Security would no longer be based on how much we had in the bank, but on how well we were nourishing chi for ourselves and our loved ones. This is the true source of joy and creativity.

The Importance of Love

The best way to nourish our chi is through acts of love and kindness. Compassion, gratitude, heartfelt prayers, and giving of ourselves to others augments chi like nothing else. We can see this in the glow of a baby suckling at her mother's breast. The child receives tremendous nourishment and nothing else will suffice. Body contact is vital to the establishment of good chi. When we share our homes with others, when we offer them a cup of tea, eye contact, and some conversation, we open up our energetic currents and unblock stagnancies. In the modern world, we can become truly cut off from this source of love as we live our lives isolated, separated from community. Churches, temples, and ashrams all offer a place to rekindle the basic connections, our ability to love and in turn nourish our core fountain of chi.

The beauty of viewing the world in this way is that it requires a great deal less money. Those living simply have the ability to cook and prepare meals mindfully. It is simple to open up the windows and sweep the dust out. It costs nothing to give and receive kind words, attention, and love. Mother Teresa was a perfect example of someone who glowed with tremendous energy amid the most poverty-stricken area in the world, Calcutta. Her open heart stirred the greatest source of energy in her and in the lepers and sick people she served. Service in the name of love and the divine accesses the full potential of our energetic selves. This is truly richness and wealth.

Quality, Not Quantity

An energetic worldview is based on quality, not quantity. It views the moment and how we interact, breathe, cook, eat, and love as the essentials of life. In our society, we often choose making money over having time. We believe that if we can make more money, then we can have nicer things, a better life, and a higher status in life. But when we lose time to work, it becomes difficult to live an energetically fulfilling life. It requires a great deal of time to nurture our relationships with love. It requires time to prepare our meals thoughtfully and lovingly. It requires time to honor the divine with ritual, prayer, and meditation. It requires time to sweep and clean our homes.

When we live energetically with awareness of chi, we start to appreciate the little things in life. The bloom of a flower, the smile of a friend, sipping tea, and the taking in and out the breath are seen as a path to wealth and happiness. As our days and years slip away as we prepare for some bountiful future, we lose sight of the gifts that we are experiencing now. Even if the experience is difficult, it is our experience and one that only we can appreciate. There is always the ability to mend, to breathe fresh chi into a situation, or to sprout wings from where we are, even in the most dire of circumstances. When we talk of faith, we talk of the belief in a never-ending supply of root energy, a wellspring upon which we can always draw.

The Four Elements—The Carriers of Core Energy

When we study the four element tradition, we are studying the prime carriers of essential chi: earth, air, fire, and water. We can draw on these sources of chi at any time in our natural environment, and they can help nourish and restore us. If we are weighted too heavily in certain elements, we can find a natural elemental remedy to draw in that missing part. The fire in the hearth carries root, warming chi that can sustain us and strengthen our own internal fire element. Bathing in a cool pool of alpine water strengthens our internal water element. Breathing in fresh air on the crags of a mountaintop connects us to the core of the air element. Meditating deep in the cave of a hill connects us to the best and most unadulterated properties of the earth element.

Each of the elements has a lesson to teach, a path of wisdom. The earth element teaches us the need to become quiet, patient, and steady in our lives. The air element teaches us the ability to use our words and our breath in healthy and positive ways. The fire element teaches us to laugh and play, to create and express in life. The water element teaches us to feel things deeply and powerfully, to take our experiences into our soul and envelop their meaning in our heart.

Each one of us may need different lessons and teachings at different times of the year and different times of our life. By paying attention and respecting our own energetic currents, we can learn what we need and what is best for us. Ultimately, the goal of four element medicine is to bring us into balance and harmony so we can grow and thrive optimally. Like a tree that needs adequate supplies of soil, rain, sunlight, and fresh air, humans also need the best expressions of earth, water, fire, and air to develop and become wise and happy creatures. By looking at our astrological chart, we can see which expressions are emphasized and which are lacking to help us understand what aspects of nature may best heal us. In the four element medicine tradition, the tools for healing are all around us, free of charge, free to anyone willing to take the time and have the desire to live in balance.

1. Albert van Helden, trans., *Siderius Nuncius, or, The Sidereal Messenger,* by Galileo Galilei (Chicago: University of Chicago Press, 1990) 8.

2. Anthony Aveni, *Conversing with the Planets: How Science and Myth Invented the Cosmos* (New York: Kodansha America, Inc., 1992) 183.

3. Zolar, *The History of Astrology* (New York: Arco Publishing, Inc., 1872) 3.

4. Ibid, XIII.

5. Aveni, 42.

6. Irvine Loudon, *Western Medicine* (New York, Oxford University Press, 1997) 29.

7. Zolar, 49.

8. Jim Tester, *A History of Western Astrology* (New York, Balantine Books, 1987) 24.

9. Loudon, 43.

10. Tester, 159.

11. Elizabeth Brooke, *An Astrological Herbal for Women* (Freedom, CA: The Crossing Press, 1992) 15.

12. Edain McCoy, *The Sabbats* (St. Paul, MN: Llewellyn Publications, 1999) 11.

13. Ibid, 227.

14. Ariel Guttman and Kenneth Johnson, *Mythic Astrology: Archetypal Powers of the Horoscope* (St. Paul, MN: Llewellyn Publications, 1993) 12.

15. Heinrich Daath, *Medical Astrology* (Santa Fe, NM: Sun Publishing Co., 1992) 63.

16. Henry M. Pachter, *Paracelsus: Magic into Science* (New York: Henry Schuman, Inc., 1951) 128.

17. Nicholas Culpeper, *Culpeper's Complete Herbal* (1652) 160.

18. Nicholas Culpeper, *The English Physitian* (1652) 223.

19. Graeme Tobyn, *Culpeper's Medicine: A Practice of Western Holistic Medicine* (Rockport, MA: Element Books, Inc., 1997) 169.

20. Hans Rhyner, *Ayurveda: The Gentle Health System* (New York: Sterling Publishing Co., Inc., 1994) 5.

21. Carl Jung, *Psychological Types* (New York and London: Bollingen Series, 1923).

22. Carl Jung, *Synchronicity* (New York and London: Bollingen Series, 1927) 86.

23. Dane Rudhyar, *The Pulses of Life* (Berkeley, CA: Shambhala Publications, Inc., 1970) 12.

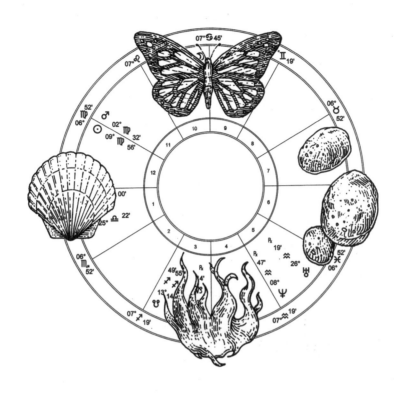

Part 1

Diagnostics

2

Techniques of Balancing and Nourishing

Out of the body of wisdom that emerged from Western historical astrological surroundings were the concepts that four elements, namely fire, water, air, and earth,
underlie all of creation, and that these elements are associated through the planets
with our fundamental archetypes and with ways in which we are subject to excesses
or deficiencies that affect our health. It is this earlier Western astrological tradition
that I like to term four element medicine. In this second chapter of the book, I will
look at the overall diagnostics underlying this system. In the third and fourth chapters, I will expand on these concepts more thoroughly, showing the different ways
in which they enable us to balance and nourish our health. Thus the goal of the
book is to introduce the reader to a system of four element medicine through
which we can harmonize our natural constitution through an understanding of the
placement of the planets.

In my life, I have lived in many different environments: cities, towns, and rural
settings. Each has its advantages. The city offers a wide range of cultural, employ-
ment, and entertainment possibilities, but country living offers the peace and soli-
tude of a natural setting. At the moment I am living in the city, and there are times
when I get overwhelmed by the cars, the lights, the pollution, and the fast-paced
movements of the people all around me. It is at these times that I need to go out
into the woods and ground myself amid the trees and plants. If I can, I find a small

river or brook to sit next to and allow the peaceful, quiet burbling to calm me and reduce my anxiety.

Perhaps you have also found ways of balancing your life with natural means. For example, if you feel slow and lazy, you might take your bike out into the open air and breathe in the fresh scents around you. If you desire grounding, you may decide to pick a few herbs from your garden and cook a nourishing, home-cooked meal.

Balancing and nourishing are at the core of what this book is about. These are the two main methods of harmonizing our lives and bringing about individual health and stability. When we become out of balance, we tend to focus excessively on one area and become extreme in our lifestyle and behavior. In four element medicine, these imbalances can appear in a number of different areas. Excesses or deficiencies of elements can bring about energetic and physical imbalances in us.

Since ancient times, astrologers have looked to the sky to see what constellation the planets were moving through. Each constellation is related to one of the four elements (Scorpio with water, Taurus with earth, etc.), and the planets can be seen as moving through a fire sign, an earth sign, an air sign, or a water sign. By looking at where the planets are at a person's birth, it is easy to delineate how much of each element that person carries throughout his or her life. Some people with a number of planets in Aries and Leo would be naturally fiery people. Those with a lot of planets in Gemini and Aquarius would be more likely to have air-element characteristics. For example, you may have a chart that is strong in the earth element but weak in the fire element. In this case, it may be wise to balance the excess earth and nourish the deficient fire in your makeup.

An astrological chart is a snapshot of the placement of the planets at our birth. Each planet is located in a sign, a modality, and a certain element. Each element, modality, planet, and sign is in turn related to parts of the body and to health concerns and processes. By reading the chart, we can understand our own physical and emotional vulnerabilities and how best to balance and nourish our constitution for optimal health. Before reading this book, it is especially important to know what parts of our chart are lacking and what parts are emphasized.

One of the best ways to analyze the astrological chart is by using a table of weights. For this book, it is important to know four factors; namely, the makeup, strengths, and weaknesses of the following factors in your chart:

1. the elements
2. the modalities
3. the planets
4. the signs

The elements (fire, earth, air, and water) are the basic primordial substances that underlie all of creation. The modalities are the ways in which these elements are expressed and directed (cardinal, fixed, and mutable). The ten planets (astrologers refer to the Sun and the Moon as planets as well) express our characteristics and our fundamental archetypes. The twelve signs describe how the planets function and manifest themselves in our lives. By understanding which of these basic aspects predominate, we can work toward balancing excesses and nourishing deficiencies in our lives.

Table of Weights

A table of weights is a simple system to determine what predominates in a chart and what is lacking. This is a system that I created and it may differ from other people's systems. The table of weights can apply to any of the four main aspects of a chart. First, you need to obtain your astrological chart. Then examine the element, sign, and modality that each of the planets are in. Here is the point system:

Sun	4 points
Moon	4 points
Ascendant	4 points
Mercury	3 points
Venus	3 points

Mars	3 points
Jupiter	2 points
Saturn	2 points
Uranus	1 point
Neptune	1 point
Pluto	1 point

To start with, you can find out which element each of your planets is in. Then add up all the points for each of the elements.

The Four Elements and Their Associated Signs

Fire—Aries, Leo, Sagittarius

Earth—Taurus, Virgo, Capricorn

Air—Gemini, Libra, Aquarius

Water—Cancer, Scorpio, Pisces

When you have made all your calculations, you can then see which elements are strong in your chart and which are lacking. Often a person has two strong elements; sometimes he or she shares three elements equally. Very rarely is there an even balance between all four elements. By studying your astrological makeup, you can determine the strength of the elements in your chart and can see which elements need to be balanced and which elements need to be nourished.

Balancing the Elements

Most of us have an emphasis on one element over the others. This emphasis helps define our personality, our vision, and our drive in life. However, if we emphasize these characteristics too much in our lives, we may eventually feel emotionally and physically out of balance. For example, people with a lot of fire in their chart may like to act in a theater troupe and enjoy after-hours parties with the cast. For a short while, this may be fine, but if these fire types continue to do this for extended periods of time, they may burn themselves out. Characteristics of burnout for fire types include insomnia, confusion, fatigue, and hot conditions like inflammations and rashes. The following table describes the excesses and deficiencies of each element, as well as a balanced expression in each of the elements.

The Four Elements and Health

Excess Earth *Energetically:* Getting stuck in a rut, workaholic, melancholy, uncreative, unimaginative, unstimulated

Physically: Heavy, slow metabolism, depression, sluggish digestion, coldness

Earth Deficiency *Energetically:* Up in the clouds, flighty, unfocused, anxious, confused, impatient, too fast

Physically: Nervous-system disorders, anxiety, skin rashes, asthma, poor breathing, excessive heat

Earth in Balance *Energetically:* Slow, patient, direct, willful, sure, steady, calm, grounded

Physically: Strong bones, teeth, and digestion, healthy, vigorous

Excess Water *Energetically:* Overly sensitive, impressionable, lack of boundaries, moody, confused, lost, susceptibility to drugs and alcohol

Physically: Water retention, edema, bloating, poor digestion, mucus and sinus problems, allergies, sensitivities, heaviness, urinary infections, mental disorders (schizophrenia, depression)

Water Deficiency   *Energetically:* Lacking empathy, self-centered, callous, insensitive, unthoughtful, narrow-minded

Physically: Dryness, rashes (eczema, psoriasis), brittle bones, poorly lubricated muscles and tendons, difficulty stretching, low libido

Water in Balance   *Energetically:* Sensitive, caring, compassionate, artistic, loving, psychic, aware

Physically: Moist skin and body, bendable, flexible, adaptable

Excess Fire   *Energetically:* Wired, "on," flamboyant, overly extroverted, manic, overly flirtatious, megalomaniac

Physically: Burnout, exhaustion, heat conditions, rashes, dryness, confusion, insomnia, hair falling out, adrenal depletion

Fire Deficiency   *Energetically:* Lethargy, listlessness, lack of spark, uncreative, undirected, unimaginative, without zest, warmth, or joie de vivre

Physically: Cold, depressive, sluggish circulation and digestion, stagnant energy, heaviness, fatigued

Fire in Balance   *Energetically:* Confident, happy, buoyant, warm, generous, creative, shining, playful

Physically: Athletic, strong, vigorous, good circulation, good digestion, lack of stagnancy

Excess Air   *Energetically:* Hyper, overly social, cerebral, detached, unemotional, insensitive, cold, flighty, anxious

Physically: Nervous-system disorders, tics, tremors, hyper-metabolism, thin, restless, insomnia, false heat

Air Deficiency	*Energetically:* Listless, fatigued, lack of humor, dull mind, removed, melancholy, heavy
	Physically: Poor breathing, tired, asthma, poor circulation, stagnancies, low blood pressure
Air in Balance	*Energetically:* Sociable, playful, intelligent, humorous, light and quick, agile mind
	Physically: Breathing properly (not too slow or fast), good circulation of breath and oxygen to all parts of the body, healthy lungs and mind

Therapeutics: Balancing and Nourishing

To find balance and healing for people with an emphasis on a certain element, it is helpful to look at two healing modalities. Since ancient times, there have been two fundamental systems of healing, both of which are efficacious and useful. The first is known as a balancing cure and is put into practice by healing an illness with an opposing remedy. In the second century, for the famous Roman physician Galen, the basis of medical treatment was that contraries are cured by contraries. What this means is that if an illness is hot and dry, then it will be cured by a treatment that is cool and moist. And if the disease is cool and moist, then the treatment is hot and dry. This is the basis of balancing therapies, in which the cure is opposite from the illness. Balancing cures are used primarily when illness has struck and unhealthy symptoms are arising. Nicholas Culpeper, the famous seventeenth-century physician who used astrology in his practice, recommended the following:

> *"You may oppose ailments by herbs of the planet opposite to the planet that causes them; as ailments of Jupiter by herbs of Mercury, and the contrary; ailments of the Luminaries (sun and moon) by herbs of Saturn, and the contrary; ailments of Mars by herbs of Venus, and the contrary."*[1]

Another more preventative therapy is through the use of nourishment. Nourishing remedies are ones that promote the healthiest and most balanced expression of an element in our chart. For example, if we want to strengthen our earth element, we may want to choose naturally grounding, building, and calming therapies to help nourish this part of ourselves. If we are lacking in a certain element, we may want to develop that part of ourselves through the use of nourishing therapies. If we are experiencing a weakness in an area ruled by Venus, for example, we could pick healing modalities that strengthen the function of Venus. Culpeper said of this:

> *"Also there is a way of bringing relief by sympathy, so every planet overcomes his own ailment—as the Sun and Moon by their herbs relieve the eyes; Saturn the spleen; Jupiter the liver; Mars the gall, etc. And Venus all ailments influenced by her."*[2]

In the case of a fire type who is strong in the fire element but weak in the earth element, it may be wise to use both of these modalities. On a long-term basis, it is a good idea to nourish the earth element while balancing and avoiding the extremes of a powerful fire element. Eating well-cooked, warm meals slowly in a relaxed atmosphere will help strengthen the earth element. Avoiding late-night parties, drugs, smoking, and stimulants will also help balance the fire element and reduce the threat of excess fire symptoms like mania, exhaustion, and burnout.

These are simply lifestyle choices that we can make, and chapter 12 is devoted to balancing and nourishing lifestyle therapies. There are also a number of other natural therapies that we can choose to help balance and nourish ourselves at a core level. Our environment is filled with expressions of all the elements, planets, signs, and modalities, and these natural manifestations can help heal us energetically, physically, and spiritually. Perhaps the excessive-fire type may want to work with a grounding animal totem such as a buffalo to increase feelings of calmness and steadiness. By watching, observing, and keeping paintings and pictures of this animal around, the excess-fire type can gain a deeper sense of spiritual balance in his or her life.

Sometimes it can be helpful to gently nourish an element that is emphasized in our chart. By choosing a stone, a bird, or an herb that expresses a strong element in our chart, we intend a healthier relationship with that element. For example, Aries individuals may want to work with a cardinal or a hawk to gain an understanding of a healthy and natural expression of their sign. Libras may want to wear an emerald to radiate their beautiful Venusian energy out to the world. This can be very healing as long as we do not overemphasize our element to the point of imbalance.

Both balancing and nourishing therapies are effective paths for healing the extremes of our chart. Nourishing medicine works well on a regular, day-to-day basis. It acts as a preventative therapy and helps strengthen our essential nature. Balancing medicine works best if ill health has progressed to the point of requiring remedial measures.

Balancing the Elements

Fire   Work with the earth element to ground and center.

Work with the water element to cool down and develop emotional awareness.

Water   Work with fire to stimulate energy and develop confidence.

Work with air to become more communicative and objective.

Air   Work with the earth element to find grounding and centering.

Work with the water element to develop emotional awareness.

Earth   Work with fire to stimulate energy, and become more creative and confident.

Work with air to become more lively, communicative, and interactive.

Modalities

There are three main modalities, and each describes the way an element is directed. Cardinal describes a directed and willful expression of energy. The fixed modality describes a magnetic and stable form of energy, and mutable describes an adaptable and fluid expression of energy. Each of these modalities is discussed further in chapter 3.

Modalities and Their Associated Signs

Cardinal   Aries, Cancer, Libra, Capricorn

Fixed   Taurus, Leo, Scorpio, Aquarius

Mutable   Gemini, Virgo, Sagittarius, Pisces

After looking at the breakdown of the elements, you can then look at your modality makeup. Again, use the table of weights listed previously. Add up your totals to find your individual breakdown. Once you have determined which modality or modalities dominate and which are lacking, you can work with the modalities through nourishing and balancing therapies. As with the elements, we often express one or two of these modalities the most, while one or two are lacking. If one modality dominates too strongly, natural imbalances will develop that can be detrimental to health and well-being. When this takes place, we look for ways to balance the excesses of our main modality (or modalities) while strengthening our weak modality (or modalities) with natural remedies.

Balancing the Modalities

Cardinal   Work with fixed energy to bring solidity and calmness.

Work with mutable energy to allow more fluidity and flexibility.

Fixed   Work with cardinal energy to gain direction and purpose.

Work with mutable energy to bring fluidity and adaptability.

Mutable   Work with cardinal energy to gain intent, will, and purpose.

Work with fixed energy to bring solidity, grounding, and surety.

The Planets and Our Health

To help strengthen and nourish ourselves at an optimum level, it is important to know which planets are especially strong in our chart. A strong planet often implies that the excesses of that planet can cause energetic and physical health problems. Balancing therapies often are advisable to use in this case. Someone whose Mars is strongly accented may tend to be more forceful, directed, and robust, and be more susceptible to illnesses such as high blood pressure, rashes, inflammations, and headaches. To help balance this strong Mars, it may be helpful to nourish the more receptive, warm, and gentle attributes of Venus. Venusian herbs such as yarrow and elder would help reduce heat and induce sweating to clear toxins. Wearing stones such as emerald or jade would help relax and soothe the energy in the wearer. Spending time in nature observing the quiet beauty of doves or swans may help release some of the intensity and fierceness of an excessively strong Mars.

Sometimes it can be helpful to nourish a planet that is dominant with sympathetic medicine. The same person who has a strong Mars may want to wear a Martian stone such as a bloodstone or ruby to express a powerful, beautiful, and balanced expression of that planet. This can act to direct and contain its powerful energies in ways that are not overly destructive and damaging. When nourishing a dominant planet, it is important to be careful not to exacerbate the excesses of that planet's energy.

Rules for Determining the Strength of Natal Planets

There are a number of factors that must be considered when determining which planets are strong:

1. Planets are strong when they are in the sign they rule.
2. Planets are strong when they are conjunct the luminaries (the Sun and Moon) or the Ascendant.
3. Planets are strong when they are found in the angular first and tenth houses.
4. A planet is strong as the ruler of the rising sign.
5. Planets are strong when there are a number of planets in the sign that they rule.
6. Planets affect our health when they are conjoined or make difficult aspects with planets that affect them. Saturn, Uranus, Neptune, and Pluto can all have a powerful effect on the inner planets and the luminaries.

7. Planets affect our health when they are placed in the fourth, sixth, eighth, and twelfth houses. They especially affect health when placed in the sixth house.

8. Planets are strong in their exaltation, and can affect our health when in their detriment or fall.

In this table, the planetary ruler describes the sign with which the planet is most closely associated. When a planet falls in the ruling sign, it is automatically stronger and more powerful. Detriment refers to the sign in which the planet is least comfortable; this is the opposing sign from the ruling sign. Planets in this position are weaker. Exaltation and fall are both ancient terms describing the signs that planets are stronger and weaker in, respectively.

Signs	Rulership	Exaltation	Detriment	Fall
Aries	Mars	Sun	Venus	Saturn
Taurus	Venus	Moon	Mars	Uranus
Gemini	Mercury	——	Jupiter	——
Cancer	Moon	Jupiter, Neptune	Saturn	Mars
Leo	Sun	——	Saturn	——
Virgo	Mercury	Mercury	Jupiter	Venus
Libra	Venus	Saturn	Mars	Sun
Scorpio	Pluto (Mars)	Uranus	Venus	Moon
Sagittarius	Jupiter	——	Mercury	——

Capricorn	Saturn	Mars	Moon	Jupiter, Neptune
Aquarius	Uranus (Saturn)	——	Sun	——
Pisces	Neptune (Jupiter)	Venus	Mercury	Mercury

Balancing Planetary Energies

Sun
- If there is too much self-centeredness and egotism, work with Neptune to bring in compassion and sensitivity.
- If there is a feeling of mania and excessive enthusiasm, work with Saturn to bring in seriousness and gravity.
- If there is too much extroversion and expression, work with the Moon to bring in quietness and receptivity.

Moon
- If there is too much quietness and receptivity, work with the Sun to draw out expressive and extroverted qualities.
- If there is too much passivity and yielding energy, work with Mars to be assertive and direct.

Mercury
- If you are too focused on the details and the minutiae, work with Jupiter to be expansive and open-minded.
- If there is too much rational and logical thinking, work with Neptune to open up more psychic and right-brained channels.

Venus
- If there is too much receptive, magnetic, and attracting energy, work with Mars to be directing, forceful, and intending.
- If there is laziness, langor, and sloth, work with Mars to gain energy and vitality.

Mars
- If there is too much aggression and a dominating mindframe, work with Venus to be gentle, loving, and peaceful.
- If you are too forceful, direct, and single-minded, work with Neptune to draw out the beauty and transcendence in everyday life and to relax the energy.

Jupiter
- If expansive, visionary, and prophetic qualities are strong, but detail-oriented, rational, and logical qualities are lacking, work with Mercury.
- If there is a tendency toward excessive exuberance and indulgence, work with Saturn to limit and set boundaries, to focus and be grounded.

Saturn
- If heavy, melancholic, and depressive qualities are strong, work with Jupiter and the Sun to brighten and lift your spirits.
- If you are too practical, earthbound, and rigid, work with Uranus to break up the monotony and Neptune to increase imagination, creativity, and fancy.

Uranus
- If you are too ungrounded, unstable, electric, and wired, work with Saturn to bring in surety, stability, and grounding.
- If you are too mental and heady, work with the Moon and Neptune to bring in receptive, psychic, and artistic ways of looking at life.

Neptune
- If visionary, transcendent, and spiritual qualities are overwhelming, work with Saturn to bring yourself down to earth and make visions practical.
- If right-brained, artistic, and psychic qualities are dominating, work with Mercury to become more logical and rational.
- If you are too passive, open-hearted, and without boundaries, work with Mars to increase forceful, direct energy.

Pluto
- If you are too intense, obsessive, and dark, work with Jupiter and the Sun to bring in qualities of joy, peace, and laughter. Work with Venus to bring in relaxation, comfort, and joy in the moment.

Rules for Determining the Strength of Signs

There are a number of factors that must be considered when determining which signs are strong. Signs are strong . . .

1. When there are a number of planets in that sign.
2. When the Sun, Moon, or Ascendant is in that sign.
3. When they rule the angles (first, fourth, seventh, and tenth-house cusps).
4. When their ruling planet is strongly placed. (For example, if a Pisces native has natal Neptune in the tenth house conjunct the Moon.)
5. When they rule the sixth-house cusp. In this case, the effect can be detrimental to your health.

Using the table of weights shown previously, you can add up the point value of planets in each of the signs in your chart. Make sure to note the sixth-house cusp, as the sign on this cusp and its ruling planet can point to health problems. Some signs will be strong, and others will be minimally important or not emphasized at all. You can focus on the health effects of those particularly strong signs. Again, use the balancing and nourishing ways of healing illnesses associated with that sign. The best way to do this is to work with the ruling planet of the sign and use the table for balancing planetary energy. For example, if Pisces is strongly emphasized, look to the ruling planet, Neptune. Depending on which aspect of Neptune needs to be balanced, you could work with Mercury, Mars, or Saturn therapies to help balance the extreme expressions of Neptune.

Final Comments

Putting together all the factors to determine what health areas need to be addressed can be difficult and confusing when looking at an astrological chart. Often one or two aspects of the chart will pop out. Perhaps the horoscope is dominated by planets in water signs; or perhaps the planet Uranus holds a prominent position (conjunct the Sun in Aquarius, for example). Focusing on one or two factors is the key to success here, instead of scattering your attention by including all aspects of the chart. In the next two chapters, I will explore more in-depth the four fundamental factors—elements, modalities, signs, and planets—to provide an understanding of how these features affect our health and well-being.

---

1. Graeme Tobyn, *Culpeper's Medicine: A Practice of Western Holistic Medicine* (Rockport, MA: Element Books, Inc., 1997) 162.

2. Ibid., 163.

3

Elements and Modalities

When I have time, I like to hike out into the mountains and experience the pleasures of the natural world. The hills lie before me, and I may see a passing robin, a crow, or even a hawk up in the sky. As I enter the woods, I can smell the rich scent of pine sap mixed with the moist dirt from the ground. I take a deep breath of air and let the clean oxygen circulate throughout my body and into my pores, refreshing and enlivening me. I leave behind the hurried pace of city life and become entranced with the slower and deeper rhythm of the earth.

It is here that I find the greatest degree of healing. The smells, tastes, and sights of this world remind me of my own natural state and my connection to the vast web of creation. An herb collected in these hills retains the freshness of the land, the spirit of the place. Each cup of water that I drink from the streams draws me into a deeper connection with snowcaps, glaciers, rainfall, and the fish running through the rivers. These are what I like to call essential experiences, because they bring me back to the essence of the land, the essence of the rivers and the lakes, the essence of myself.

The Four Elements

For millennia, many traditional societies associated these essential experiences with underlying elements in life. Experiences could be categorized according to these basic building blocks. Astrologer Stephen Arroyo writes:

"Many cultures throughout the world include the four elements in their philosophical, religious, or mythological traditions. Most of these traditions postulate one primary energy which then manifests as 'stepped down' energy currents known as the elements, a process resembling the working of an electric transformer. This primary energy has been called by many names: prana, vital force, Qi, and others. The essential characteristics of this energy have been identical for all cultures, although the names given to the primary force and to the elements themselves have varied."[1]

In Indian medicine, the building blocks of the physical constitution are known as doshas. There are three doshas in their system: vata, pitta, and kapha. Vata refers to light and quick energy, with a restless and bright quality. Pitta refers to strong and directed energy, pushing forth assertively and sometimes aggressively. Kapha refers to steady and heavy energy, weighted and solid. Medical theories of illness and healing can be categorized by these doshas in Indian thought. Therapy consists primarily of balancing the doshas through herbs, dietary changes, meditation, yoga, and oil massages.

In Chinese medicine, there is the concept of five elements: wood, fire, earth, metal, and water. Each of these elements is related to a season, an organ, certain emotions, and has many other associations. By using the five element approach to medicine, a Chinese medicine practitioner can see a correlation between anger, liver problems, diseased eyes, and a greenish color to the skin. All of these relate to the wood element, and a practitioner would work to balance this element. A five element practitioner primarily studies the pulse, the tongue, the quality of the voice, and the disposition in order to make health assessments.

In Western traditions, the essential system of categorizing life is that of the four elements: fire, earth, air, and water. These elements form the basis of all of creation, whether that be a rock (earth), a windy day (air), the sun (fire), or a deep lake (water). As in Chinese medicine, these elements are related to planets, seasons, and natural processes, as well as to human organs and emotions. In the four element medicine tradition, humans are made up of the four elements, and an astrological chart is partly a description of our elemental makeup. By understanding our core elemental makeup, a health practitioner can determine the underlying constitution and places of strength and imbalance.

In the next section, I will discuss the four elements in terms of health. Each element is related to functions of the human body. When our chart shows an emphasis on a particular element, certain functions may be more vulnerable and may need more care. Likewise, if we are lacking in a particular element, we may need to augment that element through natural healing methods.

Elements

Fire

People with a lot of fire in their chart tend to be robust, creative, expressive, and dynamic. There is a spark to these people, and they are often the initiators and the artists in our environment. They have an almost childlike desire to be admired and appreciated and may wither if they are not given love and attention. Fire types often have a great deal of enthusiasm and may need a fair amount of freedom to channel their energy. Ultimately, fire types are channeling the heat and essential divine spark of life. Their work is to direct this energy in creative, and not destructive, ways.

In medical astrology, the fire element is connected to the heart, blood, and circulation. These are all functions of the body that can get overheated and overtaxed. When there are too many toxins, circulation can become sluggish and certain parts of the body become overheated, while others receive little warmth. Excess heat and stagnation can result in heart disease, ulcers, and chronic inflammations. The regulation of body temperature is ruled by the fire element. To maintain health, we need to stoke the internal fires. Proper exercise, diet, rest, and intake of fluids ensure the right balance of heat in our system. This is akin to building a campfire, which needs wood in certain amounts and at the right time, or else the fire blazes too hot or goes out.

Fire helps us move, create, and express. In terms of our health, fire helps us digest, move heat, and sweat out toxins. In the stomach, Ayurvedic medicine calls the digestive fire energy *agni*.[2] Strong agni helps digest all the food that comes in and breaks it into smaller particles. If there is too much fire in the stomach, however, we can get indigestion, heartburn, and ultimately ulcers. Fire is an essential ingredient to proper assimilation of food, which, in turn, gives us good energy levels. If we overeat, then we dampen the fire, and food stagnates in the stomach; the agni is squelched. If we eat only cold and raw foods, then we also weaken the agni and lose the ability to assimilate food properly.

Fire is also essential for removing toxins. When we are sick, we get a fever. Higher temperatures in the body help burn out invading microbes. It is the body's way of fighting off illness and disease—by increasing the natural fire. The body then naturally sweats, evaporating moisture with toxins through the skin. The fire element also comes out when we are angry. Our face gets flushed and we feel energy rise to our heads. We literally become hot and fiery.

People with a lot of fire in their chart have a tendency toward excess and burning the candle at both ends. They need to make sure they get enough rest, fluids, and down time to recharge their batteries. People with too little fire in their chart can tend toward a lack of passion and "get up and go." They may need to eat a more stimulating diet and do more invigorating and aerobic exercise to help move their energy.

Water

People with a lot of water in their chart tend to be in touch with subtle emotions, deep feelings, and the nuances of life that other types may not catch on to. These folks sense their environment so powerfully that they can pick up on a lot of what's going on underneath people's interactions. Often they are more in touch with fear, sadness, and the deepest sensations of love, passion, and desire. Because they are so intuitive and often psychic, they can get overloaded by the intensity of life and may need quiet time to themselves to find some peace. These people often make great healers, musicians, and mystics. Ultimately, they need help defining themselves and their boundaries so that they don't lose themselves to other's needs.

In medical astrology, water is connected to all the fluids in the body besides blood. These include lymph, mucus, semen, and interstitial fluid. These fluids allow our immune and sexual systems to function properly. A proper balance of water in the body allows us to flow and move gently and gracefully. If we look at plants that have been well watered, their leaves are full and lush, and the stalks hang easily and strongly. There is life and glow to these beings. Conversely, if they have been overwatered, the plants become dull and sagging, and the leaves may rot and die.

We can observe our own water balance. Does our skin feel brittle and cracked? Is our hair dry and thin? Are our lips parched and our energy levels low? The modern world has a tremendous problem with dehydration as we take our fluids in many other ways—coffee and soda pop, primarily. These substances dehydrate and leach the vital minerals from our bodies. Water or herbal tea is the best way to receive liquid nourishment.

Our immune system functions by the interplay of our lymph and cellular water concentrations. Again, if we are too dry or moist, our immune system's equilibrium will not function at its highest potential. When this occurs, we are more susceptible to colds and flus, chronic ailments, and illnesses. Emotional constipation in the form of buried feelings, jealousy, hatred, and especially grief can function to break down our immune system and damage our internal organs. Water serves as a cleanser, helping wash out toxins and foreign particles from our body, thereby aiding our immune system and our overall health.

People with a lot of water in their chart tend to be emotional, artistic, psychic, and moody, and may be working on a lot of deep, subconscious levels. The excess of water may lead to immune-system and water-balancing problems. There may also be damp stomach conditions, which can lead to improper digestion and assimilation, and may also produce excess mucus, affecting the lungs and the throat. Reducing sugars and starches and increasing aerobic exercise will help reduce excess-water complaints.

People with too little water in their chart can suffer from dry complaints including brittleness of hair, nails, and teeth, dry coughing, and lack of internal moisture leading to arthritis, osteoporosis, hardening of the arteries, and poor fluid metabolism. This type would do well to increase liquids in the form of soups, teas, and pure water and also take plenty of time to rest and relax.

Air

People with a lot of air in their chart are often associated with the mental realm. These are the thinkers, the talkers, and the socialites in our midst. They tend to be more detached and objective in their association with the world and can often seem both friendly and distant. These folks have a great capacity to draw groups of people together and often have many friends because of their love of connection and interaction. For some people strong in the air element, there can be an overemphasis on the thinking and talking function, which can make it more difficult to reach deeper levels of emotion and sensitivity.

In medical astrology, the air element is connected to the nervous system and the lungs in the human body. The intake and exhalation of breath is the primary way for the human body to replenish oxygen and rid ourselves of carbon dioxide, a substance that is toxic to humans in high doses. Oxygen in the form of air vitalizes and nourishes every pore and cell of our body, allowing us to feel relaxed and enlivened. When we breathe, many of us do so from our upper chest in short, shallow gasps. This type of breathing, over extended periods of time, leads to fatigue, nervousness, and a lack of vitality. When we breathe from our abdomen, we get full, rich, and deep breaths that nourish our entire system, allowing our nervous system to function optimally.

The nervous system is our main defense against the stresses of the outside world. Ruled by the air element, it is our primary way of operating and functioning in the world. It acts as our antennae, taking in information and energy from the outside world, then sorting and processing it. If it is strong, then we can manage stress well, and handle adversity and crises with more ease. When our nervous system suffers due to poor diet, poor breathing, or a lack of rest and exercise, we become agitated, depressed, and unable to cope with life's demands. In our modern world, we are barraged with so much sensory input that we often feel overwhelmed, stressed, and nervous. Many of us have to shut down a fair amount of our senses so that we can survive and operate functionally in the world. Cellular phones, pagers, televisions, computers, fluorescent lights, and microwave ovens all impact our nervous system and can impair our internal air element if they are overused.

People with an emphasis on air in their chart often feel overstimulated, nervous, and excited, and may have difficulty finding grounding and connecting on intimate emotional levels. They may need to do centering exercises, meditate, and burn off excess energy through aerobic exercise. People with a lack of air in their chart tend to be more emotionally and sensually aware, perhaps becoming overly impassioned by circumstances without the ability to stand back and view things rationally and objectively. They may need to do breathing exercises, tai chi, or even stand out in windy places to draw in some of that air they lack.

Earth

People with a strong emphasis in earth signs tend to be practical, grounded, solid, and weighted in this physical reality. They tend to be oriented toward work, goals, money, and the physical senses (especially touch). These are the sensualists who often like to garden, sculpt, and give and receive massages. These are also the builders and the doers on the planet; these folks often help establish businesses, co-operatives, foundations, and projects. They are usually loyal, headstrong, and literally down-to-earth people. Their practical nature can sometimes leave them a little too weighted, and they can get stuck in ruts and feel bogged down. They need a little stimulation and spark to get them out of their routines.

In the human body, the earth element is linked to the digestive system as well as the basic structure of the body and the skeleton. The digestive system involves the intake and processing of food. Food is the building block from which all humans grow and thrive. Like an herb planted in good soil, a good diet helps us grow and be strong, and vitalizes our being. When we are malnourished, our skin may sag and look sallow, our eyes look dull, we feel more cramps and pains, and ultimately we are more prone to illness and disease.

Since industrial times, we have had an increasingly disastrous relationship with food. With the advent of processed chemicals and the widespread use of unrefined sugar, additives, and pesticides in our diet, we have become increasingly overweight and prone to illnesses such as cancer, ulcers, liver, and heart disease. Our relationship to the earth element has been difficult on both an external and internal level. As we continue to clear cut, strip mine, pave, and industrialize at breakneck speed, we also poison our bodies with excessive consumption of an unhealthy diet. Repairing this relationship is fundamental to the health of our bodies as well as the planet.

The earth element is found at the most basic level in the structure of the skeleton. The skeleton supports the rest of the body and is a storehouse for marrow, where red blood cells are formed. Bones contain the elements calcium, phosphorus, and sodium, which are essential for good health.[3] When the skeletal structure has been strengthened through proper diet, exercise, and stretching, the bones can properly support the muscles and tendons in the body.

When we get in touch with the earth element, we see that the body has the capability to give us deep pleasure and sensual gratification. We can strengthen our own earth element when we take the time to cook ourselves a delicious meal, really tasting each morsel as we savor, chew, and then swallow. We nourish the earth element when we stretch our body fully. We can experience earth when we gently take a friend or partner in our arms, and hug them, touch them, and massage them. When we extend our hands to give and receive, our bodies become enlivened and joyful, truly experiencing the bounty of the earth's riches.

People who have a lot of earth in their chart tend to get weighed down and stuck in patterns and habits. They may need to recharge their energies from time to time so that they don't get in a rut. On the other hand, these people are great builders and sensualists, and are able to savor and give lovingly of the gifts of the earth. People with a lack of earth tend to be ungrounded and a little flighty, or tend to rush off in a number of directions without accomplishing much. They may need grounding stones, herbs, and food to help strengthen their earth element.

Modalities

Another key component in studying astrology and health is the modalities, the three qualities that describe how an element is expressed. The four elements have three ways of directing their essence, making up the twelve signs. These three ways are known as cardinal, fixed, or mutable—the modalities. Each modality has its strengths and weaknesses and affects our health and well-being in different ways.

Cardinal

The cardinal modality is expressed by the signs Aries, Cancer, Libra, and Capricorn. This energy is like an arrow shooting forward. Cardinal energy is direct, forceful, and straightforward. People with a lot of cardinal energy tend to be directed, ambitious, and willful. They have the power to set their intent and move toward their goals. These are the leaders, makers, and doers in life. They make things happen when they direct their energy toward an intended outcome. Negatively, they may be pushy, demanding, and overwhelming toward others who have a different timetable or agenda.

Cardinal people need to temper their strong and forceful energy with some stabilizing and grounding energy. They need to learn to relax, let others do things, and not try to accomplish everything at once. They have the ability to direct their strong will toward accomplishing many goals. The important thing is to decide if their goal is absolutely important and if it outweighs the concerns of other parts of their life. For example, a cardinal businessman may be gifted at building a company from scratch and making it very successful, but he may have neglected his health and family. A spiritual adept may become a world-famous tai chi instructor, but not have any time for his own creative endeavors or private affairs. If people with a lot of cardinal energy can take the time to balance all their affairs and become more well-rounded, then life will become more fruitful and fulfilling.

Healthwise, cardinal energy people tend to overtax their bodies, demanding too much and moving too fast. This tends to burn them out, similar to fire-type people. The burden they place on their bodies causes them to contract illness quickly and strongly. All of a sudden, a cardinal-energy person may develop walking pneumonia, or have a heart attack, or develop rashes and boils. This is due to the body not being able to regulate itself properly. Too much energy is being expended and not enough is being retained for rest or more peaceful activities. Because cardinal energy generally implies a strong constitution, these people can usually get back on their feet in short order if direct, simple, and efficient remedial measures are taken.

Fixed

Fixed energy is found in the signs Taurus, Leo, Scorpio, and Aquarius. Unlike cardinal energy, fixed energy draws life and activity to it instead of shooting out. People with a lot of fixed energy in their chart tend to be stubborn, steadfast, solid, grounded, and stable. They tend to get in ruts and sink into repetitive states that are difficult to escape from. Fixed-energy people may have a hypnotic and power-ful presence that seems to draw people and activity toward them. Depending on their state of mind and attitude, this could be good or bad. If their mind frame is greedy, jealous, angry, and spiteful, they will usually draw people with the same at-titude toward them. That is why it is essential for fixed-sign people to develop a positive mindframe and to surround themselves with warm and supportive friends.

Fixed-sign people occasionally need a little push to get motivated, to move their energy; otherwise they can stagnate and become listless. Fixed energy is akin to the heaviest boulders firmly rooted to the ground. Imagine them like mountains: they have found their spot and are not going to move unless necessary, thank you very much. Once their energy is harnessed in a particular direction, inertia often takes place and they do not like to stray from the course. That is what makes them tena-cious warriors and wonderful spiritual adepts. They plot their course and stay with it through hell or high water. They can build up tremendous power in their aura that is magnetic and awesome in strength. But if it is not harnessed occasionally, and directed toward a goal, it can become destructive and damaging.

In terms of health, fixed-energy people have perhaps the strongest and steadiest disposition of the three modalities. They are usually slow, sure, and solid. However, once they have contracted an illness, it is often very difficult to cure it, as the sys-tem becomes fixated on this new pattern. The illness usually comes from stagna-tion and a repetitive, damaging lifestyle, whether that be through diet, emotional attitude, a lack of exercise, other causes, or a combination of factors. To counteract these problems, fixed-energy people need to stimulate themselves out of their stag-nated condition (which can be very hard for them to do; they may prefer to stay in the diseased state rather than change). Stagnant conditions that can affect fixed-en-ergy people are obesity, chronic lung and chest complaints, depression, chronic fa-tigue syndrome, and cancer. All of these illnesses require some degree of detoxifi-cation, cleansing, and energy movement.

Mutable

Mutable energy is found in Gemini, Virgo, Sagittarius, and Pisces. This energy is the most flexible and adaptable of the three energies. There is a liveliness to this energy as it bends and shapes, and moves and flows between different conditions. It is the chameleon of the three modalities. We find mutable energy in water, as it easily changes from ice to water, then evaporates, only to return as rain. Water can shape its way around anything, spills through our fingers, and washes down a mountain easily and quickly. Mutable energy is found in the activities of a bee, who spends just enough focused time gathering nectar from a flower, then speeds off in another direction to communicate with other bees or explore new terrain.

This quickness and adaptability serves mutable-energy people well as they tend to be intelligent, quick-minded, and adaptable to a number of different circumstances. They can shape themselves according to the place and time in order to best fit in. Their curious minds gather a lot of information and process it either mentally, physically, or emotionally. Mutable energy wraps and weaves the intricate parts together. Gemini gathers information, Virgo cuts away what is not important, Sagittarius elevates it to a philosophical level, and Pisces uses the information to merge with a higher spiritual plane. These are the shapeshifters, the organizers, the seekers, and the weavers between the microscopic and macroscopic levels.

On a physical level, mutable energy tends to work quickly, but not have an excessive amount of force. Mutable people have perhaps the weakest constitutions of the three modalities and tend to take on whatever illness is around them. Therefore, they often get colds and the flu or minor illnesses. If they take a rest from their busybee activities, they can usually restore their energies, but they need to remember that they are not as constitutionally able to handle as much stress as the other two modalities are. They need more calm, sedation, and nourishment to keep them well. Mutable people tend to contract nervous-system and immune-system illnesses like fibromyalgia, anxiety, arthritis, Lou Gehrig's disease, tics, tremors, and paralysis. With proper attention and care, these can be averted, however. Therapies for mutable people include moving toward a slow and steady routine with medicines that are gentle and nourishing.

---

1. Stephen Arroyo, *Astrology, Psychology, and The Four Elements* (Reno, NV: CRCS Publishing Co., 1975) 87.

2. Hans Rhyner, *Ayurveda: The Gentle Health System* (New York: Sterling Publishing Co., 1994) 64.

3. Richard Mabey, *The New Age Herbalist* (New York: Macmillan Publishing Co., 1988) 212.

4
Planets and Signs

When we look out into the night sky, we can see the twinkling of the same stars that have been seen by humans for thousands of years. Circling our solar system is a band of stars known as the zodiac. The zodiac is comprised of twelve different patterns known as signs. From the vantage point of the Earth, the planets move around the zodiac in an orbit around the Sun. To early Egyptians and Babylonians, five main planets could be observed along with the Sun and the Moon. These included Mercury, Venus, Mars, Jupiter, and Saturn. The outer planets, Uranus, Neptune, and Pluto, are not visible to the naked eye and were only discovered in the past few hundred years. The modern-day names of the planets come from the names of Roman gods and goddesses, which were based on earlier Greek, Egyptian, and Babylonian deities.

In ancient times, these planet gods were worshiped much as Christ or Allah are worshiped today. Early astrologers assigned characteristics and personalities to each planet. These gods and goddesses related to each other amicably or tempestuously depending on their individual natures. The movements of the planets across the sky described a majestic cosmic play that we could know and understand if only we observed it closely. Rituals and offerings were regularly made to please and praise this celestial pantheon. In early Egyptian hermetic philosophy, the planets and the signs were further deemed to be related to physiological processes, temperatures, plants, animals, and stones. Even today in India, Vedic astrologers still prescribe gems, mantras, and rituals to help harmonize us with the planetary influences and mitigate the effects of negative celestial events.

Though we no longer perceive the planets as gods and goddesses, it might be helpful to return to a deeper reverence of these immense orbs. In modern psychological astrology, these planets express complex archetypes, metaphors, and mythologies. In four element medicine, they are also related to physiological and natural processes that can be seen and felt everyday. The planet Venus can be seen in a dove luxuriously cleaning itself, and the Sun can be felt as a piece of amber, a golden jewel that correlates with that shining star. The planets connect with aspects of our health: Jupiter with our liver function, Saturn with our bones, skin, and teeth, and so on. By relating to these natural expressions of the planets, we create a divine connection to their essence. Essentially, we are practicing a sort of sympathetic magic where we are physically and experientially contacting our core essence, the underlying divinity.

At birth, the planets shine at a certain point and relate to each other in a way that imprints on the essential nature of the newborn as she takes her first gasp of air out of her mother's womb. In studies carried out in the twentieth century, scientific evidence has shown a remarkable correlation between planets and physical characteristics. In many astrology books, the planet Mars has been associated with the color red. In a study undertaken by Judith A. Hill and Jacalyn Thompson, these two researchers looked for Mars to be prominently located (to be within thirty degrees on either side of the Ascendant.) Hill writes:

> *"We [Hill and Thompson] completed the collection of our goal of 500 redhead birth charts in 1988. The initial findings of statistical consultant Gary Antonacci were highly significant. Exactly 27.2 percent of the 500 redheads tested were born when Mars was within 30 degrees of the Rising Point, or within our suggested Strong Zone. Males with bright red hair were born 30 percent of the time with Mars so placed. Three non-redheaded control groups demonstrated that what is normal in the population at large, stands somewhere between 16.9 percent and 19.4 percent. The probability of the redhead result occurring randomly is less than one chance in one-million."*[1]

This profound study implies a sympathy between these massive planets and something as mundane as hair color. In my practice, I have seen people with Neptune prominent in their chart who have sensitive, emotional eyes, with a tendency toward a stuffy nose from allergies and toward immune-system problems (Neptune is often associated with immune-system problems). The planets correlate with human constitution and expression as well as with the natural world. Nature provides a perfect depository for healing the imbalances formed at our birth. By understanding the planets, we can learn how to heal ourselves preventatively, before illness develops.

The Planets

Sun

The Sun is the central radiating force in the astrological chart. It is the masculine principle and our driving, active, yang self. Someone with a strong Sun (in Leo, in an angular house, conjunct the Ascendant) tends to be a leader, a shining and powerful force who can direct people and who often heads projects, is expressive, dynamic, and at the forefront of activities. The Sun sign, position, and aspects show our overall health, constitution, and energy. In terms of the physical body, the Sun rules our heart, arteries, and thymus gland, and is linked to the eyes. The heart radiates blood and nourishment to all parts of the body and keeps us stable and secure. When the solar function is inhibited, we may feel off balance, erratic, confused, and depressed. When the solar function is functioning well, we are charismatic, happy, and content.

Ruler: Leo

Detriment: Aquarius

Exaltation: Aries

Fall: Libra

Influence: Hot, dry, vitalizing, and constructive

Moon

The Moon signifies our emotional core, our family and past. Its sign, placement, and aspects show where we feel at home, most comfortable and instinctually aware. People with a strong Moon placement tend to be compassionate, nurturing, and emotional, as well as cyclical and occasionally moody. The Moon rules the breasts, the stomach, and the balance of fluids and hormones in the body. The Moon is also related to the digestion and assimilation of food. When our digestion is in balance, we are full of good energy and feel vital and alive. When our lunar function is in balance, we relate to the world easily, feel emotionally secure, and are compassionate and nourishing to those around us. When our lunar energies are compromised, we may feel insecure, unsure, and unconfident. We may want to curl up and hide.

Ruler: Cancer

Detriment: Capricorn

Exaltation: Taurus

Fall: Scorpio

Influence: Cold, moist, and assimilative

Mercury

Mercury relates to our mental, verbal, and intellectual aspects. Its placement shows us how we think and communicate. Strongly Mercurial people tend to be communicators, writers, and thinkers. Theirs is a world of ideas and thoughts. They like to express and interchange with others and to gather new information. In medical astrology, Mercury is related to the lungs, the larynx, and respiration, the act of breathing in and out. This is because Mercury is connected to the air element. Our relationship to Mercury is supremely important today as our world functions through proper communication and information exchanging. The lungs and breathing ensure proper vitality and nourishment to all the blood vessels of the body. The circulation of oxygen in the system through respiration helps us be clear-headed and lively. The exhalation of carbon dioxide helps us expel toxins and poisons from our system. Mercury is also related to our nervous system. This vital function allows us to take in and process information from external stimuli. Because of this, the nervous system is most easily affected by outside stress and can be destabilized by stimulants, a poor diet, and a lack of rest. Mercury is also associated with the hands and arms. Excessive Mercurial energy can cause nervousness and anxiety, while a balanced expression of Mercury includes the ability to be communicative and expressive while still listening well to others.

Ruler: Gemini and Virgo

Detriment: Sagittarius and Pisces

Exaltation: Virgo

Fall: Pisces

Influence: Changeable and variable

Venus

Venus rules our more receptive and loving side. It also rules our sense of beauty and aesthetics. Its placement shows us how we relate in these realms. People who are strongly Venusian often are attracted to wealth, beauty, and comfort. These folks like the pleasures in life and enjoy giving and receiving love. In medical astrology, Venus rules the kidneys, the female reproductive organs, the throat, and the thyroid gland. The thyroid gland helps in the regulation of metabolism of chemical-balancing agents. The kidneys help in the regulation of fluids, the detoxification and elimination of poisonous substances. The kidneys are also related to the emotion of fear in Chinese medicine. When toxins build up in the system due to stress or poor eating habits, this can adversely affect the kidneys and ultimately lead to more fearfulness. Venus also has a special relationship to our sexuality, and people with a strong Venus in their chart are often charismatic, attractive, and desirable people.

When our Venus is afflicted, we can feel stressed and awkward, as if we were out of sync with the natural flow. We may feel an inability to give and receive warmth and love and may feel isolated and cold. Venus is also related to our blood-sugar levels. If our Venus is being stressed by a difficult transit, then we may feel a strong desire to overconsume sugary and starchy substances or deprive ourselves of these things. When our sugar levels are out of balance, we become moody, irritated, confused, depressed, and stressed. When Venus is out of balance, we can become self-indulgent, overly luxurious, and complacent. When Venus is in balance, there is a sense of comfort and ease in the moment, a feeling of peace, beauty, and contentment.

Ruler: Taurus and Libra

Detriment: Scorpio and Aries

Exaltation: Pisces

Fall: Virgo

Influence: Warm and moist

Mars

Mars rules our more assertive and directed side. It rules the part of ourselves that aims for what we need and then goes out and gets it. People with a strong Mars are the leaders and warriors in our world. They are often physical and powerful looking and can direct and channel their energies toward a goal and reach it through their strong will.

Physically, Mars rules over our overall strength, muscles, blood, adrenal glands, and head, as well as our libido. Mars has a strong relationship to our fight-or-flight mechanism. It helps us assert boundaries and defend ourselves against unwarranted intrusions. When our Martian energy is weakened, we have difficulty creating firm boundaries and expressing our will clearly and surely. We become more prone to fear, depression, and anxiety. Our adrenals can become overstressed from this fear and can become depleted. An overly strong Martian energy can make a person aggressive and even violent. The system can become overly heated, the body becomes flushed, and anger and intense emotions arise easily. When Mars is in balance, there is a sense of strength and power, but it is used in focused amounts and only when necessary. In this case, exertion is balanced with equal amounts of rest.

Ruler: Aries and Scorpio

Detriment: Libra and Taurus

Exaltation: Capricorn

Fall: Cancer

Influence: Hot, dry, and inflammatory

Jupiter

Jupiter rules our expansive qualities. When we are magnanimous, generous, and warm-hearted, we are acting in a Jupiterian way. Those with a strong Jupiter are often explorers, wanderers, and seekers. These are the people who are joyful, bright, and boisterous. They know how to be the life of the party and stir up energy. Jupiter can also make us excessively extroverted and dominating and at times unaware of when to be quiet, slow down, and reserve our energy (that behavior is ruled by Saturn). Jupiter rules over the liver and the pancreas. It is also the planet that helps us regenerate tissue and grow new cells for healing wounds. Jupiter is a strong and beneficial planet and helps us be buoyant and cheerful. Often, Jupiterians enjoy the good life, eating and drinking for pleasure. This can overly toxify the liver, which must assimilate and help process all foods entering the body. When our Jupiter energy is adversely affected, we become dull, lifeless, stingy, and selfish. When Jupiter energy becomes overly dominant, the body can get excessively hot and the liver can become damaged. In balance, Jupiter is energetic and giving without being too dominant and overarching.

Ruler: Sagittarius and Pisces

Detriment: Gemini and Virgo

Exaltation: Cancer

Fall: Capricorn

Influence: Mild, temperate, warm, and moist

Saturn

Saturn rules over our more cautious and conservative side. When we prepare, slowly develop, consolidate, and draw our energies inward, we are acting out the Saturn myth. Saturn helps us slow and define limitations; it ground us. It helps us make a firm commitment with loyalty to people and places. Saturnians can set goals and achieve them through steady, disciplined effort. Physically, Saturn rules the foundational structures of the body—the bones, teeth, nails, and skin. When our Saturnian energy is adversely affected, these structures can become stressed and damaged. When our Saturnian energy becomes excessively dominant, we can become strict, hard, and rigid. Diseases like arthritis, stiff joints, and depression are more likely to afflict us. A balanced expression of Saturn includes the wisdom to slow down, make good plans, and then direct our energy steadily without being too uptight or rigid in our efforts.

Ruler: Capricorn, and Aquarius (traditionally)

Detriment: Cancer and Leo

Exaltation: Libra

Fall: Aries

Influence: Cold, dry, contracting, and obstructive

Uranus

Uranus rules the nervous system, sparks our mental energy, and helps us be creative, unique, and imaginative. Uranus takes us on new and unusual paths and has an electricity about it that leaves us charged up and sometimes blows our fuse. People with a strong Uranus tend to be innovators, revolutionaries, and eccentrics. These people get us out of ruts and change the molds of our perceptions. They are often strong individualists and move to their own beat. Like Mercury, Uranus is linked to the nervous system in medical astrology. When our nervous system is functioning optimally, we are secure, grounded, and serene. We can handle stressful situations and act from a centered place. When our nervous system gets overly wired (when we have drunk a lot of coffee or are undergoing a stressful Uranus transit, for example), we lose clarity and surety. We become excessively sensitive, nervous, and confused. A balanced expression of Uranus includes the ability to channel progressive and unique ways of thinking and behaving without becoming unrealistic and out of touch with society.

Ruler: Aquarius

Detriment: Leo

Exaltation: Scorpio

Fall: Taurus

Influence: Cold, dry, and magnetic

Neptune

Neptune rules our transcendent side. When we feel heightened, mystical, drunk, ecstatic, or enraptured, we are experiencing Neptune's realm. Neptune opens our perceptive doorways and allows hidden feelings and vibrations to surface. People with a strong Neptune in their chart tend to be visionary, sensitive, or psychic, and sometimes have difficulty maintaining boundaries. They can be strong agents of service and can channel great spiritual energy, but can also get lost and confused through the use of drugs, alcohol, and unhealthy life patterns. In medical astrology, Neptune rules the immune system, the protective barrier between the external and internal world. The immune system helps us fight off disease and prevents infection. When we are too open and vulnerable (maybe during a powerful Neptune transit), we can be harmed by exterior conditions. Neptune also rules the pineal gland, which is instrumental in directing the functioning of the immune system. Neptune helps us be imaginative and spiritual, but can also make us weak and vulnerable. A balanced expression of Neptune is both sensitive and transcendent without being lost and confused.

Ruler: Pisces

Detriment: Virgo

Exaltation: Cancer

Fall: Capricorn

Influence: Warm, moist, and hypnotic

Pluto

Pluto is a powerful planet that has the effect of intensifying anything it comes into contact with. Plutonian energy is deep, penetrating, transformative, and often very heavy. People with Pluto strong in their chart tend to be powerful and intense. Because Plutonian people are more in contact with the underlying pain, passion, and darkness in the world, their work is to release and let go of deep emotional wounds and transform their pain into love. Pluto also has a strong relationship to the theme of power, and often Plutonian types need to work through issues of control, sharing, and letting go. In medical astrology, Pluto rules over reproduction, the sexual organs, and regeneration of the system through healing. Primal instinctual urges are ruled by Pluto, and this planet has a way of taking over our lives when we are under its transit. Boils, eruptions, life-threatening illness, and powerful, cathartic healing experiences are all ruled by Pluto. Pluto is also connected to the sexual organs, the reproductive system, and the eliminatory systems. These are systems where deep transformation takes place: sexual energy can be encapsulated as a fetus, food is excreted as waste, and love can be brought down to earth via sexuality. When we become overly Plutonic, we can become obsessed, neurotic, and dark, choosing destructive impulses. When we balance the extremes, we learn powerful lessons from these experiences and develop a greater ability to love deeply and authentically.

Ruler: Scorpio

Detriment: Taurus

Influence: Warm, dry, transformative, and penetrating

Signs of the Zodiac

The planets move through sets of constellations known as signs. The signs that ring our solar system are known as the zodiac. Over time, mythologies developed throughout many parts of the world in relation to this celestial belt. The zodiac defines the essential play of emotions, temperaments, qualities, and potentials that humans are capable of. Each sign is related to deep archetypes common to all cultures. By understanding this panorama of archetypes, we develop the wisdom of knowing the possibilities and frustrations hidden in each of us.

In the zodiac, the sign of Gemini has long been associated with the twins. In ancient times, pairs of gods were often found at the gates of Babylonian, Egyptian, and Assyrian temples and houses. In Egypt, many people celebrated the worship of the bull, associated with Taurus in astrology. The Egyptian god Osiris was often depicted with a human body and a bull's head. In Greek and Roman mythology, the sign of Capricorn was often associated with the nature god Pan. Pan represented a lusty, wild creature of the forest with horse's hooves and often carrying a flute, which he played to entrance lovers and celebrate life.

These ancient associations of gods and the stars show the powerful interweaving of religious thought and astrological observation. The zodiac was also powerfully associated with the turn of the seasons. In *Mythic Astrology*, Ariel Guttman and Kenneth Johnson write:

> *"Though each sign has its own particular mythic resonance, the zodiac as a whole constitutes one great proto-myth. The sun's journey through the year is a drama of birth (spring), activity (summer), death (autumn) and resurrection (winter)."*[2]

The movement of the Sun through the different signs also describes a movement through the seasons and points to the essentially cyclical nature of life. The constellations themselves embody different themes and mythologies that are constantly revisited and give us a sense of timelessness. When we interact with the zodiac by looking at our chart, we enter a cosmology that has never changed. People thousands of years ago were acting out the same passion plays of greed, jealousy, undying love, loyalty, and betrayal that we experience today. When we connect to the zodiac, we connect to universal archetypes that encompass all of human experience.

Because the zodiac is associated with the turn of the seasons, astrology also points to our relationship with the natural world and its associated cycles. The patterns of birth, growth, decay, and death that are integral to human life are also part of the life cycles of plants, animals, and birds. In the next chapter, I will explore the seasons and the holy days of the year, and their importance to practicing four element medicine.

Each sign is associated with a season and a mythology, and also with aspects of our health and well-being. When we study a person's astrological chart and see dominant signs, we may notice correspondences in his or her health patterns. Each of the signs has a planetary ruler, and these planets can also give us clues to a person's health and strengths and vulnerabilities in those areas.

When I was younger, I watched a musician play music and sing in a band. He was getting older, but his voice held an awesome strength that was rough and sweet, strong and fragile at the same time. This man was a Leo and he was singing the last song of the night. The way he sang the song was so impassioned and so honest that it felt like his heart was breaking. Just then I had a vision and felt his heart skip a beat, stutter, and then stop. It was as if he was actually singing his heart out to the point where he was giving everything, his last drop of blood for this song. At that moment, I could see that he would die soon, that his Leo heart was beyond repair and that it was giving out, that he had reached the end of the road. This connection between Leo and the heart became crystal-clear to me. Less than a year later, this man had a heart attack and died, but it came as little surprise to me.

These correspondences of the signs with aspects of health are more than folklore; they are relationships that can be experienced and intuited on a very real level. When we take the time to see these connections, we can learn how to prepare ourselves and take care of ourselves in the best way possible in order to avoid illness and disease.

To understand the signs, its helpful to see them as part of a cyclical continuum, beginning with Aries and ending with Pisces, and then starting over again. Each sign represents a developmental stage of life and a stage of growth. As the first sign of the zodiac, Aries represents the seed being planted and the first breath of life of a newborn. After Aries, the sign of Taurus represents a deepening embodiment, a growing understanding of our physical abilities and senses. Gemini represents the process of inquisition and curiosity as we stretch out into the world. In Cancer, there is a sense of deriving security and comfort from the world around us and especially to the family structure that has been created. Leo describes the process of separating from the family structure to develop an ego and a sense of self-importance. Virgo describes the process of winnowing out the negative and destructive aspects of our nature in order to prepare for the sign of Libra, when we merge with a lover to create a partnership. Scorpio expresses the path of developing deeper intimacy, viewing the shadow aspects of our nature, and learning to work with the darker parts of our soul. Sagittarius describes the process of finding meaning after the exploration of the darkness of Scorpio. After the process of exploring the darker aspects of life, and finding a sense of personal meaning, we now come to the sign of Capricorn. This is the sign that leads us into the larger world and helps us build lasting structures in the world. Next, Aquarius teaches us to move out into the community and build bridges between groups of people. Pisces is related to growing older and the process of dying. There is an emphasis on letting go and encompassing greater spiritual and metaphysical realities at this time. We turn from the world of humans and reconnect to a more cosmic reality. This cycle begins again with Aries after we return to the beginning point through Pisces. By viewing each sign as part of a continuum, it is easier to see the zodiac as a complete system and indivisible. Each sign naturally comes from the one before and leads to the next. This natural cycle of birth, growth, and senescence that is encapsulated in the zodiac mirrors the processes of life on earth.

Aries

At the beginning of the zodiac we have the sign of Aries. It is a cardinal fire sign and is associated with dynamic, expressive, directed, and willful qualities. Because it is a fire sign, there is an element of playfulness, creativity, and joie de vivre in this sign. Like a newborn child, the path of Aries is to reach out into the world and understand it. They are the pioneers, the leaders, the creators, and the project initiators. People with a lot of Aries tend to have their own ideas about things and may lead a very self-oriented path. One of the most important lessons for Aries to learn is to share with others and to learn skills of cooperation and partnership.

Aries rules the head, and people with a lot of Aries in their chart often have a prominent facial or cranial feature. They can also be prone to headaches and head injuries and need to be more aware of this part of their body. Because it is a fire sign, Aries is prone to fiery ailments like inflammations, eczema, ulcers, and circulation problems.

Aries is ruled by the planet Mars, which can sometimes signify an angry or tempestuous disposition. In Chinese medicine, anger is connected to the liver. When anger is repressed or comes out too frequently, it can cause toxicity to the liver. This lowers our energy and makes us feel tight and constrained. To counteract this, many people with this condition turn to sugar and alcohol to help expand and release that stress. The sugar and alcohol, in turn, further damage the liver and make us feel even worse once the effect of the chemicals has worn off.

Ruling Planet: Mars

Element: Fire

Modality: Cardinal

Physical Rulership: Head

Taurus

Taurus is a fixed earth sign with characteristics of steadiness and firmness of disposition, with a sensual and down-to-earth approach. As Ariens are the initiators, Taureans have the ability to make plans concrete and set down firm foundations. There is a very real connection to earth matters for most Taureans. They are often engaged in physical labor or handling money, wealth, and land. These people are sensualists, basking in the glow of the warm sun, enjoying or giving a deep back massage, breathing in deeply the aroma of a meal, and drinking deeply a draft of wine. Taureans know how to enjoy life. Though Taureans are adept at finding value in the physical world, much of their work in life comes in releasing their attachment to the things they are holding on to. Because everything changes and is impermanent, Taureans often need to learn powerful lessons in letting go and becoming comfortable with change.

Taurus rules the throat and the thyroid gland. The throat and entire neck area can be sensitive for Taureans, and they sometimes suffer from sore throats, laryngitis, or tonsilitis in extreme conditions. In Hindu philosophy, the throat chakra is the area from which we are creative and express ourselves. When this area is stressed, we become tight, listless, and quiet. It can be literally difficult to get out what we are trying to say.

Taurus is also ruled by the planet Venus, and this reveals Taurus' very sensual and romantic side. Taureans enjoy touch, feel, and pleasure, and when their energy is good, they can be very adept at giving and receiving it. The Venus rulership also shows a strong connection to sexuality, and Taureans can often be very flirtatious and sensual. Their sexuality and fertility is tied in with their creative and passionate juices. When in good spirits, their sensual/creative side will be turned on, and they are capable of tremendous positive outflow. If their energies are in some way suppressed, then their sensual/creative side may feel turned off and there can be frustration and disappointment.

Ruling Planet: Venus

Element: Earth

Modality: Fixed

Physical Rulership: Throat, neck, and thyroid gland

Gemini

This is the sign of the twins, signifying the dual personality that often exists in Gemini. Gemini is a mutable air sign that usually is seen in people who are talkative, sociable, and have many different interests. These people bounce from one place to another, skimming along easily like a butterfly, and drawing attention with their quick minds and often humorous take on life. They are often smart and attentive to details, and can be found among many different groups of people, talking, laughing, and picking up new information from a wide variety of sectors.

Gemini rules the arms (including the hands) and lungs, and Geminis are often prone to bronchial complaints. With their love of anything to do with their hands, you can often catch a Gemini smoking, which can further exacerbate any lung problems. In Chinese medicinal philosophy, the lungs are associated with the feeling of grief. Geminis have a tendency to avoid heavier emotions, which can become stored in the lungs as grief. Though herbal and lifestyle remedies are helpful, it may be important to explore the deeper emotions of grief to fully heal the lungs. The ruling planet of Gemini is Mercury, and this planet is associated with the nervous system. Because Geminis have a tendency toward being quick, impatient, and doing several things at once, their nerves can be frayed if they do not take care of themselves.

Geminis are mental and verbal beings, and they often have problems exploring the emotional realm. Though they can be fun-loving and jovial, they need help exploring their secret dark side. Gemini is the sign of the twins, the split and dual personality. To fully actualize the potential of Gemini, there needs to be a fusing of both the shadowy and light sides of their nature. In ancient lore, the ruling planet of Gemini, Mercury, was associated with the god Hermes. Also known as the winged messenger, Hermes was associated with healing. Hermes carried a long staff, known as the caduceus, with two serpents twisting around it. In Hindu philosophy, there are two currents that entwine the spine, known as the ida and pingala. These currents are also known as coiled serpents arising from the base of the spine, where powerful kundalini energy is generated. It is said that when kundalini is raised in a disciplined and wise manner, the energy goes from the spine up to the crown chakra and is capable of generating enlightenment. If kundalini is raised improperly and impatiently, the energy can be so powerful that it destroys the nervous system and causes one to go mad. On a spiritual level, the sign of Gemini has to do with balancing the twin serpents and generating kundalini energy in a positive and healthy manner.

Ruling Planet: Mercury

Element: Air

Modality: Mutable

Physical Rulership: Arms, hands, and lungs (nervous system)

Cancer

Imagine a mother sitting in her home gently rocking her newborn child. Her entire essence and effort is going into caring for her precious baby. The infant suckles at her breast, and the mother gently swaddles him in warm clothing to keep him safe and comfortable. This image describes an aspect of Cancer that is the warm and loving nurturer. Because Cancer is a water sign, it is associated with a depth of emotional compassion, empathy, and a powerful sensitivity. Cancers function best when they are in a warm and loving community and family. Their sense of security and confidence grows, and they can become powerful members of their clan, providing care and assistance for the well-being of their loved ones. Cancer is associated with the moon and its cyclical patterns, and Cancers, too, can have a cyclical pattern to their emotional states, varying from easygoing to crabby and moody. When Cancers are mistreated and malnourished, they can become frustrated and depressed, and can snap and bite at people like a crab. They also have a tendency to be overly protective to the point of smothering their friends and family.

Cancer is associated with the breasts and the stomach in medical astrology. When Cancers become insecure and moody, they have a tendency to worry, which affects their stomach and digestion. They are likely to have gastric upsets and allergies to certain kinds of food. They are often sensitive to a number of different kinds of food, including chocolate, milk products, and wheat. Because Cancer is associated with the Moon and with the emotional realm, they also tend to become overwhelmed and hypersensitive. If they feel threatened or fearful, they will often retreat and may become unduly shy and reticent.

Ruling Planet: Moon

Element: Water

Modality: Cardinal

Physical Rulership: Breasts and stomach

Leo

Leo is the sign of the long-maned, proud, and noble lion. Leos are often generous, warm-spirited, playful, and flirtatious. They have a romantic and excitable personality and can be truly fun companions. Much of the path of Leo is to learn to express their full and radiant selves out to the world as a way to help others see their own beauty and to lift their hearts. Because Leos often shine so brightly, there is a danger that they can get caught up in their own self-expression and become selfish and narcissistic. The path of Leo is to learn to develop their talents and gifts without becoming too self-absorbed.

In medical astrology, Leo is linked to the heart, and a Leo in balance is open-hearted, generous, and displays great integrity. The heart is essential for pumping blood throughout the body, yet in our society it is often under great strain physically. Western society suffers from a high degree of heart disease due to a diet rich in fats and lifestyles devoid of exercise. The heart is also the center of our emotional well-being. When we feel warm, open, and kind-hearted, our lives seem to run smoothly and harmoniously. When we get caught up in the emotions of jealousy, fear, greed, and hatred, we become petty and our heart chakra starts to close down. The heart is also connected to the eyes, and we can see the state of someone's health by looking into these orbs. When we are healthy, our eyes are radiant, shining, and full of life and spark.

Leo is also a fire sign, and fire-sign people tend to have more issues with heat and the maintenance of temperature in the body. Fire types are prone to hot conditions such as eczema, rashes, ulcers, heart disease, and flushed and scaly skin. Leo is also a fixed sign, and Leos tend to get illnesses that have more staying power and are more difficult to eradicate. In general, the Leonine constitution is very strong, but fixed energy solidifies any problems that might arise. There may be difficulty in breaking patterns and habits that have developed.

Ruling Planet: Sun

Element: Fire

Modality: Fixed

Physical Rulership: Heart

Virgo

This earthy sign is the sign of the virgin, the immaculate maiden who wanders amid beautiful valleys of corn and wheat. The Virgo gently harvests the crops and separates the wheat from the chaff, taking what is bad and discarding it. Virgos tend to have a very discriminating and analytical mind, which they can use to elevate and purify themselves, helping them become more nourished and stronger. But they can also be cutting and harsh, critically picking out faults and putting themselves and others down. When they are in balance, Virgos are of service to their community, willing and able to help their loved ones grow and thrive through their hard work ethic. They use their quick minds and nimble hands to sort through their environment and nourish the garden before them with the most loving care.

Being an earth sign, Virgos are often adept at earthly activities such as business, building, gardening, knitting, or making and fixing things. They are adept organizers and bookkeepers, and are usually a little finicky, with a love of cleaning things. Sometimes their habits can be overly precise and orderly, and they can have a hard time just letting things be as they are. Virgos may sometimes need to release their need for control.

Virgo is connected to the intestines, and this is an area that can be weak for Virgos. Generally, Virgo is the sign of purity and health, but Virgo's analytical mind can start to gnaw and worry about problems. In turn, this affects their intestines and can make them feel weak and disabled in their digestion. Virgo is also ruled by Mercury, which is linked to the nervous system. It is for this reason that Virgos are sometimes prone to nervousness and anxiety, often due to some part of their lives being out of harmony. To offset these tendencies, Virgos would do well to learn skills to relax their mind and body, as well as allow for some acceptance of the imperfections in life.

Ruling Planet: Mercury

Element: Earth

Modality: Mutable

Physical Rulership: Intestines (nervous system)

Libra

Now we come to the sign of the scales, the sign of balance and relationships. After moving through the sign of discrimination and purification, we come to the sign of merger, the joining of two lovers in harmony. The problem is, it is very difficult to have complete harmony and balance in life. Libras struggle with this and often search for a romantic partnership as a way to meet these challenges and strive for a perfect union. As the sign of partnership, Libras can have difficulty balancing devotion with the need for independence. This push/pull struggle can leave them either excessively demanding and loving or excessively cool and distant. Libra is concerned with balance in all aspects of life, not just romantic love. Finding balance in all our endeavors can be very difficult. One of the major lessons in life for Libra is balancing the needs and requirements of work, family, and creative life while still maintaining good health.

Libra is an air sign, and Libras tend to be sociable and enjoy being part of their community. They are often refined and enjoy the pleasures of life. Because this sign is ruled by Venus, Libras may enjoy aesthetically pleasing surroundings and pleasurable activities such as making art, writing poetry, wearing fine clothes, and making delicious meals with friends. There is sometimes an element of superficiality to Libras that is common to all air signs. Though they possess a fine wit, intelligence, and affability in social settings, they sometimes come across as cool and reserved on a more intimate level.

Libra is linked to the kidneys, the abdomen, and the lower back. The kidneys are easily compromised by too much stress, improper diet, and not enough rest. In Chinese medicine, the kidneys are linked with the emotion of fear. Fear causes the adrenal glands to secrete adrenaline and cause a fight-or-flight reaction. Adrenaline is extremely helpful in dangerous situations, but if it is secreted on a regular basis, it will slowly deplete the kidneys' reserves of strength and will cause premature aging, fatigue, anxiety, and depression. Libras need to learn to balance their ambitions with periods of rest and relaxation so that their kidneys can stay strong and healthy.

Ruling Planet: Venus

Element: Air

Modality: Cardinal

Physical Rulership: Kidneys, lower back, and abdomen

Scorpio

This powerful and intense sign comes after the gentle and refined sign of Libra. Scorpio asks us to go beneath the surface and explore the deep currents of our past and our emotional life. Scorpio has long been associated with transformative activities such as sex, death, and magic. Scorpios seem to be more prone than others to powerful and life-changing experiences. These experiences often cause Scorpios to enter dark and difficult passages. The path of Scorpio is to take in the wisdom from those dark places and come through the other side reborn and renewed, like a phoenix rising from the ashes. Ultimately, the lesson of Scorpio is to come to a place of love and compassion after fully comprehending the heavier and darker emotions of sadness, fear, jealousy, greed, and anger.

Scorpios tend to be magnetic and penetrating. Their power comes from their fixed stability and their knowledge of the wide range of human potential. One of the keys to helping Scorpios unfold is to learn to use and wield power well. Because of their powerful magnetism and strength, they often have the ability to manipulate and dominate others. Their true lesson comes in learning to release their need for control and to share themselves authentically with others. This requires a degree of vulnerability that is hard for Scorpios (and all of us) to develop. Though often shy and reticent, once known, they can become deeply powerful and loyal friends who are capable of intimacy even while remaining totally honest with their expression. Scorpios also tend to get stuck in ruts and are prone to obsessions and addictions. These habits can be their undoing if they are not careful.

Scorpio rules the sexual organs, and there tends to be a mystery about Scorpio's sexuality and their prowess. In actuality, it is because Scorpios have the ability to be so intensely intimate that they have a powerful reach into the soul of a partner. Scorpio also rules over the reproductive organs and the eliminatory organs (colon and rectum). Emotionally, Scorpios need to be able to transform their sexual energy into love, while physically they need to transform the food they eat into waste without becoming constipated.

Ruling Planet: Pluto

Element: Water

Modality: Fixed

Physical Rulership: Sexual and reproductive organs, colon, prostate gland, and rectum

Sagittarius

This fiery sign is noted for its playfulness, exuberance, and extroversion. Sagittarians have a desire to explore life in all of its fullness, sometimes to an excessive degree. These are the travelers, the adventurers, and the partygoers. They like to take a bite out of life and live with joie de vivre. But there is also a quieter side to Sagittarius. They enjoy the philosophical realms and studying the deeper meaning of life through higher education. This is the sign of the guru and the teacher, the one who has traveled far and wide and is able to impart deep wisdom at a later age. Sometimes Sagittarians become so caught up in their travels and explorations that they lose track of the basics in life. Their minds can get so scattered by their many interests that they become ungrounded and may lack a foundation and a center to their lives. They may also become so interested in a life of leisure and having fun that they lose sight of their greater goals. One of the main lessons for Sagittarius to learn is to become centered and focus their energies on single tasks instead of scattering their energies without aim or purpose.

Extroverted Sagittarians are usually expressive, garrulous, and love a good conversation or debate. They can be blunt or exaggerate from time to time and are sometimes insensitive and dictatorial. In general, however, a healthy Sagittarian is warm and friendly, with a love of life that is infectious. They like to live life big, and they are usually willing to pay for the ride for others as well.

Sagittarius rules the liver, the thighs, and the sciatic nerve. The liver can be compromised by an excessive lifestyle that includes too much alcohol, drugs, refined and fatty foods, late-night eating, and not enough rest. Liver toxicity can erupt in the form of bad skin, ulcers, fatigue, and anxiety. In Chinese medicine, the liver is related to the emotion of anger, a fiery feeling. Sagittarians are sometimes prone to this emotion when they get excited and frustrated. For Sagittarians, the greatest health risk comes from their proclivity toward excess. Because they like to exert themselves and take on many different activities, their energy can get used up quickly and they can find themselves depleted and overburdened. They need to balance their exuberance with gentler and more relaxing pursuits.

Ruling Planet: Jupiter

Element: Fire

Modality: Mutable

Physical Rulership: Liver, hips, thighs, and sciatic nerve

Capricorn

This earth sign is ruled by Saturn, a planet known for imposing restrictions and limitations as well as melancholy. But Capricorn is also associated with industriousness, ambition, and direct and sometimes pushy energy. Capricorns tend to want to become successful, to become great in their chosen profession, to "get to the top." On their way up the mountain, however, those with this sign strongly accented in their chart often meet formidable obstacles and have difficulty reaching their goals. Life can become a struggle for Capricorns even though they constantly apply pressure and force to every situation in order to work through their problems. The more force they apply, the harder and more insurmountable the problem can become. It is at these junctures that Capricorns often have a breakdown; they literally come apart and fall down. In order to get on their feet again, they need to lose some of their self-centeredness, some of their "I know what I'm doing," and adopt some humility. They need to bend their knees and surrender to a greater process. Ultimately, this is a spiritual lesson where Capricorns surrender themselves to a higher power. By doing so, Capricorns can then ascend mountains and reach their goals more easily.

Capricorns tend to be somewhat intense, driven, and have a touch of sadness about them. People born under this sign can appear a little cold and aloof, but actually there is a tremendous sensitivity and passion in them. They are powerful influences on a community and can be strong assistants in building businesses, cooperatives, and helping projects thrive. They are usually somewhat reticent, but love their friends intensely and are loyal. They are the leaders and builders in their community and often have a strong will that helps them endure any hardship.

In terms of health, Capricorn is linked to the skin, the bones, the teeth, and especially the knees. Symbolically, the knees are where you bend and kneel when problems become too difficult. The skin, bones, and teeth form the very foundation of the body, and their nourishment is essential to the health of their overall being. When Capricorns are rigid and inflexible, their joints and bones take on these characteristics as well, which can lead to health problems. Capricorns are prone to bouts of melancholy and depression and need good friends who are cheerful to lift them up.

Ruling Planet: Saturn

Element: Earth

Modality: Cardinal

Physical Rulership: Skin, bones, teeth, and knees

Aquarius

People who have this air sign prominent in their chart are often known for their unusual approach to life and their orientation toward the community, even while maintaining a unique vision of their own. This explains the problematic nature of Aquarians, for while they seek company and are usually able socialites, they are also often detached, a little cool and removed. Their rebellious nature helps them be pioneers, freethinkers, and revolutionaries, even though they can also be dogmatic and stubborn in their ideas. These folks are often quirky and will bring an element of spontaneity and surprise into a group setting. They can spark new mindsets and can be truly exciting people to hang out with. Though they are adept at connecting on a social level, it can be harder for them to relate at a feeling level and express themselves emotionally. This can make it difficult for partners who want to be intimate with them. Aquarians are also community builders, and their path is to increase the harmony between all people. Aquarians can have a hard time reconciling their unique and rebellious mindset with their desire to work with groups. One of the main lessons in life for Aquarius is to merge these seemingly contradictory characteristics.

Physically, Aquarius rules the circulation and the ankles, but is also aligned with the nervous system, because its ruling planet, Uranus, is connected to this function. The nervous system is delicate and is easy to deplete and damage. It helps us process all external stimuli as well as our own thoughts and perceptions. Aquarians are more likely to feel overwhelmed from time to time, and this in turn can cause them anxiety, confusion, mania, and depression. The nervous system is especially compromised by electrical activity in the form of computers, televisions, cellular phones, and power lines.

Ruling Planet: Uranus

Element: Air

Modality: Fixed

Physical Rulership: Ankles, circulation, and nervous system

Pisces

This dreamy water sign is associated with imagination, romanticism, idealism, and a love of transcending the mundane experiences of everyday life. This desire for transcendence comes in many ways for Pisceans. For some, it may mean religious and spiritual worship or a love of music, movies, and theater. For others, it may mean a descent into the world of drug or alcohol addiction. Pisceans often have an "old soul" quality about them. Because it is the last sign of the zodiac, there is a sense of Pisces wanting to return back to the beginning point, the source and center of all creation. This spiritual yearning can lead some Pisceans to get lost and confused and forget about the necessities of everyday life. They can become so caught up in the beauty of a flower, the majesty of an operatic aria, or the taste of whiskey that they forget the basic chores and tasks necessary for leading their daily life. Ultimately, the lesson for Pisceans to learn is to channel their essential spiritual nature into selfless service to the community and the world. When they act as conduits of compassionate service, they gain a sense of purpose and grounding that can guide their lives.

Pisceans are known for their soft beauty and their deep, mysterious power. These are the monks, the musicians, the lovers, and the drunkards. Because Pisces is a water sign, they tend to feel things on a deep and core level. If they are strong, they can translate this gift into compassion, empathy, and artistic expression. If they become weakened, this intense sensitivity can become debilitating, and they can become prone to emotional disorders, confusion, fatigue, and depression. Pisceans are good mimics and channelers. They are strongly affected by the people around them, and it is smart for Pisceans to pick good, healthy friends to augment and strengthen them.

Physically, Pisces is linked to the feet and the immune system. The immune system is our primary defense mechanism against disease and illness. In Pisceans, the immune system can be depleted by both physical and emotionally toxic situations. When Pisceans keep company with primarily negative and cynical people, it can have a harmful impact on their immune system, which in turn will cause them to fall sick more often. Pisceans are primarily emotional and sensory-oriented people. A good home atmosphere and loving people around them will go far to ensure the health of a Pisces. Pisceans also do well with frequent periods of rest and isolation to avoid outside stimuli and to recharge their batteries. Pisceans also need an outlet for their creative and imaginative side. By drawing on the wellspring of their unconscious through artistic mediums, Pisceans can release emotions and feelings that may be deeply buried. By doing this, intense energy can be expressed instead of remaining in the body and causing disease and illness.

Ruling Planet: Neptune

Element: Water

Modality: Mutable

Physical Rulership: Feet and immune system

---

1. Michael Theroux and Brian Butler, eds., *The Astrological Body Types: Face, Form and Expression*, illustr. Judith A. Hill (Bayside, CA: Borderland Sciences Research Foundation, 1993) 169.

2. Ariel Guttman and Kenneth Johnson, *Mythic Astrology: Archetypal Powers of the Horoscope* (St. Paul, MN: Llewellyn Publications, 1993) 183.

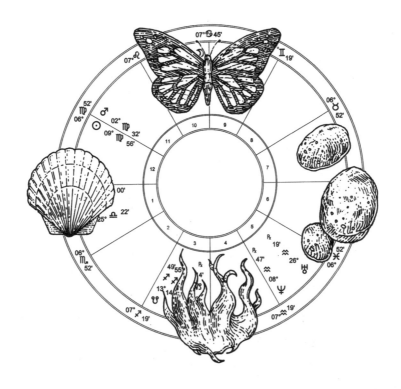

Part 2

Foundations of Practice

5

Groundwork: Ritual and the Cycles of the Moon and the Seasons

Dating back to the last Ice Age and long before modern civilizations flourished, prehistoric man carved notches on the bones of reindeer and the tusks of mammoths to represent the phases of the moon. It is hard to imagine the awe and reverence these early people undoubtedly had for the heavens and its cycles. Shamanic and animistic rites and rituals were performed in concordance with the movements of the stars. Although we know little of these early ceremonies, we know that they formed the basis of religious philosophies that developed after them.

As civilizations grew and developed throughout the world, observatories and temples were built to study the stars and to conduct ritual work associated with the heavens. In Mesopotamia, structures as tall as 270 feet high, known as ziggurats, were built to observe the stars. In southern England, the famous monument known as Stonehenge was built in part to observe the equinoxes and solstices as well as to provide a setting for carrying out religious rituals.

In Babylon and Egypt, religious ceremonies were held at fixed times when the planets moved into a certain alignment. The ceremonies were presided over by priests whose knowledge of astrology enabled them to understand the planetary configurations. Rituals were often carried out to bring successful outcomes in battle, or to protect rulers and chieftains against possible harm. Many such ceremonies involved animal sacrifice and sometimes even human sacrifice.

In most cultures, the stars, the sun, and the moon were worshiped as powerful deities, each carrying individual characteristics and attributes. In Egyptian cosmology, when the stars and the sun set over the horizon, they descended into the underworld and were born again each day when the sun rose. In Babylon, the planet Venus was known as Ishtar, the mistress and goddess of vegetation during the growth season. In Greece, the planet Mercury was known as Hermes, the winged messenger.

For ancient peoples, astrology helped them understand and determine the will of the gods. Rites and rituals could be performed to appease these gods according to the most judicious moment as seen in the stars. If a Roman soldier was going to war, he could express allegiance and prayers to the war god Mars. Done at the right time, this soldier would believe that he was gaining the favor of Mars and could perform more bravely and heroically in battle. To this day in India, an entire sect of priests known as Brahmins memorize complex Sanskrit odes to offset or mitigate the negative influences of planets/gods like Saturn and Mars or to draw forth the positive influences of planets/gods like Venus and Jupiter.

Over time, astrologically oriented religious ceremonies fell out of favor in the West as Christianity became the dominant model for worship. Appeasing the gods and pagan rites and rituals based on astrology were seen as blasphemous and heretical in the eyes of God. These forms of worship continued, however, in secret and in underground societies throughout Europe. Common folk kept the ancient pagan holidays and incorporated them into their worship of Christianity. Easter egg hunting, dressing up for Halloween, and celebrating Christmas near the winter solstice are all based on the ancient pagan practice of honoring the seasons and honoring our place in the cycles of the universe.

Today we are revisiting the idea of performing astrological and seasonal rituals as a way of connecting ourselves to nature and the universe. For many of us in the modern world, we live in a twenty-four-hours-a-day, always-open, nonstop society where business goes on no matter what season or time of day it is. We work behind computer terminals in closed buildings with fluorescent lights, and shop at stores where we can get anything we want all year round. Because of these modern "advancements," we have slowly and subtly lost some of our connection to the basic rhythms of the earth. Seasonal and lunar rituals are ways of rediscovering our place in the web of creation, of re-attuning ourselves to the natural cycles of life.

Practicing regular seasonal and lunar ritual work helps us form a foundation for any four element healing work we may do. Because the four elements are based on the seasons, we have a chance to honor the elements throughout the year. Honoring the elements is a powerful way of establishing ourselves as a part of nature. When we use herbs and stones, and work with animals, we can see ourselves as part of a united, natural framework. Ritual work helps lay the foundation for using four element medicine and helps nourish our spirit at a core level.

Preparing for Ritual

The first thing to do before beginning ritual work is to clean the space. All clutter and garbage should be removed so that the space feels quiet and tidy. This preliminary cleaning helps remove any unwanted energy, both physical and emotional, that has been dormant in the area. If you are inside, open up the windows to allow fresh air to come in. Sweep the place with a broom so the space feels fresh and alive. Burn some sage or incense to purify the space of negative influences and to enliven the energy for sacred ritual. This initial work is highly important, for it lays the groundwork for later spiritual work to take place.

Preparing the Altar

Once you are prepared, you can start with the core of the ritual practice—honoring the four elements. Each element has a number of correspondences and can be honored by creating an altar. First, divide the altar up into four directions (use a compass if you need to) and designate the elements along with the directions. Then begin by gathering sacred objects that signify the element to you. For some people, it may mean placing feathers and flutes in the east for the air element; for others, it may mean placing an image of Buddha meditating and a picture of a raven there. In later chapters, I list the corresponding element for each animal, bird, stone, herb, and food. I also give some corresponding ritual objects in the following table. Take the time to find what you are most connected to and place those objects in the appropriate place on the altar. After you've finished making the altar, each direction should have a number of sacred objects that signify each particular element.

Elemental Correspondences

Earth   *Season:* Winter

Time of Day: Midnight

Holidays: Yule (winter solstice) and Imbolc

Direction: North

Signs: Taurus, Virgo, Capricorn

Planets: Venus, Saturn

Colors: Brown, green

Physical Correspondences: Stomach, spleen, intestines, bones, teeth, skin

Ritual Objects: Stones, salt, drums, animal fur and figurines, plants

Associations: Work, food, nourishment, path, grounding, center, money, gardens and crops, stability

Air   *Season:* Spring

Time of Day: Dawn

Holidays: Ostara (spring equinox) and Beltane

Direction: East

Signs: Gemini, Libra, Aquarius

Planets: Mercury, Uranus

Colors: Yellow, sky blue, white

Physical Correspondences: Nervous system, lungs

Ritual Objects: Feathers, knives, athame, bells, wind instruments (flutes)

Associations: Vision, sight, communication, language, thought, breath

Fire   *Season:* Summer

Time of Day: Noon

Holidays: Midsummer (summer solstice) and Lughnasadh

Direction: South

Signs: Aries, Leo, Sagittarius

Planets: Sun, Mars, Jupiter

Colors: Red, bright yellow, gold

Physical Correspondences: Heart, blood, liver, circulation

Ritual Objects: Wand, candles, pipes, incense, burning pot

Associations: Playfulness, passion, sex, self-expression, creativity, dance, joy, laughter, spark of life

Water *Season:* Fall

Time of Day: Dusk

Holidays: Mabon (fall equinox) and Samhain

Direction: West

Signs: Cancer, Scorpio, Pisces

Planets: Moon, Neptune, Pluto

Colors: Blue, blue-green, silver

Physical Correspondences: Lymph glands, fluids in the body besides blood, immune system, urinary and reproductive systems

Ritual Objects: Bowls, water, cups, cauldrons, shells, silver (Moon)

Associations: Dreams, intuition, imagination, psychic work, trance, death, love, emotions, intensity, transformation

At this point, participants in the ritual should ready themselves by going into a meditative space. This can be done by playing quiet music, gently singing, chanting, or meditating. This helps clear the mind of mental clutter and prepares you for ritual work. Some thought should go into what the purpose of the ritual is and how you will proceed. I prefer to leave some spontaneity in my rituals and allow them to unfold with only a bare outline. The more rigid I make them, the more they seem to lose some of their magic. Some of the best rituals I have performed have happened spontaneously while I was out in the woods with some friends.

Casting the Circle

Now that the space has been cleansed, your altar has been created, and you are in a meditative space, you can then begin the ritual by "casting the circle." Casting the circle is a way of securing the space you have created and warding off any negative or undue influences. It further draws you out of the world of the mundane and into the world of the witch and the shaman. Casting the circle is quite simple. Simply stand a few feet away from the altar (often in the eastern direction) and draw a circle around the altar by walking around it. You can use a wand, a ceremonial knife (athame), or just your fingers to do this. Visualize a stream of energy coming out and creating a wall of white or blue energy around your ritual space. At this point you are "between the worlds," ready to honor the elements.

Honoring the Elements

It is at this point that you can "call the quarters," specifically thanking and honoring each sector of your altar. Remember that each sector is a physical representation of the seasons, certain emotions, qualities, and perceptions. When you call the quarters, you are reminding yourself of your place in the fabric of the seasons, the time of year it is, the phase of the moon, and your relationship to the natural world. This is a time to ground, honor, and give thanks. The element of earth may be especially powerful for you at a certain time because it is the winter, or because you are working with issues around nutrition and diet. Or the fire element may be especially poignant because you are taking dance classes, or have just felt the spark of falling in love. This is a time to honor the elements and personalize them, to see how they relate to your everyday life. When you see the connections, you may start to see the deeper wisdom of the elements, the deeper relationship of them to your life and path. If you are not by yourself, take turns honoring the elements, or pick specific people to give thanks to each quarter.

Thanks and Prayers to Spirit

After honoring the elements, it is now time to go a little deeper into the ritual work. I begin by giving thanks and prayers to the central Source, the Great Spirit. I also like to honor the twin aspects of this divinity in the form of the God and the Goddess. The God and the Goddess represent the masculine and feminine energies and have been worshiped in many forms. The God has been worshiped as Lugh in Ireland, Shiva in India, Oluksak in Inuit culture, and Ogun in West Africa. The Goddess has been worshiped as Kuan Yin in China, Mother Mary by certain Catholics especially in Latin America, Kali in India, and Yemaya in West Africa. These are just a few of their names. Though it can be helpful to call on a specific god or goddess, it is important to understand the significance and attributes of any deity you call in. It is not necessary to mention any specific names, but to just have an idea of how the archetypal feminine and masculine images impact your life, what they mean to you, and how they help you be strong and thrive. One way to do this is to honor the masculine and feminine expressions in your own life. This may mean mentioning and honoring a grandmother who has passed away. You could also describe a beautiful river or a mountain you are connected to. In this way, you are calling in the divine expression of the male and female that is close by and personal.

When to Do Ritual

Rituals can be conducted at any time of the year, but they are especially powerful during New and Full Moons and during one of the eight sabbats during the year. The sabbats, or holy days, include the solstices and equinoxes and the four midpoints in between. These are points during the year when the focus of energy in the skies is particularly potent. I liken this to watching the sun set or rise. It is a particularly magical and entrancing time of the day, when the energy of the world seems quieter and more pregnant with power.

This is a good time to honor the particular time of year it is. You may be carrying out your ritual under a Full Moon in Capricorn, a New Moon in Aries, or during the winter solstice. Whenever it may be, you can work with the particular energies that are happening at that time. Each point of the year has a different set of correspondences and a different kind of power associated with it. By knowing these different associations, you can channel your work accordingly. One way to work with the different sabbats is by acknowledging the sign the Moon is in and the ruling planet of that sign. For example, you may be experiencing health problems with your blood. It may contain toxins you want to release. You can amplify any healing ritual or spell you make concerning your issues by choosing to carry out a ritual under an Aries Moon, or at least when the Moon is in a fire sign.

Planetary Correspondences

Sun   *Element:* Fire

Sign Ruler: Leo

Physical Correspondences: Heart, eyes

Associations: Ego, self-expression, strength, purification, play, dance, logic, left brain, conscious-mind identity, protection, purpose, father

Moon   *Element:* Water

Sign Ruler: Cancer

Physical Correspondences: Hormonal, menstrual cycles, fertility, digestion, breasts

Associations: Emotions, receptivity, cycles, creativity, mystery, nighttime, occult, subconscious, nourishment, mother

Mercury   *Element:* Air

Sign Rulers: Gemini, Virgo

Physical Correspondence: Nervous system

Associations: Intelligence, cleverness, wit, short travel, communication, messages

Venus   *Element:* Earth

Sign Rulers: Taurus, Libra

Physical Correspondences: Kidneys, throat, blood-sugar balancing, weight

Associations: Love, romance, beauty, wealth, prosperity, sensuality, artistic expression, fertility, clothing, jewelry, adornments, yin

Mars

Element: Fire

Sign Ruler: Aries

Physical Correspondences: Blood, muscles, adrenals

Associations: Power, strength, direction, purpose, assertiveness, aggression, anger, lust, ambition, yang

Jupiter

Element: Fire

Sign Ruler: Sagittarius

Physical Correspondences: Liver, sciatic nerve

Associations: Royalty, generosity, philosophy, higher education, long travel, luck, beneficence, expansiveness

Saturn

Element: Earth

Sign Ruler: Capricorn

Physical Correspondences: Skin, bones, teeth

Associations: Contraction, limitation, reservation, fear, grounding, shaping form, endurance, perseverance, loyalty, wisdom, solidity, lasting structure

Uranus

Element: Air

Sign Ruler: Aquarius

Physical Correspondence: Nervous system

Associations: Electricity, technology, eclectic, unusual, progressive, unique, rebellious, revolutionary

Neptune

Element: Water

Sign Ruler: Pisces

Physical Correspondences: Immune system, water balance

Associations: Imagination, dreams, psychic work, the sea, compassion, service, transcendence, music, drugs and alcohol, movies, theater

Pluto   *Element:* Water

Sign Ruler: Scorpio

Physical Correspondences: Eliminatory and sexual organs, prostate

Associations: Intensity, sex, death/rebirth, transformation, power, underworld, hidden secrets, penetrating, dark

Sabbats—The Holy Days

In all cultures throughout the world, holidays (holy days) are celebrated throughout the year for religious and secular reasons. For thousands of years, certain days have been noted as being especially important for conducting ceremony and ritual. In the four element tradition, these holy days are known as sabbats. There are eight sabbats, each divided by a little over six weeks between them. There are two equinoxes, two solstices, and four cross-quarter points. These sabbats have a long and rich history throughout the world. In Edain McCoy's book *The Sabbats*, she writes:

> *"It is estimated that the Sabbats have been observed in various places and in various forms for at least 12,000 years."*[1]

The sabbats were initially accorded importance primarily because of their significance in relation to agriculture and hunting. As nomadic tribes began to settle down, the sabbats took on greater religious and ceremonial importance. The word sabbat comes from the Babylonian word *sabbatu*, meaning "heart-rest." Ultimately, these holy days have been seen as times to relax and enjoy festivities with the community. They have been times to honor the gods and goddesses of each individual society.

Today when we honor the sabbats, we can see them as part of the Wheel of the Year, each holiday significant in a seasonal, emotional, and spiritual way. The sabbats link us to the natural world. When we gather holly and pine trees for the winter solstice, carve pumpkins for Samhain, or go Easter egg hunting at the spring solstice, we honor the ancient traditions of our ancestors and the experience of the environment around us. We integrate our human existence with the warp and weft of nature. Each sabbat also evokes emotional reactions and experiences. The smell of spiced apple cider can return us to thoughts of childhood, the family, and the warmth of a fire on a cold, snowy day. A traditional Maypole dance at Beltane reminds us of fertility and our sensual and sexual energy. Dressing up at Halloween reminds us of the world of spirits and our ancestors. This may be a time of grief or cherished memories.

When we honor the turn of the year, we ground ourselves in the four elements of the natural world as well as the four elements that constitute our health and well-being. By honoring and celebrating these times, we grow closer to the environment and can assist our own process of growth and healing. The sabbats are times to grow closer to the community, and renew, transform, strengthen, and nourish ourselves.

The Seasons and the Sabbats

Winter

Winter is associated with the the earth element and the direction north. The winter is a good time to come into contact with the silence that lies across the land. Deciduous trees are bare, the summer birds are gone, and seeds lie dormant, ready to unfurl in the springtime. This is a quiet and meditative time, a time to rest and hibernate, to sleep and dream more. The earth element is related to our foundations. This is a good time to learn skills of silence, conservation, mindfulness, and endurance.

During this powerful time, you may experience fear and depression. The weather can turn cold, the rains are stronger, and the wind blows harder. For our ancestors, the winter was a difficult time of waiting and surviving. But it is also a time to turn inward and strengthen our roots. If we have been living superficially and been putting down only shallow roots, then the winter can be difficult and may ask you to go inward and take a closer look at how you are living life. The earth element asks you to create a steady foundation, a strong platform from which to grow when the spring arrives. This may mean weeding out difficult emotions and exploring the darker feelings you may have.

Now is the time to work with your earth totems, to realign yourself with your path, your ground, your diet, your body, the physical tools you work with, and the money you are making. Now is the time to eat hardy, warm meals and to keep strong by being physically active, meditating, working with rocks and bones, and fixing your house up, shoring up the foundation.

Yule

In the Northern Hemisphere, the winter solstice sabbat falls near the traditional Christian holiday of Christmas, near December 21. Christians celebrate this day as the birth of Christ, but in actuality, this day was borrowed from ancient societies who celebrated the solstice. The significance of the two holidays merge as well. The birth of the son (Jesus) is related to the return and birth of the sun, as the days prepare to grow longer and the light to become stronger at this darkest point of the year. In Celtic tradition, the God dies six weeks prior at Samhain and then is reborn at Yule time. Death and rebirth are also concepts that were borrowed by Christian mythology. This is a time of celebration, when light conquers the dark and there is renewal and hope.

The "return of the light" has been heralded by traditional societies with many different customs. Placing lights (originally candles) on Christmas trees and houses is a way of luring the sun back so that the light may wax again. The evergreen tree is a symbol of everlasting life. Making wreaths by gathering evergreen boughs and cones creates a wonderful, aromatic decoration that also signifies the circular nature of time. "Jingle" bells were traditionally meant to drive away the darkness and the evil spirits associated with them.

Imbolc

Imbolc is the midpoint sabbat between the winter solstice and spring equinox and falls in the time of Aquarius, around February 2. Groundhog Day is the modern

Ericka

What's up Cuz

How R u doing? Fine I hope and

in the best of Health, Tell reka I said

What's up and I Love her O.K. It's

2 letter's in her, They name's are on them,

I put 2 stamps in here just get the enuoples

please and send them off O.K. Thank u very

much and thanks 4 being there 4 my MOM

Love U always Cuz onion.

This is they info and u can use ur address
for a return address please O.K.

Tiffany Elkins   Valencia Williams
20110885130 unit 03 B 381   201909097 unit 04 A 322
P.O Box 089002   P.O Box 089002
Chicago, IL 60608   Chicago, IL 60608
          Divison 4   Divison 4

          O.K. Thanks

equivalent, where a groundhog is watched when he comes out of his hole. If he sees his shadow, then spring will come early; if he does not, then there will be six more weeks of winter. In Europe, the Celts celebrated Imbolc by honoring the goddess Brigid, the waiting bride for the Sun God. Brigid has been associated with healing, poetry, creativity, and fiery activities like metal-smithing. Imbolc is truly in the dead of winter, and for many peoples, the weather is cold and intense. Brigid is a symbol of fire and the light returning to the earth.

This is a good time to honor the returning light by celebrating the creative and fiery side of our nature. When we make fires, light candles, sing songs, and write poetry, we are making sympathetic magic to bring back the sun. This is a good time to initiate and release. If you want to make a commitment, choose this time to start the process. If you have old, negative feelings that you have stored through the winter, write them down on paper and burn them in the fire or with a candle.

Spring

Spring is associated with the element of air and the direction east. It is a time of new beginnings, new visions, and new paths. We can see the small shoots of ferns, the blooms from violets and Indian plum in the early days of spring, and then a roaring, rushing cavalcade of greenery and lush plant life that follows throughout these months. This vibrant, fresh time teaches us about the possibility of renewal, suggesting that all of us can enjoy resurrection from difficult times. This is a time to take walks through the woods and smell the fresh air and scent of the trees. The aroma of the land gives vitality and nourishment.

Air is related to eyesight, vision, and setting intention. Like an eagle high above on its perch, it uses its powerful eyes to gather information and make decisions. When it spies its prey, it descends rapidly and effortlessly aims for its goal. This precision and clarity is something that is available to us during the spring. Air is also related to our words and thoughts. When we weave our language to affirm, honor, celebrate, and pray, we can direct our intent like an eagle aims for its prey. Our words are powerful and have the effect of tearing ourselves and others down, or of strengthening and nourishing ourselves and others. In Buddhist thought, one of the precepts for a good life is right speech. When our words are true and come from the heart, we are strengthening our own internal air element.

This time of profound growth and renewal is a good time for cleansing fasts, removing toxins from our system, and allowing for our health to get stronger. This is also a time to get in touch with our air friends, the birds. Work with feathers this time of year and take the time to go bird watching. These creatures have a lot to teach us when we watch and listen.

Ostara

The spring equinox, or Ostara, coincides with the beginning of the astrological wheel and the first degree of Aries, around March 21. The light and dark are now equally balanced, and this is the initiating point of the zodiac, signifying the start of a new cycle. The winter is now over, and there is joyous celebration as the spring plants begin to come out again. Ostara was the German name of the virgin Goddess in ancient times. One of the most famous symbols of Ostara is the egg. The egg is a symbol for the seed of creation, the potential in all of us. Easter egg hunts are simply a ritual of searching for the lost inner self and returning to wholeness and light. From Ostara, we get Easter, the Christian holiday of resurrection. In this story, Christ is crucified on the cross and then returns to life three days later. This is very similar to earlier pagan stories of deities returning from the Land of the Dead to be reborn again at springtime.

One of the most famous stories relating to this time of year is that of Persephone, who was abducted by Pluto and taken to the underworld. Her mother, Demeter, the goddess of nature and the harvest, searched for her child and mourned her absence. While her daughter was gone, Demeter forbade the earth to bear fruit and froze the land into an eternal winter. When it seemed that everyone would perish because of Demeter's sorrow, Zeus sent the messenger god Hermes (Mercury) down to the underworld to bargain for Persephone's release. Finally, Persephone returned to the earth, but only after a compromise had been reached. She had to spend three months (the winter) every year in the lower world with Pluto and could have the other nine months above.

During this time, you may want to think about the theme of death and rebirth yourself, the concept of resurrection. If you have had a difficult winter and explored many dark and heavy emotions, now is the time to release the stagnancy of the cold season, shake it off, and be reborn again. Clean your house and your altar, breathe fresh life and light into your bedroom, and open yourself up to the fresh, new spring.

Beltane

At the midpoint between the spring equinox and the summer solstice is the holiday of Beltane, around May 1. Also known as May Day, this sabbat signifies the holy merger of the God and the Goddess and is often honored with fertility rituals and Maypole dances. The Maypole is a symbol of the male phallus and is planted deeply into the earth, the symbol of female sexuality. Brightly colored ribbons are then gathered by a group of dancers circling the Maypole, and their dance weaves the cloth into an intricate and beautiful web around the pole.

This is often a time of joyous revelry, merrymaking, and feasting. The sexual union of the God and the Goddess is often literally enacted by lovers at this time, and the energy of the union helps strengthen the crops for the coming year. If you have a partner, you can use this time to rekindle your romantic attraction to each other, to stoke the fires of your passion. Lovemaking can help strengthen and deepen your relationship.

Traditionally, a giant bonfire was built to honor the holiday. Wood from the fire was often used to purify and bless households. Smudging with sage, cedar, and pine can also be used to bring health to the home. You can use this time to release old, negative, toxic emotions and strengthen your living and working spaces to make them more vital and alive. Houses and homes can become deadened and heavy just as much as living organisms. It is our job to help keep our homes strong and energetically nourishing.

Summer

Summer is associated with the fire element and the direction south. This is a time of buoyant, expressive energy when we can spend long hours outside, enjoying the warm and sunny weather. This is a wonderful time to go camping, hiking, fishing, and traveling. This is also a good time to explore our creativity through dance, art, and music. We are vital, beautiful expressions of the original drop of light from the sun. Now is the time to direct and express that bright spark.

Fire also is related to our passionate and sexual energies. Because we are often more extroverted at this time of year, the summer can be a time of romance and connection. We feel more attractions and our libidos may be stronger. Our sense of sexuality is often damaged in our culture by magazine and television ads that tell us what we should look like. Our modern-day association with thinness has created legions of people unhappy with the shape of their bodies. In truth, our vitality and beauty come from the spark in our eyes, our passion for life, how we treat our bodies and souls, and how we laugh, love, and glow. The summer can be a wonderful time to come back into contact with our essential self—the beautiful, divine, and sexy creatures that we are. When we are bold and express ourselves from the heart, our radiance shines brightly.

Midsummer

The sun reaches its peak of power at the summer solstice, around June 22. The sunlight now starts to wane and the days begin to grow shorter. This holy day has been venerated by most cultures as a day of celebration and ritual. Because the sun is at its peak during this time, Midsummer is often devoted to celebrating the sun and the fire element. In Celtic tradition, tribes would "light balefires all over the lands from sunset the night before Midsummer until sunset the next day."[2] This has also traditionally been a time to bless the crops for the first harvest at the next holiday of Lughnasadh.

With the sun so powerful, now is the time to honor the fullest expression of our own light by being creative, dynamic, sexual, playful, and expressive. Now is the time to honor our rich, radiant selves by dancing, making music, and celebrating life to the fullest. The fiery sun is related to our own beating and pulsating heart, and this is a good time to be active, raise our heartbeat, and walk out under the sun's healing rays. The heart is connected with the emotions of joy, elation, and love. Ultimately, this time is perfect for turning on our heart's ability to emote and express love. Now is a good time to raise our energy through rituals of ecstasy, such as dancing and making love, to generate heart warmth and to honor this powerfully solar time.

Lughnasadh

This holy day falls during one of the hottest parts of the summer in the Northern Hemisphere in the sign of Leo, around August 1. This is the midpoint between the summer solstice and the fall equinox and has traditionally been seen as a first-harvest holy day. Lughnasadh refers to the ancient Celtic sun god Lugh. In the Northern Hemisphere, many crops such as wheat, barley, and corn were ready to be reaped from the fields, and this was a time of feasting and celebrating the fertility of the crops. Although there is fertility and abundance, it is also a time when the sun represented by the God is waning in power and the first hints of fall come across the land.

Harvest time is a time to show gratitude for abundance and to celebrate our connection to the land. It is a time to give thanks for all the bounteous riches of the earth and to explore our relationship with food and sharing. We often have so many issues about our diet, how much we eat and how others eat, that we can lose track of the enjoyment of a meal. This is a time to sumptuously enjoy the pleasure of the grain and the corn from the harvest, to celebrate the earth by truly enjoying each morsel with thanks and praise.

Fall

Fall is associated with the water element and the direction west. This is a time for deep inner work and transformation. The Chinese associate the fall with the emotion of grief. There is a sense of loss and letting go at this time of year. There is often tremendous beauty in the changing leaves of the trees that reminds us of the glory of a fading sunset. This is a powerful and magical time when we can deepen our wisdom and our sense of inner beauty, when we can explore the deeper, dark mysteries and occult wisdom. Fall is associated with dying and death and is a good time to work with these themes and to honor our ancestors who have passed before us.

Water is the element associated with emotion. This is an introverted time after the dynamism of the summer, and there may be more intense feelings this time of year. Our modern world sometimes does not honor dark and intense emotions and seeks to shut them off with television, long work hours, and drugs and alcohol. But heavier emotions like depression and sadness are just as necessary to the human experience as joy and love. Sometimes it is important to delve into these feelings to explore their roots. Often they can tell us about our past, the way we live and see life, and how we are treating ourselves. Looked at with compassion, dark emotions can be teaching and nourishing tools to help us grow and shed the parts of us that are no longer necessary, like a snake sheds its skin.

This is also a time of preparation for the cold and dark of winter. We may need to stock up on provisions, shore up the house for winter storms, and be quieter and less extroverted to protect our health. This is a time to take baths, talk with friends by candlelight, and go to bed earlier to ensure plenty of rest. Though we may be feeling intense emotions, it is important not to let them become more extreme than they need be by nourishing ourselves optimally. Home-baked bread, warm soups, casseroles, and healing herbal tea will help us relax into the present moment and let go of stress and disease.

Mabon

At the time of the fall equinox, around September 22, the day divides into equal parts of light and dark. In the next twelve weeks, the light will wane to its lowest level in the Northern Hemisphere. This is the second of the harvest sabbats and is again a time to honor the abundance of food with feasting, dancing, and celebration. At this time of the year, there are more berries and fruits that are ready to be eaten. One of the most famous symbols of Mabon is the horn of plenty. In this symbol, a large horn is filled to overflowing with the bounties from the harvest. The horn represents the masculine energies and the harvest represent the riches of the Mother.

This is also a time to recognize that there is growing darkness across the land and we are at the balance point tipping over toward winter. Mabon helps us remember that life is always in balance, that there is always an equal and opposite force to our actions. Many religious texts describe this natural law. In Vedic texts, it is explained as the Law of Karma. The Bible describes it as "You reap what you sow," or "Do unto others as you would have them do unto you." Mabon is the start of the sign of Libra, the sign associated with balance and equilibrium. This is a good time to look at our priorities and how we organize our lives. If we have been giving too much energy to our work at the expense of our family life, we may want to tip the scales, or vice versa.

Samhain

Also known as Halloween, this holy day is celebrated in the time of Scorpio, around October 31, and is often called the "Witch's New Year." In Celtic tradition, the Sun God dies at this time, marking the end of the year before rising again at Yule. Samhain is traditionally seen as a time when the "veil between the worlds lifts," and there is much intersection between the world of spirits and the world of humans. Because of this, there is a sense of deep mystery and power surrounding this ritual time. Halloween is often associated with images of ghosts and skeletons, witches and magic.

Samhain is a powerful time to honor our ancestors and to connect with the past. Creating an altar that contains pictures of family members who have passed away, or making art or writing a poem that commemorates those who are no longer here are beautiful ways of honoring this sabbat. By drawing on our past, we see ourselves as part of a vast continuum of which we are but a small part. Our nature and characteristics have been forged by the people before us, and it is important to understand both the positive and negative aspects of that history. For many of us, there is a tremendous amount of suffering and pain that has come before us, and part of this time could be devoted to drawing that forth and shedding light on it. Slavery, the Indian wars, and the Holocaust are all part of our collective past, and these atrocities need to be remembered and acknowledged so that they will not happen again. Samhain is associated with the death of light in Celtic tradition, and often this is a time of grief and mourning. Grief allows us to cleanse our souls and see the world more clearly. Sadness and tears are appropriate responses to the pain we have inflicted on our environment and the people around us.

On another level, Samhain is also a time of magic and sorcery, a time for delving deeper into the mysteries of life. This is a wonderful time to practice magic and to increase our psychic skills. Samhain offers us a doorway into the unseen worlds, and rituals performed at this time can be particularly potent. Because the veil between the worlds is thin, we can shapeshift and contact spirits more easily. It is important to be careful around this time, and to avoid doing work that is more powerful than we can handle.

In modern times, Samhain is now celebrated as Halloween. When we dress up for Halloween, we honor the different archetypes in our consciousness and can access a different framework. As a child, I fondly remember dressing up as Batman, a robber, Charlie Chaplin, and a mouse for Halloween. Half of the fun came in dressing up, the other half in getting the candy from the neighbors' homes. For one time in the year, we were allowed to be someone we were not, to take on a role and play a part. We could be sweet angels, rock stars, or the most villainous and evil monsters. For a few moments, we could be someone we could never be in real life. We could literally change our identities.

As we grow older, we wear the costumes and disguises less and less and our personalities begin to become more established and defined. All the goblins, wizards, and clowns become internalized as we try to play a role that is safe and likeable in the world. This lunation is a good time to play with some of those characters nestled deep in our psyche and bring them to light. When we see ourselves as multidimensional people, we broaden our experience to include a wider panorama of possibilities. Perhaps there is a monster inside of us that needs to say something. Perhaps there is a famous movie star inside of us who needs some attention and laughter. As we play with roles, we acknowledge our shadow selves and lift the veil between the mundane world and the world of fantasy, imagination, and possibility.

The Esbats—Lunar Rituals

Besides the eight major sabbats that are celebrated each year, there are thirteen Full Moons that traditionally have been celebrated as well. These are known as esbats, or times for lunar ritual. Traditionally, sabbats were times when major community events would take place, while esbats were times when small groups of people would gather to perform healing and magical rites.

Though esbats are specifically associated with Full Moons, rituals can take place at any time of the month. New Moons are associated with times of death, beginning, and renewal. Waxing Moons are associated with strengthening, nourishing, and building energy of some sort. This would be a wonderful time to help someone who is frail or weak build and gain health. Full Moons are times of fruition, when there is a great deal of energy on the planet. This makes them the perfect occasion to conduct many rituals, cast spells, empower tools, herbs, stones, and make magic. Waning Moons are a good time to let go and to banish negative energy, such as losing weight or quitting addictions and bad habits.

In the next section, I will discuss the power of the Moon in all the signs of the zodiac. It is especially powerful to carry out a regular ritual during the Full Moon in each of the signs once a month, but it may also be important to perform a ritual during the month when the Moon is not full. I will also discuss additional ways to make use of the Moon cycles for healing and developing strength and wisdom.

Lunar Ritual and the Phases of the Moon

New Moon   Initiating, beginnings, setting down intentions, new plans and practices

Waxing Moon   Building energy, developing strength and health, increasing money

Full Moon   Fruition, expression, practicing magic, empowering tools

Waning Moon   Releasing, banishing, losing weight, letting go of bad addictions and habits

Aries Moon

The Moon in Aries is a time to initiate, lead, and direct energy toward an intended goal. Now is a good time to invoke warrior energy and develop courage, strength, and will. Ruled by Mars, this Moon is a good time to work with anger and frustration. Unexpressed anger can become damaging and destructive to the community around you as well as to yourself, so use this time to release and vent anger. It is also a good time to do ritual work on the Aries/Libra axis. Themes of personal needs/security balanced with shared needs and responsibilities can be addressed during this Moon time.

In terms of health, Aries is connected to physical vigor and energy. Now is the time to renew and strengthen vitality as well as burn out toxins and strengthen the adrenal system. Repressed anger can damage the liver, so it may be wise to perform ritual work connected with healing the liver and gall bladder functions as well.

For ceremonial work, use red cloth, red candles, and basil and clove essential oils for invigorating and stimulating energy. If you can conduct the ritual outside, try to light a fire to symbolize Aries' relationship to the fire element.

Taurus Moon

This is a wonderful time to relax, center, and take time for pleasurable sensual activities. Try taking a bath or getting a massage before any ritual to help put you in a Taurean mindframe. This is a good time to ground yourself and get in touch with your body. If you have been moving fast and it has been difficult for you to slow down, call on the energies of the Taurus Moon to release your impatience and anxiety. This is a good Moon for working on issues of your body image and weight, your physical and inner beauty, your self-worth, and your relationship to money, savings, and wealth. This is also a powerful time to simplify and clarify what things are valuable and important in your life. If you can, utilize the Taurean connection to the throat and sing for a portion of the ritual. Allow the singing to help build and release energy.

In terms of health, this is a good time to work on healing nervousness, strengthening your inner stability and strength, and nourishing your throat, your thyroid glands, and your sexuality. You can also work on blood-sugar imbalances or try to lose or gain weight if you need to.

For this ritual, light green candles and gather Venusian figurines, plants, and rocks to symbolize the earth element. Music, flowers, and food also symbolize the sign of Taurus. Rose oil is wonderful for strengthening love bonds and stimulating the heart chakra. Ylang ylang stimulates sensual and sexual energies, and lilac is a lovely aromatic oil for increasing beauty, harmony, and gentle qualities in a ritual.

Gemini Moon

The Moon in Gemini is a good time to work with themes of communication, connection, and social relations. Ruled by Mercury, Gemini is connected to our speech, our thoughts, and how we use our language. If you have been overly critical and negative with your words, you may want to use this ritual time to re-center yourself and be more mindful of what you say. Words are at the core of ritual, magic, and prayer. This is a good time to develop verbal skills through writing in a journal, making blessings, and reciting poetry or telling stories. This is also the sign of the messenger, and you can take a look at what your essential and divine message in life is and seek to cultivate that message to its utmost.

In terms of health, you may want to take this time to perform healing work for the lungs, the nervous system, and the arms and hands. It is also a good time for breath work in the form of meditation, tai chi, or yoga. By drawing in good oxygen, you can vitalize your entire system and strengthen your nerves as well. This is also a good time to chant, write poetry, and do journaling work as a way of expressing your Mercurial side.

Try gathering yellow or white candles and feathers to symbolize the sky and the air element. Work with chimes and bells to augment the ceremony as well. Their sounds can help clear the space and bring meditative clarity to the ritual. Lavender is a lovely aromatic oil for stimulating and soothing the nervous system simultaneously. Hyssop oil will help open the lungs and allow your breath to be deep and strong. Peppermint and thyme oils are also wonderful for stimulating the best qualities in Gemini and releasing any stagnancy and confusion, replacing it with clarity.

Cancer Moon

The Moon in Cancer has a strong relationship to home and hearth. If you carry out a ritual during this time, make sure you thoroughly examine your house and clean and sweep away any trash or residue. Open the windows and bring in fresh air to clear out stale smells and emotions. Warm your home with a good fire or by turning up the thermostat. Some gentle music will help set the mood as well. Cancer is connected with mothering and nurturing qualities. This is a good time to have close friends and family present to show the depth of your love. If you have family issues and concerns, you can conduct a ritual to help heal rifts and past hurts. You may feel a greater degree of emotion than usual under this Moon. Allow these feelings to come, and let the ritual be a time to process anything that is stagnant in you or causing undue stress and worry.

In medical astrology, Cancer is connected to the breasts and the stomach. Reduce stress and nourish these parts of the body by gently stretching and rubbing your belly in a clockwise manner. Bathe in hot water and rub your stomach with healing aromatic oils. I find that jasmine oil is tremendously helpful for Cancers, as it reduces worry and tension and is gentle and uplifting.

For ritual work, gather blue candles, shells, crab claws, coral, bowls of water, and pictures of oceans and lakes to symbolize Cancer. Allow this to be a deep and nourishing time for your emotional life. You can release emotional pain through crying, as the tears help dissolve tension and strengthen your connection to the water element.

Leo Moon

This fiery Moon is a wonderful time for play, music, dance, and romance. The Leo Moon is a good time to stimulate creativity and allow your dynamic and expressive side to come out. If you are feeling dull, lethargic, and tired, the Leo Moon is a perfect time to recharge your battery, strengthen your sense of adventure, and rekindle your fire. Leo rules the heart chakra and our sense of warmth, generosity, and love. If you have been feeling cold and closed off, the Leo Moon reminds you that you can be silly and take risks. Leo is ruled by the Sun, the shining star that symbolizes your golden and radiant self. This is a good time to strengthen your self-confidence and charisma.

Healthwise, Leo is connected to the heart and spine. A few yogic sun salutations, a long day in the sun, or kindling a warm fire in the fireplace are all wonderful ways to prepare for a Leo Moon ritual. Dancing is one of the best ways to raise the heart rate, throw off toxins, and transform depression into joy. Take a few minutes before and during the ritual to dance with a bright, shining Leo heart. Another way to work with this Moon is to be dramatic and do some role playing and performance. This is a time to bring out the kid in us, so doing work with the inner child can be really helpful during this Moon.

To prepare for the ritual, gather red and gold cloth and candles and find pictures of lions and the sun. Amber is the best essence to use with the Leo Moon, as it strengthens calmness, confidence, and radiance. Neroli essence brings in the sweet smell of oranges, helping you laugh and smile during the ritual.

Virgo Moon

The Virgo Moon is the one most associated with health. This is a good time for cleansing and purifying as well as for conducting powerful healing rituals. Ultimately, Virgo has to do with service, and if you have been feeling a little too self-centered, this is a good time to do work in the community that is positive and compassionate. Virgo teaches us to release negative habits and replace them with healthier, more nourishing ones. If you need help with this, pick a Virgo Moon for doing the work. Ultimately, Virgo has to do with the mundane, day-to-day activities of life. If you are feeling overwhelmed and impatient, this is a good time to do a ritual on becoming more mindful and peaceful in your daily rhythm. Washing dishes, taking the dog out for a walk, or cleaning the house can be beautiful, holy tasks. A ritual at this time can help you remember to acknowledge the extraordinary in the simple things in life.

In terms of health, Virgo is connected to the intestines. Often this is an area where anxiety and worries cause discomfort and disease. Go to the deeper issues and release the mental struggle that is at the root of any physical discomfort. Make sure that excessive self-criticism is not harming your creativity and confidence.

For the Virgo ritual, make sure you clean your altar and your space thoroughly before starting. This includes yourself. Wash your clothes and then take a bath and put on fresh, clean clothes. Make sure all the plants are watered and well tended for the past few days, so they are bright and healthy. This will add to the strength of any ritual. Purify the space with sage or incense and make sure you feel emotionally comfortable with anyone with whom you do the ritual. Finally, use cleansing essences such as thyme, rosemary, and fennel to charge, vitalize, and purify the environment. Use green and dark-blue candles and dark-blue cloth for setting up the altar.

Libra Moon

This beautiful and artistic Moon is ruled by Venus. The Libra Moon is a time when you can conduct ritual work around issues of relationships and balance in all areas of your life. If you are centering too much attention on yourself, or are giving too much of your energy away to your partner, try to bring a balance back to your life. If there have been power struggles, anger, and wounds with your partner, work with the Libra Moon to ask for healing. It is also a good time to prioritize your different activities and to carve out time for creativity, play, work, and family time. This can be very difficult in our busy, modern world. Allow your intent and your prayers to guide your path.

When the Moon is in Libra, it is a good time for artistic pursuits, so make paintings, draw pictures, and write poetry. Libra has to do with balance and symmetry, so refining your home environment to be more beautiful and pleasing is a great way to work with this Moon sign. The art of feng shui involves decorating and designing the house so that all its aspects lead to inner harmony and peace. This is a good time to simply rearrange the decor of the house, to move a few desks and tables around to make the energy in the house flow better.

Libra rules the kidneys. If you have been experiencing a lot of stress from trying to balance all the different facets of your life, this can tax your kidneys, the source of your energy and vitality. When the kidneys are taxed, you can feel tired, depressed, and anxious. Utilize the Libra Moon to strengthen and nourish your kidneys at a core level.

Libra is the sign of the scales. Try to use symmetry and balance in your altar for your ritual. White, light-blue, and yellow candles and cloth are wonderful Libran colors. Leaves, feathers, and pictures and figurines of lovers and partners would be helpful for the altar as well. Essence of rose will help open your heart and draw you closer to your lover. Raspberry essence will help strengthen your sense of beauty, joy, and creativity.

Scorpio Moon

This is a powerful and transformative time of the month and is a wonderful time to delve into deep emotional realms. Scorpio often brings up the darker emotions of fear and self-hatred and asks that we take a deep look at ourselves. In this space, we can also realize that we have amazing inner beauty and powerful gifts to share with the rest of the world. Much of the ritual work comes in transforming these inner demons into beautiful jewels of love and faith. Intentions and prayers are deeply powerful at this time and can help set a tone for the weeks and months to come.

Because this is a water Moon, it is an intensely emotional time, and you may need to cry, vent, and rage to fully express the depth of your feelings. Part of the work lies in acknowledging that the darkness is part of the path and to learn greater acceptance and self-love. Scorpio has a deep connection with the hidden and shamanic realms as well as the realm of the dead. Death reminds us of the brevity and beauty of every moment in our lives. Use this time to carry out powerful spell and magic work and to delve into the hidden recesses of your unconscious. You may want to do some release work by writing down a few things you want to let go of on a piece of paper. During the ritual, simply ask that those things be released, and burn the paper up in a fireplace or in a small pot.

In terms of health, Scorpio is connected to the reproductive and sexual organs and the process of elimination and detoxification. If there has been trauma and pain associated with these powerful and vulnerable areas, this is a wonderful time to find release through painting, writing, acting, and dancing.

To create your altar, try placing on it images of ancestors and loved ones who have passed away. Put offerings of corn and grain and whatever food they liked before the images. Black cloth and maroon, dark-blue, and black candles are appropriate for this Moon time. Try to sink deeply into a meditative state and get very quiet before starting this ritual. Make sure the ritual is done only by candlelight so that the unseen worlds and spirit helpers will want to assist your work. Oil essences that are helpful for this ritual include sage, a sacred and purifying herb that will strengthen meditative and spiritual work, and patchouli, for working with sexual and reproductive issues.

Sagittarius Moon

This fiery Moon is a wonderful time to bring joy, creativity, and adventure into your life. If you have been feeling stuck, depressed, or too intense, work with this Moon to draw luck and play back to you. Ruled by Jupiter, this is a time to drink wine and make merry, to extend yourself, and to seek greater expansiveness and expression in your life. Fiery Moons are good times to generate energy on many levels. Fire helps warm the body and circulate the blood and chi. Drumming, singing, and chanting will stimulate the fire energy to activate and draw power from your roots and extend it outward. This energy can go toward creative endeavors like painting, writing, and acting, as well as toward developing sexual and charismatic energy. Since laughter is the best medicine of all, allow this ritual to be spontaneous, raucous, and even silly. Loosen up, and your body will relax and your health will become stronger.

Sagittarius rules the liver in medical astrology. If you have been overdoing it and have been overly expansive and indulgent, your liver may feel stagnant, and you may be experiencing frustration, anger, and irritability. Choose prayers and make intentions for drawing your energy inward somewhat and reducing overconsumptive behavior. On the other hand, if you have been too emotionally constrained, this can also damage the liver, and you may want to choose this time to kindle the fires and become more expressive and extroverted.

In creating your altar, choose red and purple cloth and try to light a number of red candles to stimulate the fire energy. The laughing Buddha and the Fool card from the Tarot are two of the best images I know for Sagittarius. By working with these images, we can learn to regain some of the play and innocent wonder in life, to not take things so seriously. You can also bring wine and libations as offerings to Spirit during the Sagittarius Moon. Sandalwood incense gives off a fiery and stimulating smell that is wonderful for Sagittarius rituals. You can also try juniper and cedar essences, as they have a deep, rich aroma that is invigorating and warming.

Capricorn Moon

The Capricorn Moon is a time of consolidation and foundational work. This is a time to build and strengthen the core of the body and spirit. Prayers and intentions can be made for setting your will and using discipline to accomplish goals. In the Tibetan Buddhist tradition, they call this "building the diamond body." If there has been weakness and confusion, the Capricorn Moon is a time to develop clear and direct paths for overcoming obstacles and moving through difficulties. Ultimately, the spiritual message of Capricorn is to bend the knees (ruled by Capricorn) and serve and surrender to Spirit. By releasing our own ego's attachment to needing power and approval, we gain true power by aligning ourselves with the strength of Spirit.

In terms of health, Capricorn is linked to the foundational structures of the skin, bones, knees, teeth, and nails. This is a good time to build strength in these areas through yoga or martial arts. Envision your entire body strengthening and building at this time of the month.

When creating your altar, dark-green, maroon, and black cloth are great for creating a base. Choose green, brown, and black candles to symbolize the earth element. Bring images of structures and buildings that are holy and long lasting to the altar. Plants and stones are always wonderful for Capricorn Moon work as well.

Essence of pine is strengthening and rejuvenating, and reminds us of one of the holiest and strongest natural structures in the world. You can also try cedar and sage to cleanse and strengthen the environment for doing ritual work.

Aquarius Moon

This is a good time to be unusual, eclectic, and revolutionary in your intentions and prayers. Choose this time to allow for electric and sudden flashes of brilliance and creative ideas to come to you. Aquarius is also connected to the principle of community, and this is a wonderful time to develop prayers for integrating with the community and drawing people closer together. You may have new and crazy ideas that you want to implement. Now is a good time to do that as well. Aquarius is connected to technology. Think about your relationship to technology in your life—your car, your computer, your television, your phone, and even your mop and your rake. Try to establish a healthy, balanced relationship with technology, where you can utilize it, but it does not dominate your life and put an undue burden on the environment.

Now is the time to pray for a healthy nervous system. Healing energy work such as acupuncture, reiki, and polarity work all will help you rebalance and strengthen your nerve channels. Yoga and tai chi are wonderful for developing internal fortitude and stronger nerves.

During the Aquarius Moon, lay out a light-blue or white piece of cloth and burn unusual and eclectic types of candles for your ritual. Gather feathers, bells, gongs, and chimes to symbolize the air element. You can meditate on smoke from incense as well. If you want, place pictures of gatherings, groups, and circles on your altar. This will help you meditate on your connection to the community. Eucalyptus essence will stimulate your mind, and cinnamon and clove will help your circulation during this ritual time.

Pisces Moon

This is a beautiful time to do dream work and uncover the hidden doors to the realm of imagination, visualization, and metaphysical experiences. Explore any dream images or archetypes with which you have been working. If you have been working with spirit and animal allies, call on their power and bring them in close. Pisces has to do with surrender, faith, and service. If you have been experiencing struggle and pain in your life, this may be a karmic experience, and you may need to surrender to the process. Ritual work will help put you in touch with the spiritual Source so that you can give yourself over to that power. When you work as a vehicle of service to Spirit, your life can become unblocked and freed up. Release your need for control and flow with the gentle and beautiful waters of the Pisces Moon. Allow this ritual to be a time of meditation and merging with the oceanic underlying Spirit. Here you will find answers. This is a time to sing and pray, to channel the wisdom of your guides and affirm it in your intentions.

Pisces rules the immune system and this is a good Moon to strengthen this part of the body. Bathe, sweat, and purify your body of toxins and be quiet and gentle with yourself. Drink lots of water and avoid pollutants at this time of the month. Feel the healing current of the Moon in your depth work and allow it to wash over you and cure you of disease.

For this ritual, find candles and cloth that are blue and blue-green. Use water to wash your stones and ritual objects and to clean the altar space. Find images of Poseidon, mermaids, the sea, and ships on water. Gather seashells and seaweed to place on the altar, and make music and sing during this ritual. If you can sing some of your prayers and your spells, the magic will be even stronger. Use essence of lotus for meditative and spiritual work, and frankincense and sage for purifying the environment and readying it for psychic and trance work.

---

1. Edain McCoy, *The Sabbats: A New Approach to Living the Old Ways* (St. Paul, MN: Llewellyn Publications, 1999) 3.

2. Ibid., 153.

6

Connecting with the Natural World

Last summer I hiked with some friends through the Olympic National Forest and walked alongside a streambed under towering, old-growth hemlocks. The deep and musky aroma of the rainforest and the steady pace of our hike enchanted me and left me in a sort of trance. My thoughts about life at home and the outside world diminished and I fell into the slow rhythm of the woods. In the midst of our walk, a black bear leaped in front of our path, just a few yards ahead. Normally these creatures are not too dangerous if you give them ample berth, but they have been known to attack humans if they feel threatened or if they are just in a bad mood. Obviously, we had stumbled across the bear's path and had made it nervous and scared. It leaped in front of us and then loped quickly up the hill to our right. We stopped in our tracks and watched as this amazingly swift creature turned to stare at us from about twenty yards away. I tried to remember all the advice about how to interact with an angry bear. Was it "Drop and play dead"? or "Act aggressive"? or just "Run like hell!"? I couldn't remember and just stood there frozen, staring at this black bear and watching it stare back at us. Slowly, we started quietly moving forward, being careful not to make any sudden movements, as if the bear were a villain with a gun. The bear just watched us walk by, its senses obviously heightened, but without any desire to chase us down.

In those few moments, I learned a lot about brown bears, how quick they are, how fierce they can be, and how they can navigate brush, boulders, and stumps with powerful leaps, hops, and zigzagging movements. I saw some of the ferocity and the dangers of the woods. I realized I needed to be a little more aware of what was around me and not to fall into a trance so deep that I failed to see a bear a few yards in front of me.

Simple skills of observation—watching, listening, smelling, touching, and tasting—are at the core of four element medicine work. They help us get in touch with the natural world and understand its intricacies. By understanding the different facets of the natural world, we gain a deeper appreciation of the elements. In my story, I saw how the bear was in touch with the earth element: he was able to scramble sure-footedly through a thicket of shrubs and trees; the air element: he moved with speed and grace; the fire element: he was angry and fierce; and the water element: his emotions were strong and intense.

By developing an appreciation for the natural world, we heighten our senses and allow for a greater connection to the lessons of the natural world and how they relate to our own astrological chart. If we lack earth in our chart, we may need to learn lessons in patience and being grounded. One way to do this is to spend an afternoon watching a beaver build a dam. It takes its time to gather all the proper materials and relay them to the precise spot along a river or stream. Watching that process reminds us of the need to be slow and deliberate in our actions.

Someone lacking in the air element may do well to watch a hummingbird in the springtime. When I lived in Ecuador, I had a chance to study a small area of trees and flowers that were filled with different kinds of hummingbirds. Their amazing speed, precision, and agility were fascinating. They literally hovered over the flowers as they dove their beaks in to receive the nectar. A few days of watching them taught me about the fragility and the beauty in life. Each hummingbird seemed to weave its way joyously through the trees, sometimes for the sake of finding food, sometimes for the pleasure and play of the activity. The joy in darting from one flower to the next reminds me of the lightning-quick expressiveness of a Gemini, the love of pleasure of a Libra, or the rapid insights of an Aquarius.

By seeing the connections of the natural world to the myth and metaphor of the zodiac, we gain tools for balancing and harmonizing our own astrological makeup. The herbs, stones, animals, and birds in our environment have the potential to catalyze growth and development of our personality, heal our physical ailments, and align us with the natural world.

In astrology, the zodiac is divided up into twelve signs. Each sign is associated with an element and a modality, and with a ruling planet. In four element medicine, all of creation can be categorized as well. A mountain has earthy and fixed qualities, a bird has airy and Mercurial properties, and a waterfall has watery and perhaps Martian properties due to its strength and virility. These concepts are fluid and changeable, depending on the mind of the perceiver. Since all of creation carries an essential force or energy, it is possible to work with different things on a number of different levels. We can take an herb that has medicinal properties, and it can enact physical and chemical changes on us. By merely admiring an herb, or by smelling it or drawing a picture of it, we can take in its essence on a different level. It may impact us on a more emotional level, which in turn may affect us on a physical level. Finally, we may have a powerful experience where we contact the spirit and the essence of an herb and truly understand it from a nonordinary standpoint. This is the realm of shamans, witches, magicians, and sorcerers. They see the herb as wholly alive and as having a personality and an expression that impacts us at a core level. In this way, we are experiencing and being affected by the medicine of an herb on an entirely different level, a spiritual level.

In this chapter, I will explore some of the methods for making connections with the natural world and making alliances and relationships with the plants, stones, and creatures of the wild.

Listening and Observing

Each creature, each rock, and each herb has its own language, its own expression that requires a special, individual relationship. Listening to and observing these beings will help you create a relationship to the natural world. Using your senses to understand the natural world will help you develop your healing skills. Be patient with this process. Try to take walks in the woods and learn the names of plants. Buy a pair of binoculars and do some bird watching on the weekends. Watch animals in their natural environment if you can. Be aware of the movements of the stars in the sky. Make connections between the natural world and the elements and planets. This is core work for developing your skills to practice four element medicine.

The skills of observing, touching, tasting, and smelling will help you arrive at a deeper connection to anything you work with. It is important to take a lot of time in these endeavors, to really get to know who and what you are working with. If you have picked up on some of the characteristics of what you are studying, whether those be assertive, peaceful, or intense, try allowing those characteristics to seep into your being. Take them on like an actor would take on a role. Start to embody their features and attributes and take their medicine into your own heart.

For example, if you are interested in the properties of jade, it would be helpful to find one of these stones in a natural setting, the original source of the material. If that is not possible, take a piece of jade that you have bought or that has been given to you and then sit with it, feel it, and observe its color and texture, its overall expression. You may start to pick up on a few things. Its green color may remind you of the forest and of the rich color of the earth. Its smooth feel may give you a sense of ease and tranquility, and its weight may give you a feeling of grounding and centeredness. The best place to observe and listen is outdoors, preferably alone and in a quiet place without distractions. This will allow you to move from a clinical to an intuitive state of mind. As you gently feel and look at the jade, your mind can begin to wander and make associations. You will start to feel the properties of the stone on a much more personal level.

For an herb, find a living specimen that preferably grows in the wild. Sit with it and see where it lives and what other plants and trees it enjoys the company of. See what kind of light and heat it likes. You may want to draw the herb to gain a deeper appreciation of it. Take a piece of a leaf (ask the herb first) or a petal of a flower and taste it. Does it taste bitter or sweet? Feel the texture of the stalk and the entire herb. Is it smooth or rough, sticky or smooth? All of these characteristics make up the essence of the herb and describe its essence, its nature, and its purpose.

For an animal or a bird, try to find one in the wild and then watch and observe it for a while. See what movements it makes, how it communicates, smells, sees, and behaves. Certain characteristics will become apparent, such as the cautious grace of a deer, the regal majesty and keen eyesight of an eagle, or the quick orderliness of a mouse. You may begin to make associations with the planets and the signs of the zodiac when you study these beings. Deer may remind you of the beautiful sweetness of Venus or the swift speed of Mercury. Eagles may remind you of the intense directness of Mars or the nobility of the Sun. Whatever it is, begin to make connections—see the zodiac in the world around you. The natural world presents opportunities for tremendous learning and wisdom.

Shamanic Techniques for Connection to the Natural World

Once you have made connections to the natural world on a physical level, it is possible to gain a deeper appreciation for nature on a deeper, more shamanic level. Indigenous cultures throughout the world have developed numerous tools for accessing the profound wisdom of the natural world. When we utilize these tools, we open the doorway to the deeper part of our consciousness, where all of the earth and the cosmos is alive and interrelated. When we access this framework, we come into contact with the essential, luminous fabric that underlies our reality. Though we live in a world of planes, trains, computers, and cell phones, there is an underlying experience that is as old as time and cannot be buried by the forces of modern life.

In the world we live in, it is easy to forget the differences and subtle nuances emanating from all of life. When many of our restaurants, the media, and clothing and chain stores have been duplicated and replicated throughout the world, we are often more used to homogeneity than diversity. The uniformity of modern culture has helped deaden our senses, making us less aware of the subtleties, the shades and colors that make everything vibrant and alive. When everything is the same, we may feel a sense of safety and security in the world wherever we may go. What is scarier is to step out into an unknown world and to truly live as explorers, experiencing the fresh and vital universe with all its chaos, pandemonium, and beauty.

Why Should I Use These Tools?

The use of shamanic tools to connect to the natural world is a way of helping us come to know ourselves on a deeper level. It is a way of linking ourselves with the natural world of plants, animals, and stones, and teaches us the connection between nature and the zodiac. These tools help us ally ourselves with our ancestors, who used these tools throughout the world, whether that be in Africa, Asia, Europe, Australia, or the Americas. They are particularly important tools in our modern world, where our contact with nature is becoming more destructive and alienated with each passing day. It is a way of healing our relationship to that which we have disfigured or destroyed.

In many tribal systems, these techniques are known as shamanism, the ability to bridge the gap between this world and the unseen worlds. In Europe, these techniques are known as magic, the ability to transform and shape consciousness through our will and the assistance of tools found in nature according to the principles of natural law. In essence, these tools have been used for thousands of years to help develop our wisdom, our appreciation of all facets of life, and for knowledge and healing. While these tools and techniques can also be used for ill intent and purpose, magic wielded poorly and for ill will inevitably has a way of returning to the practitioner in a way that is equally, if not more, damaging.

In the previous chapter, you learned the basics of ritual and the importance of time, place, and space for conducting rites and doing foundational work. Sacred nature rituals are often practiced with devotion, prayer, and supplication in mind. At the core, they are about bridging the gap between humans and the divine via the forces of the natural world. When this core practice has been developed, it is then possible to continue on into deeper layers of astrological magic and shamanism. Without the core of ritual and prayer, these later tools will be much less effective.

Shamanic Astrology

Ceremonial tools are especially important to students of astrology because astrology is the study of cyclical and circular time, and astrologers see life as being related throughout the microcosmic and macrocosmic levels. Because we are all related, these tools help bridge the gap between our worlds and teach us the language, the symbology, and the techniques for interconnection.

When we see each cobweb, each grain of sand, each human, and each planet as interrelated and part of a vast framework, we start to see that all of creation has the potential of being medicinal or poisonous, good for our energy or depleting, depending on how we work with it and in what manner we spend time with it. When we view all of creation as sacred, we begin to see the value of everything not just on a physical level, but on an emotional and spiritual level as well. A horse is no longer just seen as an animal to ride, but as a creature capable of emotion and self-expression, and possessing admirable qualities such as swiftness, endurance, and strength. We can see the nobility and prowess of a horse, and it begins to take on a deeper meaning. It is no longer just a horse, but it becomes Horse, a form of medicine on an energetic and shamanic level.

Meditation

One of the most basic techniques for connecting with the natural world is the practice of meditation. Meditation quiets the mind and eliminates distractions so we can be focused and concentrate. When we become truly quiet in meditation, we can sometimes hear the essential silence, the divinity that underlies all of creation. Developing a relationship with this Source will enable you to hear the basic hum in the natural world, the thread that ties everything together. By being able to be silent, you will also see and feel the essential nature of anything you are studying and working with.

Begin by closing your eyes, and allow your breath to become slow and steady. Maintain an erect posture and try not to slump. If necessary, sit in a chair to maintain your back's upright position. In this posture, simply observe your breath and try not to get distracted by other thoughts and concerns. Stay present to your inhalation and exhalation and allow your concentration to become focused there. You may feel emotional and physical discomfort in this state. Repetitive and negative thoughts may also arise while you are meditating. Allow them to exist and do not fight with them. Breathe them in and breathe them out. The rhythm of your breath will soon bring you into a quiet and deep place. Your body will become more relaxed and still. By meditating for a short time everyday, you increase the stillness inside and reduce the stress in your life. This will help you be more present and open in your ritual and healing work.

Concentration

Another type of meditation is concentration. Concentration helps hone our skills of being quiet and attentive so we can take in information and apprehend the essential qualities of what we are studying. To work on concentration skills, set up a quiet place to do this work. Then light a candle or place an image or figurine about two to three feet away from you. Sit down in a comfortable position and direct your attention toward your focus. Try to breathe slowly and surely and sit upright in your posture. When thoughts and worries arise, return to the object of your attention. Try not to move your head or your eyes, and sink into this space without distraction. This is very difficult to do for more than five or ten minutes for most of us. If you can, build your practice up to twenty minutes per session. This powerful technique is wonderful for honing observational and healing skills.

Visualization

Meditation and concentration help develop more complex skills such as visualization. Visualization is simply the ability to imagine and recreate an image or situation in your head with as many details as possible. Again, begin by closing your eyes and breathing deeply and slowly. Then allow yourself to concentrate on a single image. Start with something simple like the color blue or red. Next, move on to something more complicated like a bowl or a cup. Finally, focus on images of plants, animals, and birds that you have seen. Try to conjure up as many facets of their essence as possible—leaf coloring, facial features, feathering, body types, etc. When you have mastered the ability to work with visual images and maintain a calm, meditative state, you will have prepared yourself for contacting the underlying essence of the natural world.

Drumming, Chanting, and Singing: Doorways to Unseen Realms

The most powerful and ancient tool for accessing nonordinary reality is through the use of rhythm and music. In India, spiritual adepts recite sections of their ancient holy text, the Vedas, in order to achieve spiritual growth and attainment. In North America, Native Americans use drums to contact spiritual forces and ally themselves with natural earth rhythms. In Europe, monks sing hymns to God to harmonize their minds and draw their souls into deeper worship. These techniques of chanting, drumming, and singing are powerful tools for invocation and spiritual growth.

In shamanic cultures, the drum is used to open up unseen worlds and provides a doorway to the other side. Through the use of a drum or rattle, a shaman can go into a trance and visit nonordinary reality, the spiritual realms that are not visible to us everyday. Through the use of chanting and singing, he can contact the spiritual forces in those worlds, the animal and plant spirits that can enable him to heal or provide wisdom to his tribe.

In your work, it is helpful to choose a musical medium that will put you into a trance and allow you to drop down out of your ordinary awareness. This may be through using a drum, shaking a rattle, chanting a repeated phrase, or singing a familiar song. These techniques will help you deepen your process of making connections with the natural world.

Traveling, Contacting, and Shapechanging

Once you have made a connection with a plant, animal, or bird in nature and have gained some experience in meditation, concentration, and visualization, it is possible to make a deeper shamanic connection with totems in nature. It is best to pick a time and a day that relate well to the specific creature. In later chapters, I describe elemental and planetary allies for each of the herbs, birds, and animals. Choose a Moon sign that relates well to the being you are working with. If it is a plant, try to do your work near the herb and preferably outside. If you cannot be near the living herb, you need to have the dried herb near you so you can taste, touch, and smell it. If you are working with a bird or animal, try to have a physical manifestation of it in the form of a feather, a bone, a tooth, or a piece of fur. These are physical reminders and spiritual embodiments of the creatures you want to contact.

Next, create a ritual space by following the directions I outlined in chapter 5. In the context of the ritual and after you have given your thanks and made your prayers, you can choose a technique for drawing yourself into a trance. Begin by meditating to calm yourself and to drop down into your body and away from fleeting thoughts and worries. Repeatedly hitting a drum at a steady, rhythmic pace is one of the most ancient ways to alter consciousness. You may also want to try singing a song or chanting a simple set of familiar words or sounds. Once you feel completely relaxed by your chanting or drumming, you can lie down in your circle and begin to dream lucidly.

Use your techniques of visualization to see yourself and to travel to a natural setting where this animal, bird, or plant might be. For some people, this means going through a cave or a hole in the ground to arrive in an alternate world. If you do go through a hole, remember how to get back the same way you came down. In this alternate reality, you may see hills and mountains, rivers and trees. Allow yourself to walk and move through this land, and open yourself to the possibility of seeing the plant, animal, or bird you want to contact. If you are not so lucky, just keep trying this technique, and over time you may see them.

If you find what you are looking for, this is an opportunity to make a friendship at a deep level. You can ask questions about their deeper qualities, their connections to the elements and the planets, and their energetic and healing properties. Be open to them on an emotional level and be kind and friendly. They may speak to you through movements, sounds, and language. They may make physical contact with you or keep their distance. Whatever happens, be open to the experience and honor the creatures with thanks and praise. By getting to know them down here, you are increasing your ability to work with them energetically and in healing ceremonies. Make sure you return to the same place from which you started before coming out of the trance.

You may want to make an animal or bird connection while you are dancing. Dancing and chanting can put you in a trance, and you can again journey to the other world and make shamanic connections with the natural world. In the process of dancing, you may take on the characteristics of the bird or animal and can begin to shapechange. You can begin to embody the features of the creature you are connecting with. Run, lope, preen, and call out like these beings do. Allow their energy to become your own. This is a very intimate way of connecting with the natural world.

Finally, you may also want to contact these beings in the dream world. Any dream that includes animals, birds, and plants is a very auspicious dream. If you do have a dream like this, make sure you write down what happened and try to go back to the dream and understand the meaning behind it. If you want to work with a creature in your dreams, bring a physical representation of the being to your bed and make prayers and ask to see it in your dreams that night. This can be very difficult to make happen, but if you are lucky, you will receive a visitor that evening.

Do not be distressed if this does not happen. You can receive information in many other ways.

All of these techniques are powerful methods for understanding and making connections with the natural world. By making these alliances, we can call on their physical and spiritual power in our ritual and healing work. Each animal, bird, stone, and herb has a resonance with the elements, modalities, planets, and signs. By understanding our astrological chart, we can work with the natural world as an intermediary to harmonize and heal ourselves. In the next section, I will describe methods for working with the natural world for these purposes.

Tools

The use of tools in four element medicine work is essential for accomplishing your goals. We have already discussed ideas for creating an altar and developing a ritual space. When you want to focus your intent toward a specific aim, it is important to have objects that have been ritually consecrated for your work. At a simple level, you only need one main tool for each element. For the air element, this may be a very special feather. Perhaps this is a feather of the bird with which you are most in contact, your totem bird. It could also be a bell or a chime. For the fire element, you may want to choose a wand made out of a very special piece of wood, like oak or madrona. For the water element, you may want to choose a cup or a bowl. For the earth element, you may want to choose a special stone. Whatever the tool is, make sure it is personal, meaningful, and connected to nature.

These tools are at the core of any four element work you do. When you choose the specific Moon time at which to carry out a specific ritual, utilize the tool connected to the element the Moon sign is in. That tool should be the centerpiece of your energetic and healing work. Each tool needs to be especially cared for, cleansed, and purified on a regular basis so that it remains strong and potent. Try to do this on each solar sabbat. When choosing a tool to be the main representation of an element, take the time to make a ritual specific for that powerful work. Choose a good Moon sign and make prayers and ask for blessings for that tool. Smudge it and honor it by keeping it on your altar permanently.

Spellcasting

A spell is simply a prayer symbolically represented in something physical along with specific words to help direct the energy. For example, you may be experiencing lung complaints regularly and have been doing the best you can with herbs and your diet, but have not healed completely. You may want to cast a spell that specifically asks for your lungs to heal completely and fully. Since lungs are connected to the sign of Gemini, you may want to choose a Gemini Moon to conduct your healing work. Then you may gather air objects, such as a feather from a hawk (a symbol of power and the air element), a shaft of mullein (lung healer), and a reed of bamboo (strong but able to bend in the wind). After your tools have been gathered, you can start with regular ritual work, honoring the elements, and giving thanks to the Spirit. You can then consecrate the tools you have chosen by praying over them and explaining why you chose them. These physical manifestations of air can then be tied up with a ribbon or placed in a special sacred box or bowl. You can then make a prayer and cast a spell with the objects. This is unique to every individual, but it should be heartfelt. The words you say could have something to do with what you have been going through and how long you have been going through it. It can be helpful to make the words you use rhyme.

> *Breathe in, breathe out*
> *I feel no fear, I feel no doubt.*
> *Steady, strong, I will wait*
> *And let my lungs rejuvenate.*

Rhyming can increase the potency and magic in your work. *Now cast the spell.* Explain what your intent is and make prayers for a good outcome. In this case, you may want to visualize your lungs healing and strengthening. Create a mental image of a stream of white or golden light encapsulating your lungs and gently restoring and vitalizing them. Visualization and heartfelt words are the keys to good spellwork.

Finally, place the bundled tools in a private place that is meaningful to you. For me, this is the permanent altar that I have in my room. This space is always charged with good energy and helps my spellwork unfold in a good way. When you place the spell, give a timeframe for how long you want the spell to last. If your lung complaints are immediate, you may want to say one full lunation (about twenty-eight days). If you want to heal your lungs on a deeper and more profound level, you may want to work the spell for as long as a year. Whatever it is, make sure you release the spell at the end of the allotted time by unbundling the objects and releasing the energy. It is good to give thanks to Spirit for helping you at the end of your spellcasting.

Healing may then take place in an unusual way—perhaps the lung issues have to do with some underlying unresolved emotional issues. The spell may work, but not in the way you thought it would. It may bring up those emotional concerns and ask that you deal with them. I have found that spellwork is supremely effective if I am coming from a good place and have a good intention. It is much less effective when I am confused, angry, tired, or impatient. Spellwork should not be done to harm others, to get things from people, or to make you rich or famous. This type of magic inevitably backfires and can be quite damaging, so be careful how you weave your craft.

Spellwork Basics

1. *Choose the appropriate time.* Pick a Moon time that makes sense: an air Moon for healing nervous complaints, a water Moon for working with emotional issues, etc. Make sure you choose a phase of the moon that makes sense as well: a New Moon for beginnings and endings, a waxing Moon for building energy, a Full Moon for consecrating, blessing, and healing, or a waning Moon for banishing and releasing.

2. *Set your intent.* Determine what your goal is and make sure it harms no one.

3. *Gather sacred tools.* By understanding the theme of your work—i.e., healing, prosperity, protection, etc.—gather meaningful objects that correspond elementally and astrologically.

4. *Make the ritual.* Begin the process by performing the ritual and giving thanks.

5. *Consecrate the tools.* Make your tools holy by saying the reasons for which you have chosen each object, and make prayers for each one.

6. *Bundle the tools.* Take the ritual objects and place them together. Tie them with a ribbon, and place them in a special piece of cloth or put them in a special box.

7. *Raise energy.* Using the power of chanting, singing, drumming, or making music, add energy to the ritual space and draw down the power from the Source into your work.

8. *Cast the spell.* Explain what your intent is and make prayers for a good outcome. Visualize your desired outcome.

9. *Ground the spell.* Place the bundled ritual objects in a special place (a permanent altar, in the crack of a tree, in a desk meant for magic work, etc.). Give a specific time when you will release the objects from the spell. This could be a lunation, a season, a year, or whatever you deem appropriate.

10. *Close the spell and give thanks.* Always finish spellwork with thanks by honoring the Spirit.

Amulets

Another form of magic that you can perform in the context of ritual is the making of amulets. Amulets are one or a combination of sacred objects that can be worn or held near to provide protective, healing, and positive effects for the creator. Like spells, amulets are meant to aid transformation and assist in making our intentions manifest. They can be used by the creator or given to a friend who asked specifically for them. Like spells, amulets should not cause harm or assist in undue gain for the creator. They should simply be physically symbolic and magically infused tokens that assist our prayers and best intentions.

Amulets can be made in a number of ways, and I encourage you to be creative. They are most often made with a combination of herbs, stones, and metals. My favorite way of making an amulet is to bundle several natural objects into a small pouch and then wear the pouch around my neck or in my pocket. I may also hang the amulet in my house somewhere special if I'm not wearing it.

The first thing you need to do is determine what your intent is with the amulet. An amulet may be made for courage, strength, fortitude, healing (although it is best to be specific), the ability to move through a process, better income, wisdom, intelligence, or just about anything you can think of. What is most important is to align your intent with what is best for you. What is best for you and what you want are not necessarily the same. Making an amulet to win a million dollars might not be what your soul needs to experience (and probably won't work).

The timing for making an amulet is of the utmost importance. The planetary energies will help transform the mundane physical ingredients into something special, something potent, something magical. Thus, if I need courage and strength, I may make the talisman when the energy of Mars is strong in the sky. If I want to make an amulet to feel more beautiful and loving, I may want to make the amulet under the influence of Venus. Once you have associated a planet with your intent, it is best to wait until the Moon is in the sign ruled by that planet. For Mars, that would mean waiting for an Aries or Scorpio Moon. For Venus, that would mean waiting for a Taurus or Libra Moon.

The next step is to gather the particular ingredients needed to make the amulet. In chapter 7, you can read about the energetic qualities of each herb, as well as the associated sign and planet. Try to choose herbs that you feel most connected to, which will help actualize your spiritual, and not necessarily physical, goals. For a Venus amulet, you may want to choose licorice root and raspberry leaf. For a Martian amulet, you may want to choose garlic and cayenne. Two or three good-quality herbs are going to be much more effective than a whole bunch of herbs that you are not connected to.

When gathering herbal ingredients, your best bet is to gather the herbs yourself, especially under a Full Moon and especially under a Moon associated with the plant. That way you will have a special and deep connection to the herb that will transfer into your amulet. If you cannot gather the herbs yourself, make sure they are of good quality. Buy them from a health-food store you trust, and find out where they were collected, and if they were wildcrafted or farm raised. Make sure they are organic—no pesticides are allowed in this process!

Once you have assembled the herbal ingredients, you can gather certain minerals as well. In many stone stores, you can purchase high-quality stones that aren't too expensive. Refer to chapter 11 on stones to understand the energetic properties of the stones when you are making your potion. For a Martian amulet, you may want a pinch of garnet and bloodstone. For a Venusian amulet, you may want a few pieces of coral and jade.

You may also want to bring a token from an animal or bird into your amulet. A tooth that you found from a bear skeleton, a feather from a small bird, or some fur from a deer can be very potent in this type of work. Make sure that the energy of the animal or bird is of the highest quality and that the animal was not needlessly killed or desecrated in any way.

Next, you will need a particular pouch for your medicine amulet. The can be made of any material you like, but try to make sure that it is made of high-quality fabric or leather. You may want to wear this around your neck as a necklace, tie it on your pants, or wear it in your pocket. The best way is to make the amulet pouch yourself and to sew in designs specific for your intention. You can sew the glyph of the planet you specifically want to invoke—Mars for strength, Neptune for inspiration, etc.

When you have gathered all of the sacred objects for your amulet, it is important to empower them within the context of ritual. After honoring Spirit, it is important to smudge and purify the sacred objects and the pouch itself. Like casting a spell, it is important to honor each herb, animal, and stone, explaining the reason for their use in your talisman. Then place the objects in the pouch and express the intent of your amulet as you bless and purify it for wearing. You may choose to wear the amulet for a short or long period of time, depending on your need. If you wear it for a long time, make sure to strengthen and renew it during ritual occasions so that it remains strong and vital in your care. Amulets are tremendously powerful for strengthening vitality, warding off illness, and strengthening the constitution.

Potions

Once I had a dream that I was on a long journey through woods and over streams, and though I was more than halfway to the end, it became so difficult to continue that I had to lie down and rest. Overwhelmed by how much farther I had to go, I became despondent and sat by the banks of a river, sad and scared. I closed my eyes and drifted off for a few minutes, and at that moment a young girl came walking by. She came near me and pulled something out of a small rucksack she was carrying. Without a word, she brought a flask close to my mouth and beckoned me to drink. At first I was nervous and alarmed by this stranger, but her kind eyes told me there was no danger and I took a few sips and then a couple gulps due to my thirst. Immediately, a calm tranquility overtook me and a gentle glow emanated from my entire being. I felt relaxed and rejuvenated. I got up, and feeling revitalized and ready to walk the additional miles of the rest of my journey, I turned around to thank the young girl, but she was gone.

Though this was only a dream, I have had many experiences in my waking life where a liquid has renewed and refreshed me. After going hiking in the mountains for many hours, a long drink of cold stream water can be tremendously rejuvenating. When I have been tired and anxious from a long, stressful day, a cup of chamomile or nettle tea has strengthened my system. Tinctures and flower essences are other forms of liquid that are powerfully healing and strengthening.

What makes a simple liquid into a magical and transforming potion is the degree of intent and preparation, and the timing involved. Imagine the simple act of making an herbal tea. One way to make tea is simply to boil water and steep a tea bag that you bought at the corner store. Another way is by collecting the herbs yourself under a Moon that is associated with the herb (an Aries or Scorpio Moon for a plant ruled by Mars, for example) and then carefully drying them. The herb then becomes more personalized, has a greater energetic state, and is more capable of creating transformation. When making the tea, if the water is from an artesian well, a mountain stream, or has been purified of toxins, it too has a greater energetic state and potential. Boiling the water over open flames would further strengthen the tea by bringing in a natural form of the fire element. Boiling the water in a cast-iron or copper pot would also assist in creating a superior tea. Finally, choosing a good time to make tea can be very helpful for strengthening its potency. Making the tea so that the herb agrees with the Moon sign augments the energy of the tea. This is not always possible and not always necessary, however. At this point, a certain intent can be added to the tea when steeping the herbs by saying a few words of prayer. If the tea is meant for strengthening and rejuvenating, then intending that outcome will help the tea have more impact. In essence, the tea then becomes a po-tion, a magical elixir of transformation. The flames from the fire, the water on the stove, the herbs that get steeped, and the aroma from the tea combine to create a powerful alchemical mixture.

All beverages can be made within the same framework, with care taken in all steps along the way. A tincture is simply herbs steeped in alcohol until their medic-inal qualities become soaked in the alcohol itself. Choosing a high-quality alcohol is important for making a good tincture. Again, handpicking the herbs involved will help the tincture glow with strength and potency. The more steady and direct the handiwork that is involved, the more magical and efficacious the tincture will be in the end.

Flower Essences

Finally, one of the most profound ways to create transformational potions is by making flower essences. Flower essences were first discovered in the 1920s by Ed-ward Bach. Bach believed that flowers contain important energetic qualities that can help transform negative and intense emotional states that limit and contract us. By soaking flowers in fresh water and then storing them in bottles partially pre-served with brandy, these essences have the potential to assist a metamorphosis of the soul. Flowers such as sunflower could help someone regain confidence and vi-tality. Agrimony helps people find their authentic selves and release pain they are holding deep inside. Flower essences are truly transformational potions.

Making a flower essence requires preparation, timing, and good intent. Before going out into the natural world to make a flower essence, it is helpful to clear the mind and heart with ritual work, meditation, eating lightly (or fasting), and pray-ing. Choose a day when the Moon is in a sign related to the flowers you will gather. Then go out early in the day when the sun is shining. Take along a glass bowl, pure water (spring or artesian water is the best), some small, one-ounce dropper bottles, and a bottle of brandy to preserve the essences.

When you have reached the spot where you will gather flowers, make sure it is a place that seems pure and protected—where the flowers have had a chance to grow optimally. To make a flower essence, it's important to spend considerable time with the plant on a physical and shamanic level, as described in previous chapters.

By understanding their nature and developing a friendship with these plants, the medicine you make will be more potent and act on a deeper level.

Next, ask for some of the flowers from the plant and place them in a crystal glass bowl filled with pure water. Never take more than one-third of the flowers available in one spot. The flowers should cover the surface of the water, and the bowl should be placed in the sun. During the day, the magical energy of the flowers will infuse the water and give it the potency of the plant it comes from. After about four hours, the water can be decanted into a few of the dropper bottles you brought along. These bottles will be known as the "mother essences." Make sure not to touch the water when it is being decanted as that can contaminate the essences.

To make a stock essence, fill a bottle with 50 percent spring water and 50 percent brandy, and then add four drops of the mother essence to this bottle. To make a dosage bottle (or what you would use on a regular basis), take four drops of the stock and add it to a bottle filled 90 percent of the way with spring water and 10 percent of the way with brandy. The brandy stabilizes the formula and ensures its strength for up to a year. Make sure you label the bottle with the name of the herb, the date, and the time of the creation so you can know the astrological configuration at the time.

Essences work best when they are given for a two- to four-week time period. I often start taking them at the beginning of a New Moon and then take them until the Full Moon or until the next New Moon. To take them, drop four drops underneath the tongue (one for each element) once a day. There are many pre-made formulas in the stores, including Bach, FES, and Pegasus. These companies are wonderful and create truly magical essences.

In this chapter, I have discussed a number of methods for connecting with the natural world. By developing connections and alliances with the animals, birds, stones, and herbs in the environment, they can become powerful assistants in our healing work. Casting spells and making talismans are two wonderful ways to direct and channel the energy of the natural world for magical and transformative purposes. Using the foundation of astrological ritual work, we can weave our intent with the attributes and powers of nature to heal ourselves at the deepest level.

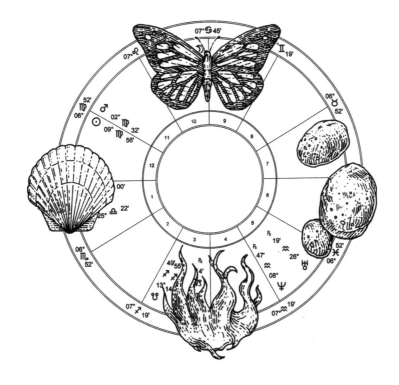

Part 3

Therapeutics

7

The Healing Power of Herbs, Plants, and Trees

Human beings have a long history of using herbs for their medicinal and healing value. In modern times, echinacea and St. John's wort have become household names and part of many people's home medicine kits. Naturopaths, herbalists, and acupuncturists all advise the use of herbs to heal anything from gout to cancer. Herbs are often found to be particularly useful in treating chronic conditions. Healers may recommend a tea made from chamomile, valerian, or skullcap to help heal nervous conditions. They may also prescribe dandelion, burdock, and Oregon grape to help with liver disorders. These simple herbs are found in our backyards, in the woods, and by the side of the road. They are simple, effective medicines that are nourishing and healing and also lack damaging side effects.

On a deeper level, herbs have long been associated with astrology, the planets, and the different signs of the zodiac. The famous English physician of the 1600s, Nicholas Culpeper, produced compendiums delineating herbs in terms of astrology. By looking at a person's astrological chart, herbs could be prescribed to offset any vulnerabilities and weaknesses he or she might suffer from. The placement of the planets at birth indicates what sort of illnesses could arise. For example, someone with a strong amount of Libra in the chart may have difficulties with the kidneys. Libra is ruled by Venus, so that person may need to balance this expression with herbs ruled by Mars, the complementing planet of Venus. Early physicians might have offered herbs such as nettle or garlic to balance the Libra energy and strengthen the kidneys.

Herbs not only have medicinal properties, but have energetic and magical properties as well. The famous thirteenth-century alchemist Albertus Magnus wrote a book describing the magical virtues of stones, animals, and herbs. In it, he writes about the herb marigold:

> *"The first herb is called with the men of Chaldea, Elios, with the Greeks, Matuchiol, with the Latins, Heliotropum, with the Englishmen, Marigold, whose interpretation is of helios, that is the Sun, and tropos, that is alteration, or change, because it is turned according to the Sun. The virtue of this herb is marvelous: for if it be gathered, the Sun being in the sign Leo, in August, and be wrapped in the leaf of a laurel, or Bay tree, and a Wolf's tooth be added thereto, no man shall be able to have a word to speak against the bearer therof, but words of peace. And if anything be stolen, if the bearer of the things before named lay them under his head in the night, he shall see the thief, and all his conditions. And moreover, if the aforesaid herb be put in any church, where women be which have broken matrimony on their part, they shall never be able to go forth of the church, except it be put away. And this last point hath been proved, and is very true."*[1]

A magical relationship to plants was common up to and throughout the Middle Ages. Plants displayed powers that could be used for supernatural means. Though this might seem strange to some, try approaching herbs from a new perspective. If you have the opportunity, go out into a field of sunflowers. See how these gigantic, beautiful herbs crane their heads toward the sun. These plants not only carry vital food and medicine, they express a personality that is unique and powerful. Sunflowers are associated with the sun, radiance, confidence, and courage. When you study these herbs and walk around them and feel their presence, you may be able to pick up on some of these characteristics. Each herb carries a particular vibration, a particular essence that makes it stand out from the rest. These characteristics and vibrations can have a transforming and magical effect on us.

Not only is each type of herb different from the others, each herb is different from any other, even if it is the same type of herb. Lavender grown in high, mountainous country will differ greatly from lavender grown in a low-lying valley. Herbs from higher altitudes tend to be hardier, stronger, and a little smaller. Herbs grown with pesticides will be markedly less vital than herbs grown organically or found in the wild. Herbs grown with love and care will differ from herbs that are factory farmed. Herbs express a unique personality, one that can be shaped and formed much as a young child develops depending on the family in which he or she is raised.

When we work with herbs in terms of astrology, it is important to develop an intimate relationship with them. We need to understand them not only from a medicinal standpoint, but from an energetic and magical standpoint as well. The best way to develop "plant friends" is to spend time with them. Herb walks, gardening, and making teas and tinctures are some of the best ways to get in touch with these herbal allies. As our knowledge of them grows on both an empiric and intuitive level, we find that their characteristics impact us on subtler and subtler levels. The smell of a rose may help us feel more serene and content as well as remind us of our romantic partner and the fire element. A tea with licorice in it may strengthen our adrenal system as well as remind us of the water element and help us release fear and emotional residue from our system.

Finally, when we have made friends with them, we can employ these herbs in our magic and prayers. When we go about procuring herbs, it is essential to take some preliminary steps. The best way to obtain herbs is by going out and harvesting them ourselves. When we do this, we can make prayers and give offerings (some hair, a semiprecious stone, some tobacco) in exchange for the herbs. This also helps us form a relationship to the place where we got them, whether that be a farm or out in the woods. The essence of that place is tied to the medicine of the herbs, so pick a good, healthy spot to harvest.

Wildcrafting (picking herbs in the wild) is a powerful form of herbal harvesting, but make sure you do not pick any rare plants like trillium or lady's slipper. These plants have a difficult time propagating and their numbers could dwindle as a result of our actions. Next, make sure you only take as much as you need. My rule of thumb is to take no more than one-third of the amount of herbs in one spot. Greedy harvesting will also impact the quality of the herbs. In terms of harvesting, here are a few tips on how to get their best medicinal value: Collect roots and rhizomes in the spring, when the sap is just rising, or in the fall, when the sap returns to the root. Collect flowers right as they bloom, not when they dissipate into fruits. Collect the fruits when they have fully matured.

Finally, try to gather herbs in the morning before their vital essence is dried out by the sun. It's also helpful to gather roots when the Moon is waning (better near the New Moon) and aerial parts when the Moon is waxing (better near the Full Moon). The best time to gather an herb is when the Moon is in the sign that rules the herb. For example, you can pick nettle under an Aries Moon to ensure a strong herb (a fire Moon such as Leo or Sagittarius is appropriate as well). This ensures that the fire energy of the plant is further amplified by the astrological conditions.

If you are growing your own herbs, try to choose a time when the Moon is waxing. This will encourage the seed to sprout and the plant to grow. The best time to plant seeds is on waxing earth Moons (Taurus, Virgo, and Capricorn). Cultivate the herbs with care and attention. Be mindful of where you plant them in terms of sun and shade. Water them appropriately and weed the beds often. Show your love and affection by saying kind words and prayers as you move around them. A compassionate gardener will harvest the best herbs.

If you are getting herbs from a farm, inquire about the kind of people who run the place. Are they friendly, caring people? Do they take good care of their herbs? Find out what kind of land they grow the herbs on. Is it low-lying or up in the hills? Is the soil dry and sandy or moist and rich? These things all go into the energetics of an herb. If you are getting your herbs from a store (like most of us do), take some time to ask the people where they receive their herbs; the closer to the place you live, the better. Herbs don't like to be stored, shipped, and trucked around. Find out how long they have been sitting in their containers; the shorter amount of time, the better. The energy of the store also will go into the health of the herb. If the store feels negative or stagnant, it's a good bet to avoid buying herbs there. Also, try buying your herbs whole and as fresh as possible. This ensures their strength and vitality when you work with them.

When you have finally procured the herbs you want, it is now time to take them home and store them. Herbs should not be kept for more than one year, as their freshness and magic dissipates. (Roots are an exception, as they can be stored for many years if it is done right.) Store your herbs in a cool, dry spot in glass jars. If they are stored in plastic, the residue of the plastic will affect the strength of the herbs.

Finally, you are ready to work with your herbs. Medicinally, I prefer to make teas with my herbs if at all possible. After that, I make tinctures with them. Tinctures are concentrated essences of the herb compressed in an alcohol or glycerin base. You can also make poultices, creams, salves, and washes with them. There are many good herb books on this subject that you can check out. Astrologically, herbs can be given for different complaints associated with your chart. Take a look at the planetary and elemental associations of an herb in the compendium at the end of this chapter. It gives ideas on what herbs are best for you astrologically.

The Magic of Herbs

Each herb can be used not only medicinally but magically. The more you know about an herb, the more effective it will be in your spells and prayers. Spend time reading about the herb, and, if you can, find a living specimen and sit with it, draw it, and write what thoughts and perceptions you have about it. Try to visit it at different times of the day and night and at different times of its growing cycle. You will find it changes expression throughout the seasons. Once it has been harvested, try holding the herb in your hand and pick up the impressions you get through looking at it, smelling it, touching it, and tasting it. The herb may be prickly (a quality of Mars), or it may have come from a bog or marsh (linking it to the water element). It may taste bitter (fire) or smell sweet (Venus). Each quality will add to the overall gestalt of a plant and will give clues as to what element, planet, and sign it may be associated with. There is no need to be psychic in this process. We all pick up impressions and qualities of everything we come into contact with. If you can sense the mood of a friend or lover, you can also sense the vibration of any herb you work with.

As you work on deeper and deeper levels, use some of the shamanic skills I wrote about in chapter 6 for contacting the herb that you are interested in. Trance-work and journeying help us contact the root essence of the plant. When we experience these plants on a spiritual level, they may tell us information we were unable to see in our everyday connection. You may find that a plant expresses a different energy from what I've described. That is fine. Our experiences are subjective and we each have a different relationship to a plant. If you discover that nettle seems more like a Moon plant or a Pluto plant, then work from that framework. This is about individual exploration and discovery. There are no rules for what is right and wrong.

When you have developed this fine-tuned connection, you may have a powerful relationship with the herb. I find that working with a plant over many years helps deepen the relationship to profound levels. You may not think of the herb as food or medicine anymore. Instead, you may see it as a vibrant, expressive force with a personality of its own. You do not need to work with a plant for many years to have an energetic relationship with it, but your connection will grow stronger and your magic may become deeper over time.

When you work with a plant energetically, you are calling on its essence and spirit to shine through and give assistance in your work. You are not just working with a part of a plant, you are working with a unique spiritual creation that can assist you at fundamental levels. Because of this, the spirit of a plant can work more effectively at emotional and spiritual levels. When you are working with herbs energetically, you are asking to transform yourself on a spiritual level.

When you read through this compendium, you will discover that each plant has a section on its energetic properties. When you are weaving spells, making prayers with the names of the herbs, making teas and tinctures, or making amulets and talismans, bring the spirit of that plant into your ritual space. Call on it to be there with you as you would call a friend on the telephone. This may seem strange at first, but will soon feel commonplace. These herbs are embodiments of planetary and elemental power. When you call on them, you are calling on the physical representations of those powerful energies. In this way, you can augment a fire spell with a fire plant, or a lunar spell with a lunar plant. The plant will amplify your prayers. Touch them and weave them into your work. When you ask for their help humbly, they will help you tremendously.

Ways to Use Herbs

Teas (Infusions and Decoctions)

Making tea is my favorite way of taking an herb. The hot water seems to extract the most nutrients and medicinally active components of the herb and delivers them in a way that is most easily assimilated. Infusions are generally made with the flowers and leafy material of an herb, and decoctions are made with the roots or woody stems and bark. Teas are made with one ounce of dried herb to one pint of water. To make an infusion, simply boil a quart of water, add the herb, and then let it simmer for twenty minutes. To make a decoction, place the roots in the water, boil the mixture, and let it simmer for at least a half hour. In both cases, decant the water and then drink one glass (half a pint) in the morning and one glass in the evening. A quart is enough for two days. Refrigerate the tea when you are not using it. Children and elders should take one-quarter to half as much medicine as adults.

Tinctures

Tinctures are made by compressing herbs into a bottle of alcohol (usually vodka or brandy) and letting the herbs soak into the alcohol for one lunation (twenty-eight days). Try adding one ounce of herb to every four ounces of alcohol. After letting the mixture sit, the alcohol is decanted and strained off from the herbs and placed into small bottles. You usually take thirty to sixty drops of a tincture twice to four times a day. Acute conditions often call for more doses (four a day) for no more than seven days, while chronic conditions call for fewer doses (two a day) for at least six weeks. Again, children and elders should take one-quarter to half as much medicine as adults. As a side note, making the tincture on an auspicious Moon benefits the medicine tremendously.

Oils

Oils are used for massages and to rub into the skin. Their medicinal components are absorbed by the skin and into the body. Making an oil is similar to making a tincture. If the herbs are leaves, crush them in your palm and then place them in a glass, sealable container. Then pour olive oil over the herbs and seal the container. Allow two to six weeks for the herbs to steep into the oil. Then decant the oil from the bottle through muslin cloth into another container, leaving the herb behind. Oils can last up to a year.

Salves and Ointments

Another way to encapsulate the energy of an herb is to make a remedy that you can apply to your skin. You can make wonderful salves that soothe and heal cuts, abrasions, and rashes with herbs such as comfrey, St. John's wort, and calendula.

Salves are topical creams that are helpful in alleviating skin problems such as acne, dry skin, and eczema, as well as cuts and bruises. To make a salve, first make an oil of a particular herb. Then pour the oil into a pot and heat up the oil while you add beeswax. Mix the two together until they are completely blended. At this point, you will need to add enough beeswax to harden the oil, but not so much that the salve is too hard. Finding the right blend of oil and beeswax is up to personal taste. When complete, pour the heated mixture into containers and allow it to cool. It will harden and then be ready to use.

Flower Essences

One of the most powerful ways to deliver the essential, energetic quality of a plant is through the use of flower essences. I described how to make flower essences in chapter 6. These powerful liquids have the capability of magically and energetically transforming our lives through their subtle effect.

Flower Arrangements

Herbs can be incredibly beneficial in the form of bouquets, dried and hanging from the wall or ceiling or in potpourri form. All of these methods allow the scent and color of the herbs to infuse a room with their magical energy. This is one of the primary ways to bring life and vitality to a house and home. It augments the spirit and emotional energy of all who live there.

In Gardens and as Houseplants

One of the most profound ways to work with herbs is to have their living presence near you. By gently and lovingly caretaking their growth and development, you can see their patterns throughout the day and throughout the seasons. Their presence improves any environment and can be a source of medicine, both physically and energetically.

Amulets

One of the most magical ways to use herbs is in amulets. This process was described in chapter 6. By gathering some of the herb fresh and then drying it, the herb can then be placed in a pouch to secure its energetic and magical healing properties.

Spells

As in your work with talismans, it is helpful to gather herbs and dry them yourself, if at all possible. Herbs are most potent when gathered from nearby. Because of their proximity, they already are in sync with the climate, the terrain, and the other plants of the surrounding environment and can more readily give of their energy.

Compendium of Herbs, Plants, and Trees

Aloe—*Aloe vera*

Actions: Aloe has a very firm, erect, and spiny exterior, and a soothing, moist interior to the leaves. Aloe has a soothing, cooling energy that helps moisten and heal burns and skin inflammations. It heals burns and skin inflammations. It also has a bitter quality that helps soothe an inflamed liver with its symptoms of ulcers, stomach problems, migraines, tension, and anger.

Planetary Allies: Moon and Neptune

Sign Ruler: Cancer

Elemental Ally: Water

Energetics: Aloe is a protective plant to be called on in times of excessive intensity and hot emotions. It helps us remain strong, cool, and unruffled.

Basil—*Ocinium basilicum*

Actions: Basil is a diaphoretic, stimulating perspiration, and thus is good for colds, flus, and fevers. It also helps in the digestion and assimilation of food. Used primarily as a kitchen herb, basil adds a beautiful aroma to any garden or meal.

Planetary Ally: Mars

Sign Ruler: Scorpio

Elemental Ally: Fire

Energetics: Basil is a sacred and revered plant in India. It acts as a fresh clearing influence that stimulates our highest selves, opens our hearts, and clears our aura. Basil works in matters of transformation, helping us through transitions and powerful changes in our lives. It is also an aphrodisiac and helps stimulate passion.

Borage—*Borago officianalis*

Actions: Borage acts as an antidepressant, lifting our spirits. It also helps induce sweating and is good for colds and the flu. Borage can increase milk production in nursing mothers.

Planetary Ally: Jupiter

Sign Ruler: Leo

Elemental Allies: Air, fire

Energetics: This herb has traditionally been known to relieve fear and be protective. The ancient physician Pliny said of this herb, "I give courage."

Burdock—*Arctium lappa*

Actions: Burdock works to cleanse the system by flushing the liver and blood of toxins as well as offering a tonic effect to the whole body. This imparts clearer skin, better digestion, more ease, and less stress.

Planetary Ally: Venus

Sign Ruler: Leo

Elemental Ally: Fire

Energetics: Burdock relieves stagnancies by cleaning the old energy out and offering gentle healing, calming the emotions, and helping us become more relaxed and positive.

Caraway—*Carum carvi*

Actions: Caraway is a wonderful culinary herb that promotes good digestion and relieves stagnancy and dyspepsia. It stimulates the appetite and helps cure diarrhea. Caraway is also known for helping with bronchitis and asthma.

Planetary Ally: Mercury

Sign Ruler: Cancer

Elemental Ally: Air

Energetics: Caraway helps reduce the stress that comes from excessive worry and mental tension. It promotes a clear and open flow of energy.

Calendula—*Calendula officianalis*

Actions: Calendula is often used as a soothing ointment to heal cuts and wounds. It also has a reputation for healing ulcers and helps us digest and assimilate food better.

Planetary Ally: Sun

Sign Ruler: Leo

Elemental Ally: Fire

Energetics: When displayed in the garden or as an ornamental bouquet, calendula helps brighten and lighten any atmosphere. It has the power to protect and draw forth our psychic resources, helping open our clairvoyant and telepathic powers.

Cascara Sagrada—*Rhamnus purshiana*

Actions: The bark of this tree helps stimulate the liver, gall bladder, and digestive system. This helps us digest and eliminate food, thus causing a laxative effect, and thereby reducing poisons and toxins in the system. It should be used only by people who are relatively strong; debilitated and seriously ill people should choose a gentler remedy.

Planetary Ally: Jupiter

Sign Ruler: Virgo

Elemental Ally: Earth

Energetics: When life or energy becomes blocked, cascara acts as an ally to push out unwanted stagnancy, release tension, and stimulate movement and change.

Caution: When ingested, the fruits and bark of this tree will cause diarrhea and vomiting.

Catnip—*Nepata cataria*

Actions: Catnip is predominantly known for its use with felines. They seem to become euphoric and drunk off the smell of this herb and will often roll about in its leaves and flowers as if in a stupor. It can also be given to humans as a mild sedative, helping calm the nerves. It is also a digestive aid and a fever reducer.

Planetary Ally: Venus

Sign Rulers: Virgo, Leo

Elemental Ally: Water

Energetics: This herb is especially designed for cat magic. It augments the connection to the lioness in all of us and strengthens our ties to any cats we may have in our homes.

Cayenne—*Capsicum frutescens*

Actions: Cayenne acts to stimulate heat and energy in all parts of the body, helping eliminate toxins, mucus, and sickness. It should only be used if the consumer is not too weak.

Planetary Ally: Mars

Sign Ruler: Aries

Elemental Ally: Fire

Energetics: Cayenne is a wonderful ally for stimulating energy and power, and warding off fear and darkness. Its beautiful, long, red shape is wonderful to look at when hanging in bunches.

Chamomile—*Matricaria chamomilla*

Actions: Chamomile is a primary nervous-system relaxant, acting to soothe and calm the nerves in a gentle but not overly sedative way.

Planetary Ally: Sun

Sign Ruler: Leo

Elemental Allies: Fire, air

Energetics: Chamomile has a light and pleasing appearance. She offers clarity and ease of vision so that good choices can be made. Chamomile relaxes the energy.

Caution: Ragweed allergy sufferers may want to avoid chamomile.

Chicory—*Cichorium intybus*

Actions: Chicory is a delightful, blue-flowered plant that helps us digest food and strengthens the liver. It also assists in removing gallstones and is a good cleanser of uric acid from the system, thus helping cure rheumatism and gout.

Planetary Ally: Jupiter

Sign Ruler: Virgo

Elemental Ally: Earth

Energetics: Chicory displays a positive and mystical radiance that is helpful for banishing negativity and promoting the ability to move easily through difficult situations. It has also been said to be able to make a person invisible. Scott Cunningham says that "chicory has to be gathered with a gold knife in perfect silence at noon or midnight on Midsummer" in order to accomplish this task.[2]

Cinnamon—*Cinnamomum zeylanicum*

Actions: Cinnamon is a wonderfully aromatic plant that warms our constitution and strengthens our digestion. It is also an astringent herb that alleviates diarrhea.

Planetary Ally: Sun

Sign Ruler: Aries

Elemental Ally: Fire

Energetics: This herb helps put us in touch with the luminous spirit world, the underlying nature of things. It stimulates energy for positive means, whether that be for healing, gaining money, or attuning to a spiritual source.

Coltsfoot—*Tussilago farfara*

Actions: Coltsfoot has a strong expectorant property that helps heal coughs and illnesses of the lungs.

Planetary Ally: Mercury

Sign Ruler: Taurus

Elemental Ally: Earth

Energetics: This plant brings peace and tranquility to any situation and is used to draw forth a nourishing and abiding love.

Caution: Coltsfoot can be toxic if ingested in large amounts.

Comfrey—*Symphytum officianale*

Actions: Comfrey helps heal wounds and broken bones primarily. It is also good for inflammations of the lungs with associated coughing, fevers, etc. Comfrey grows wild and freely and is often found in waste areas of garden pastures. Comfrey has recently been listed as a dangerous herb by the FDA due to studies showing that an alkaloid it contains may be damaging to the liver. Comfrey should be used with caution.

Planetary Ally: Saturn

Sign Ruler: Capricorn

Elemental Ally: Earth

Energetics: Comfrey is used for regeneration in times of extreme weakness and debility. It is about making things whole again, knitting the parts back together.

Caution: Comfrey is carcinogenic when ingested in large amounts.

Dandelion—*Taraxacum officianalis*

Actions: Dandelion is a fabulous liver cleanser and stimulator of bile and digestive juices. It also helps cleanse and tonify the blood.

Planetary Ally: Jupiter

Sign Ruler: Libra

Elemental Ally: Earth

Energetics: Dandelion is a great plant totem. Its nobility, strength, and sweet optimism make it a delight to know. It relieves stress and strain in the body and the emotions.

Caution: Contact with dandelion can cause dermatitis.

Dill—*Anetheum graveolens*

Actions: Dill helps relieve indigestion and flatulence and is also known to stimulate lactation in nursing mothers.

Planetary Ally: Mercury

Sign Ruler: Cancer

Elemental Ally: Air

Energetics: This tall creature with its wonderful, bisected leaves is a great ally when we need to feel clear-headed, as it stimulates our mental and communicative side. Dill helps us process life experiences without feeling overloaded. It is also a great totem for mothers who need protection and security. A bundle of it tied up in the house reduces stress and banishes negativity.

Dock—*Rumex crispus*

Actions: Dock acts as a great liver cleanser, strengthening the flow of bile to increase harmony in the digestive and eliminative functions. This weedy plant is found in gardens and waste areas and grows by underground rhizome. Unless it is completely dug up, each rhizomatous root will spring forth a new dock plant. Thus this plant retains a strong resiliency and the ability to regenerate and revitalize under even the most adverse conditions.

Planetary Ally: Jupiter

Sign Ruler: Aries

Elemental Ally: Air

Energetics: Dock is supremely regenerative and is helpful for those who need to be reborn after a difficult time. Dock cleans out negative emotions and brings new life, new love, and new hope and faith.

Caution: Avoid ingesting dock in large doses.

Echinacea—*Echinacea* spp.

Actions: Echinacea is a wonderful herbal antibiotic, used as a prime plant against colds and flu. It strengthens the body's natural immune system to help ward off infection and disease.

Planetary Ally: Jupiter

Sign Ruler: Sagittarius

Elemental Ally: Fire

Energetics: Echinacea has a beautiful purple radial set of petals that give it the look of an unfolding chakra. Echinacea, or coneflower, is a great protector against negativity and stimulates the aura to shine more fully. It helps act as a balancing agent in times of upset and distress.

Elder—*Sambucus nigra*

Actions: Elder acts primarily as a diaphoretic, helping us sweat out toxins during illness and fever.

Planetary Ally: Mercury

Sign Ruler: Sagittarius

Elemental Ally: Fire

Energetics: Elder is a wise totem, a capable guide through rough and treacherous waters that points us to the other side when we become lost. It helps in our transformations and acts as a benevolent protector. It is also used for exorcisms and banishment of negative energy.

Caution: Elder bark, roots, leaves, and unripe berries are toxic if ingested.

Eyebright—*Euphrasia officianalis*

Actions: Eyebright works primarily as a great eye wash for infections and diseases of the eye like conjunctivitis and glaucoma.

Planetary Ally: Sun

Sign Ruler: Leo

Elemental Allies: Fire, air

Energetics: This sweet, small plant is a marvelous ally for those of us needing clearer vision and direction in our life. Call upon it when making difficult decisions.

Caution: Avoid the use of eyebright without a physician's advice.

Fennel—*Foeniculum vulgare*

Actions: Fennel is used especially as a culinary digestive aid, helping increase the gastric juices that allow for better assimilation and elimination.

Planetary Allies: Mercury, Uranus

Sign Ruler: Virgo

Elemental Ally: Fire

Energetics: This tall and showy plant acts as a sentinel in the garden, banishing negative forces from entering and stimulating a positive flow of healing and communicative energy.

Caution: Contact with fennel may cause dermatitis.

Feverfew—*Tanecetum parthenium*

Actions: Feverfew is often discussed as a remedy for migraines and persistent headaches. It also alleviates nausea and improves sleep and digestion.

Planetary Ally: Venus

Sign Ruler: Aries

Elemental Ally: Water

Energetics: This is primarily a protective herb.

Caution: Contact with fennel may cause dermatitis and/or allergic reactions.

Garlic—*Allium sativum*

Actions: Garlic has a tremendous number of uses. It acts as an immune-system booster, a natural antibiotic, a digestive stimulant and carminative, a diaphoretic (meaning it induces sweating), a healer of lung ailments, and as an overall, powerful tonic for the system.

Planetary Allies: Mars, Pluto

Sign Ruler: Aries

Elemental Ally: Fire

Energetics: Have you heard of garlic strands warding off vampires? Garlic is a powerful protective ally and one that brings strength and nourishment to any space it occupies. It is a strong warrior capable of rooting out negative influences and banishing them. Garlic also helps in transformative rituals when we need help in shifting and changing our path toward one of greater harmony.

Gentian—*Gentiana lutea*

Actions: Gentian is used primarily as a digestive aid. It has a cool and bitter quality that relieves heat in the liver and stomach; it is therefore good for ulcers and poor eating habits.

Planetary Ally: Mars

Sign Ruler: Virgo

Elemental Ally: Fire

Energetics: When we get heated up by the stress of fast living and a compulsive lifestyle, gentian helps cool us down and brings more ease and harmony into our lives.

Ginger—*Zingiber officianale*

Actions: Ginger is a wonderful culinary herb that is heating and stimulating to the system. It induces sweating and thus removes toxins and impurities from the system. It has the quality of moving stagnancies and raising our energy levels.

Planetary Ally: Mars

Sign Ruler: Aries

Elemental Ally: Fire

Energetics: When we are listless, drained, or sapped by our lifestyle and the people we are around, ginger enlivens our best qualities and moves us out of ruts. There is a rawness to the root that helps draw out creativity and sexual energy.

Ginseng—*Panax ginseng*

Actions: Ginseng is a supreme tonic. There are several different kinds of ginseng: Korean, Siberian, and American. Each is a very different plant, but all three act as tonics. Korean is the most fiery and masculine, helping stimulate testosterone, which wards off fear and gives us strength and firmness. Siberian is gentler but still warming and reduces stress in the system. American is cooler and should be given to hot and fiery-type people. It is also an adaptogen, meaning it is a stress reducer. All three are powerful tonics and bring nourishment and strength to the entire system. Ginseng is wonderful for people with nervous complaints, weakness, debilities, or a weak sexual drive.

Planetary Ally: Mars

Sign Ruler: Capricorn

Elemental Allies: Earth, (fire: Korean ginseng)

Energetic Properties: Ginseng has tremendous force. When we need to be grounded, rooted, and centered, we call on ginseng. We can also call on ginseng when we need warrior courage to confront problems.

Caution: Avoid ingesting ginseng in large doses.

Goldenseal—*Hydrastis canadensis*

Actions: Goldenseal is a very potent herb to be given in times of cold and flu. It acts as an antibiotic, effectively ridding the body of harmful bacteria. It also has a bitter effect, which can stimulate the digestive tract and liver. It has a somewhat abrasive effect, however, and should be used infrequently.

Planetary Ally: Sun

Sign Ruler: Aries

Elemental Ally: Fire

Energetic Properties: Goldenseal acts as a powerful cleansing agent, removing unwanted negativity and depression while promoting health and strength.

Caution: Avoid the use of goldenseal during pregnancy.

Hawthorn—*Crataegus oxycantha*

Actions: Hawthorn is one of the best overall tonics and healers of the heart. Its astringent nature helps regulate heart rhythm, tonify the blood vessels and muscles of the heart, and strengthen and regulate the overall circulation of blood throughout the body.

Planetary Allies: Mars, Sun

Sign Ruler: Leo

Elemental Ally: Fire

Energetics: Though it is an herb of the Sun and Mars, it is not bold or flashy in its nature. Hawthorn is a more subtle ally, helping over time to bring peace, serenity, and an open heart. It is an ancient ally to the Celtic people who revere the oak, ash, and thorn as strong tree friends.

Caution: The use of hawthorn may affect blood pressure and heart rate.

Hops—*Humulus lupulus*

Actions: Hops has a soporific effect and can make us feel sedated and drowsy. It is very effective for decreasing insomnia and anxiety.

Planetary Allies: Mars, Neptune

Sign Ruler: Aries

Elemental Ally: Fire

Energetics: Hops grows as a climbing and trailing vine, emitting musky and sedating vibrations from its pores. When we need relaxation and a slightly mystical feeling, we can call on hops. It is somewhat hallucinatory and wonderful for trance and psychic work.

Caution: Contact with hops may cause dermatitis.

Horsetail—*Equisetum* spp.

Actions: Horsetail is an excellent source of silica that helps builds bones and tissues as well as heal wounds. It also acts as an astringent and diuretic, helping heal the urogenital system. It is also known for its ability to heal the prostate gland and strengthen the kidneys.

Planetary Ruler: Saturn

Sign Ruler: Pisces

Elemental Ally: Earth

Energetics: Horsetail is often found in watery and boggy areas. It helps us move out of heavy and difficult areas of our lives, and lets us gain a footing and build solid foundations. If we are feeling sunk or bottled up, we may want to work with horsetail to help us transform and move through difficulty.

Caution: Horsetail is toxic to livestock.

Hyssop—*Hyssopus officinalis*

Actions: Hyssop is primarily used for lung complaints and nervous disorders. It has anti-spasmodic actions that help relieve coughs and symptoms of bronchitis. As a nervine, it relieves anxiety, relaxes tics and tremors, and restores the nervous system.

Planetary Ruler: Jupiter

Sign Ruler: Cancer

Elemental Ally: Fire

Energetics: With its expansive and opening qualities, hyssop helps draw forth any intense emotions, such as sadness, grief, and emotional tension, and then release them with awareness and compassion. Hyssop is gentle but firm and strong in approach.

Juniper—*Juniperus communis*

Actions: Juniper berries have a good diuretic effect and help in treating cystitis and urethritis.

Planetary Ally: Mars

Sign Ruler: Aries

Elemental Ally: Fire

Energetics: This strong and aromatic tree helps enliven and purify any environment. It draws forth our fiery, passionate, creative, and sexual energies.

Caution: Avoid the use of juniper during pregnancy.

Kelp—*Fucus vesiculosus*

Actions: Kelp is a wonderful seaweed that is especially nutritive and tonifying. One of its prime functions is to heal an underactive thyroid for those who are overweight. It is also known to lubricate the joints and help with problems such as arthritis and rheumatism.

Planetary Ally: Neptune

Sign Ruler: Pisces

Elemental Ally: Water

Energetics: Dive down into the ocean and feel the cooling and nourishing effect of the salt water. All pain and turmoil are erased with the first blast of the salt spray on your face. Kelp helps alleviate tension at a fundamental level and release any emotional tension, helping us feel happy and contented in the moment. It also elevates our spiritual and psychic sensitivity and puts us in touch with the transcendent.

Kinnikinnick—*Arctostaphylos uva-ursi*

Actions: Kinnikinnick grows wild in the Northwest and has a diuretic property. It is primarily used with infections of the urinary system and can be used to help strengthen the kidneys by flushing toxins out of them.

Planetary Ally: Pluto

Sign Ruler: Scorpio

Elemental Ally: Water

Energetics: Kinnikinick is a small but not inconsequential plant. It grows by rhizome and spreads out over a wide area. It helps us release fear and tightness and helps us let go of tension.

Lavender—*Lavendula officianalis*

Actions: Lavender has a wonderful aroma that stimulates and cleanses our respiratory system. It enlivens the senses and purifies the air. Because it contains essential oils, it acts as a natural antibiotic. Lavender is used primarily as an oil and can be placed in hot baths or in pillows. It can also be applied in ointments as an antiseptic and cell rejuvenator. Lavender helps relax the nervous system and enables us to remain at ease.

Planetary Allies: Mercury, Uranus

Sign Rulers: Leo, Aquarius

Elemental Ally: Air

Energetics: Lavender's sweet, refreshing scent and lively, beautiful, purple flowers help us access our highest selves. We feel refreshed and calm with this herb. Lavender opens our hearts and makes our connections sweeter. It brings us serenity and blessings.

Lemon Balm—*Melissa officianalis*

Actions: Lemon balm is a sweet and refreshing herb, and can also be taken as a tea. This herb relieves stomach distress and calms our nervous system. Balm is slightly stimulating, but in a very gentle manner.

Planetary Allies: Jupiter, Moon

Sign Ruler: Cancer

Elemental Ally: Water

Energetics: Lemon balm is a dear friend to have. Her relaxed and jovial manner attracts friendship and success. She helps put us in touch with serene joy, peaceful wonder, and simple pleasure.

Licorice—*Glycyrrhiza glabra*

Actions: Licorice is one of the sweetest tasting of all the herbs. It is often used in herbal combinations to offset bitterness and also for its wonderful rejuvenative properties. Licorice is a kidney and adrenal-system tonifier. It helps dispel illness and poisons in the body and builds our storehouse of chi and vitality.

Planetary Allies: Venus, Neptune

Sign Ruler: Libra

Elemental Ally: Water

Energetics: When we feel washed out, depleted, and at the end of our rope, licorice is a lifeline. Licorice has a warm, resonating glow that can restore and nourish us at our core. It calms and centers us so that we can hear the eternal hum, the OM underneath.

Lobelia—*Lobelia inflata*

Actions: Lobelia is very helpful for lung and chest complaints. It helps cure bronchitis and relieves cattarh and mucus from the respiratory areas.

Planetary Ally: Uranus

Sign Ruler: Aquarius

Elemental Ally: Air

Energetics: Lobelia is a powerful cleanser and opener. When a breath of new life needs to be brought in and fear and constriction need to be dispelled, lobelia is the herb. Tightness and congestion are replaced by expansion and expressiveness.

Caution: Lobelia is an herb that has generated some controversy. The FDA recommends that lobelia not be taken in any dose, because usage of lobelia is dose dependent, and natural products can vary in concentration. In some people, a dose as small as 0.6 gram of lobelia leaves can cause rapid or irregular heartbeat, breathing difficulties, sleepiness, and muscle twitching. A dose of 4 grams or more is fatal.

Madrona—*Arbutus madrona*

Actions: No medicinal actions.

Planetary Ally: Pluto

Sign Ruler: Scorpio

Elemental Ally: Water

Energetics: The madrona tree is an ancient and primeval being. Her tremendous power comes from her gnarled connection to earth and sky. She draws down power almost electrically and channels it through her leaves and roots. Her skin peels like a snake and there is great sexual and regenerative power in her. She can shapeshift and sustain powerful emotional and psychic energies. She is truly an incredible magical entity.

Maple—*Acer macrophyllum*

Actions: No medicinal actions.

Planetary Ally: Jupiter

Sign Ruler: Sagittarius

Elemental Ally: Air

Energetics: Maple is a beneficent and joyful creature, giving fruitfulness and expansiveness of nature to all those around her.

Marijuana—*Cannibus sativa* spp.

Actions: This controversial herb acts as a strong narcotic, affecting our perceptions of time, place, and self. When taken infrequently, marijuana puts us in touch with the here and now and augments our experiences so that our senses of touch, feel, smell, and taste become more heightened, more aware. It also can have a calming and slightly ecstatic quality about it, but induces fear and paranoia in many people as well. When consumed on a regular basis, marijuana may cause greater introversion and stagnancy, and also takes a toll on the lungs, kidneys, and heart. The aura becomes weakened and grayer.

Planetary Ally: Neptune

Sign Ruler: Pisces

Elemental Ally: Water

Energetics: Marijuana is a strongly vibratory plant that enlivens any room it is in. Its power can open and expand, or bind and control those who use it as a totem.

Caution: Marijuana is an illegal, addictive narcotic.

Marshmallow—*Althaea officinalis*

Actions: Marshmallow has a moist and dry property that is soothing to the lungs and throat. It helps those who are very weak and dry and need sustenance and moisture in their system.

Planetary Ally: Moon

Sign Ruler: Cancer

Elemental Ally: Water

Energetics: Marshmallow is a beautiful, tender plant that softens and eases life when it is difficult and uncomfortable. Rely on marshmallow as a comfort and a security blanket when times are hard.

Mugwort—*Artemisia vulgaris*

Actions: Mugwort improves the digestion and helps circulate the blood in the body. It also acts as an effective nervine when ingested as smoke.

Planetary Allies: Venus, Neptune

Sign Ruler: Cancer

Elemental Ally: Water

Energetics: Mugwort is a very powerful shamanic herb, capable of tremendous healing. It is used as a smudge to purify and enliven an environment. It is very helpful for those needing to seek a vision or to gain psychic skills. It has the power to move and channel energy like almost no other herb.

Caution: Contact with mugwort may cause dermatitis.

Mullein—*Verbascum thapsus*

Actions: Mullein is primarily used as a lung healer, helping calm and repair the tissue in those areas. It acts as a nervine, which also helps relax the muscles of the lungs to stop destructive coughing.

Planetary Ally: Saturn

Sign Ruler: Gemini

Elemental Allies: Air, earth

Energetics: Mullein is a proud creature that stands very tall and erect (sometimes up to nine feet). Its firmness of character as well as its soft, velvety leaves give it a nobility of character, a charming gentleman who can help us stand firm and see clearly.

Caution: Avoid the leaves of mullein.

Nettle—*Urtica dioica*

Actions: Nettle has many incredible effects. It acts primarily as a powerful tonic, enlivening and enriching all the cells of the body. This imparts to people who take nettle often a lustrous glow, shiny hair, and soft, smooth skin. Nettle is great for problems in the lungs, like mucous conditions, and is also great for the skin, helping with problems like eczema and acne.

Planetary Ally: Mars

Sign Ruler: Aries

Elemental Ally: Fire

Energetics: Nettle is a powerful healer and rejuvenator. It picks the worst wastelands and clearcuts to grow strong. It provides a rich mineral and nutrient base for other plants and trees to grow on. Nettle energy is the proud warrior energy, strong, clear, and glowing with green power.

Caution: Fresh nettle plants sting.

Oak—*Quercus alba*

Actions: No medicinal actions.

Planetary Allies: Saturn, Jupiter (both rulerships have been noted)

Sign Ruler: Capricorn

Elemental Allies: Earth, fire

Energetics: Oak is a wise sage; it is a teacher tree. With its gnarled and twisted branches, it channels a great deal of energy and is a favorite of many witches. Oak is a great totem tree and is a strong, regal figure. Oak is protective and it heals and instills wisdom and luck to its allies. Oak is especially powerful for those who are "caught on the treadmill" and are working too hard and exhausting themselves. It helps return a sense of peace and inner strength and an ability to endure the travails of life.

Caution: Inner oak bark contains tannic acid, which is potentially toxic.

Oats—*Avena sativa*

Actions: Oats is one of the principal herbs used to heal the nervous system. It is especially helpful for restoring a person after a long illness as it is restorative and has a tonic effect. It is soothing and gentle and can be used for those who are feverish.

Planetary Ally: Mercury

Sign Ruler: Virgo

Elemental Ally: Air

Energetics: After long periods of confusion and disability, oats has the ability to bring us back from the brink and help restore a foundation. Any time we have been scattered, hurt, damaged, or depleted, oats is a great ally to return us to our essential goodness, our essential divinity.

Oregon Grape—*Berberis aquifolium, nervosa*

Actions: This herb is used specifically as a liver cleanser, akin to dandelion. It induces bile to flow and helps the digestive process. Oregon grape has an antibiotic effect that makes it helpful for strengthening the immune system.

Planetary Ally: Jupiter

Sign Ruler: Virgo

Elemental Ally: Earth

Energetics: Oregon grape is a prickly creature and a great defender. If negative energy is being thrown at someone, Oregon grape can ward it off and send it away.

Parsley—*Petroselinum crispum*

Actions: Parsley is used primary as a culinary herb, as it helps with digestion. It is also a strong diuretic and helps with illnesses of the urinary tract and kidneys.

Planetary Ally: Mercury

Sign Ruler: Libra

Elemental Ally: Air

Energetics: Parsley is a friendly little creature, designed to heighten our senses. It is often added as a garnish on the side of a plate to add pleasure and healthfulness to eating and conversation. Parsley helps confer a protective aura around the place where it resides.

Peppermint—*Mentha piperita*

Actions: Peppermint is often sipped as an herbal tea and is principally a digestive aid, but also acts to enliven the system and can work as a febrifuge (sweat inducer).

Planetary Ally: Mercury

Sign Ruler: Gemini

Elemental Ally: Air

Energetics: Peppermint is a lively and friendly plant (think Gemini) and likes to brighten up a room with its smell. It is great for increasing friendliness and talkativeness. It banishes negativity and heightens amorous feelings.

Caution: Contact with peppermint may cause dermatitis and/or allergic reactions. Peppermint oil is toxic if ingested.

Pine—*Pinus* spp.

Actions: No medicinal actions.

Planetary Ally: Mars

Sign Ruler: Capricorn

Elemental Ally: Air

Energetics: Pine has an intensely aromatic odor that is very stimulating to the psyche. Its power lies as a strong cleanser of negative emotions and energies and as a warrior defender and protector of land. It is a guardian over the woods creatures that dwell beneath and around it. In flower essences, it is said that pine can relieve us of feelings of guilt and remorse for past mistakes.

Plantain—*Plantago lanceolata* spp.

Actions: Plantain has soothing and expectorant properties that are helpful for lung infections. Plantain has diuretic properties and is used for kidney problems. It also is used externally in poultice or ointment form to soothe cuts, burns, and skin problems.

Planetary Ally: Saturn

Sign Ruler: Capricorn

Elemental Ally: Earth

Energetics: Plantain is a gentle friend, helping strengthen the system when we are dealing with grief, stress, and sadness. Plantain helps clear out old habits and ways of doing things and replaces them with fresh new pathways. It helps create a firm foundation and assists in transitions.

Raspberry—*Rubus idaeus*

Actions: Raspberry is a fabulous uterine tonic and is the prime herb taken by pregnant women to strengthen and prepare them for childbirth.

Planetary Ally: Venus

Sign Ruler: Scorpio

Elemental Ally: Water

Energetics: Raspberry is a beautiful, tangled herb with delicious berries. Its interwoven physical form represents the web of life and shows the beauty of our interconnectedness. We honor raspberry as a powerful feminine force, beautiful, rich, complex, and deep.

Red Clover—*Trifolium pratense*

Actions: Clover is a great blood tonic and cleanser that helps cool and heal skin problems. It acts as a reducer of toxins in the system. It is great for addicts, alcoholics, and smokers who are trying to quit. Red clover has been reported to help reduce tumors and may be helpful in cases of cancer.

Planetary Ally: Mercury

Sign Ruler: Leo

Elemental Ally: Air

Energetics: Red clover is known as a plant of good luck, as in four-leaf clovers. Luck means simply flowing with life in an easy and unobstructed way. Clover helps this process and should be called upon when we are weighed down or "off the path."

Caution: Contact with red clover may cause dermatitis.

Rose—*Rosa* spp.

Actions: Rose hips are taken as a great source of vitamin C, and its oil is used for its sweet and enlivening smell.

Planetary Ally: Venus

Sign Ruler: Libra

Elemental Ally: Fire

Energetics: Rose has been written about as a metaphor for centuries. The incredible beauty of a rose bloom lasts only a very short time before it withers, so it shows the ephemeral quality of life, that only a few things really matter. With its thorns, it also shows beauty and pain tied together, which is also a metaphor for life. Roses help lift our spirits and strengthen our hearts. Roses are given to show love and are truly a romantic flower.

Rosemary—*Rosmarinus officinalis*

Actions: Used primarily as a culinary herb, rosemary helps with digestion and stimulates the liver function. Rosemary has a pungent aroma that stimulates the appetite. It is also used as an incense.

Planetary Allies: Sun, Jupiter

Sign Ruler: Aries

Elemental Ally: Fire

Energetics: Rosemary is a wonderful, friendly ally that stimulates good feelings and helps purify an environment of negativity. Rosemary also helps stimulate the memory.

Sage—*Salva officinalis*

Actions: Sage has an antiseptic property that makes it great for throat and lung infections. It also works well as a carminative for indigestion, and is also a nervine.

Planetary Allies: Jupiter, Neptune

Sign Ruler: Taurus

Elemental Allies: Air, water

Energetics: Sage is used as a smudge to cleanse and enliven a space. It is a very powerful healing herb and can be called on to help solidify intent and vision. It is powerful in ritual and is capable of magically transforming our lives and emotions.

Caution: Do not take sage if breastfeeding.

Sarsaparilla—*Smilax officinalis*

Actions: Sarsaparilla is very helpful for skin conditions, helping to heal rashes, eczema, and psoriasis. It is also helpful for rheumatism and arthritis. Sarsaparilla is known for its ability to strengthen the libido and the testosterone level in men.

Planetary Ruler: Mars

Sign Ruler: Scorpio

Elemental Ally: Water

Energetics: This powerful, dense spirit has an intense and driving disposition. When we need to transform and cleanse out old patterns with force and vigor, we can call on this plant. He is strongly protective and a good warrior friend. Sarsaparilla helps us be direct, forceful, and sure.

Skullcap—*Scuttelaria lateriflora*

Actions: Skullcap is primarily used as a gentle nervine, relaxing any tense feelings, especially hot emotions like anger and hatred. It promotes an easy and detached state of mind.

Planetary Ally: Uranus

Sign Ruler: Aquarius

Elemental Ally: Air

Energetics: We call on skullcap when we need a meditative and contemplative energy, when we need balance and temperance.

Caution: Avoid ingesting skullcap in large doses.

Slippery Elm—*Ulmus fulva*

Actions: Slippery elm is used for its mucilaginous and sweet properties and is primarily taken for digestive, lung, and throat problems. It has a soothing, nourishing, and rebuilding quality, helping heal those who are weak and febrile.

Planetary Ally: Saturn

Sign Ruler: Taurus

Elemental Ally: Earth

Energetics: Slippery elm is a great totem for the home and family. It helps solidify and strengthen our familial ties and relieve any interpersonal struggle and tension.

St. John's Wort—*Hypericum perforatum*

Actions: St. John's wort is used most effectively as a mild antidepressant. It helps elevate the mood and is relaxing as well. As an oil, it can help with nerve pain as well as heal external wounds.

Planetary Ally: Sun

Sign Ruler: Leo

Elemental Ally: Fire

Energetics: St. John's wort is a beneficent healer. In these times of high stress and fast-paced lives, this herb gives us a timeout, a breather, and a natural dose of joy and pleasure. St. John's wort brings the light in, adds color to our lives, and is naturally protective against negative energy.

Caution: With external use of St. John's wort, avoid prolonged exposure to sunlight. St. John's wort is not recommended for treating severe depression, and should not be taken with other prescription drugs.

Sunflower—*Helianthus anuus*

Actions: No medicinal actions.

Planetary Ally: Sun

Sign Ruler: Leo

Elemental Ally: Fire

Energetics: Sunflower is the supreme solar plant and can be called on when our inner sun, our inner glow, is diminished. Sunflower helps broaden, magnify, and externalize our expression. We become more dynamic, healthy, and happy beings with sunflower around.

Caution: The pollen of sunflowers may cause allergic reactions.

Thyme—*Thymus vulgaris*

Actions: Thyme is used in cooking to help stimulate and promote good digestion. It also has antiseptic qualities that make it good for combating all kinds of infections.

Planetary Ally: Venus

Sign Ruler: Aries

Elemental Ally: Fire

Energetics: Thyme stimulates a better flow of our energies and helps clear out old thought patterns. It is great for obsessive types and worriers.

Caution: Thyme oil is toxic if ingested.

Tobacco—*Nicotiana* spp.

Actions: In modern times, we have a very poor relationship with this alkaloid-rich plant. Millions of people die every year from cancer and tobacco-related illnesses. This is unfortunate, because used in moderation and with sacred intent, tobacco is a very powerful and enlivening plant, used often for ritual purposes (especially by certain Native American tribes).

Planetary Ally: Mars

Sign Ruler: Libra

Elemental Ally: Fire

Energetics: This plant confers psychic and spiritual energy on those who use it well, with humility and gratitude. Tobacco helps purify and is often used in healing ceremonies by shamans who are friends with the tobacco ally.

Caution: Tobacco is an addictive narcotic and carcinogen.

Valerian—*Valeriana officinalis*

Actions: Valerian has a sedative and nerve-relaxing quality. It has somewhat of a spacey effect, like marijuana, if taken in higher doses. It reduces stress and calms us.

Planetary Ally: Mercury

Sign Ruler: Scorpio

Elemental Allies: Water, air

Energetics: When we need to access trance and psychic spaces, we call on valerian. We can draw on her power to explore our deepest depths and call up visions stored within us.

Vervain—*Verbena officianalis*

Actions: Vervain is used primarily as a nervine and relaxant, helping restore the nervous system and offset anxiety and nervousness. It also seems to help with depression and melancholy, as it has a tonic effect on the whole body.

Planetary Ally: Venus

Sign Ruler: Gemini

Elemental Ally: Earth

Energetics: When the body and mind have been depleted and we feel exhausted, vervain helps restore our emotional and spiritual health. When there has been an overabundance of energy, especially in terms of mental activity, vervain is a wonderful remedy.

Violet—*Viola* spp.

Actions: Violet is known for its ability to soothe different complaints. Violet helps cool and heal rashes and skin problems, relaxes us and acts as an expectorant for coughing, and heals urinary infections.

Planetary Ally: Venus

Sign Ruler: Libra

Elemental Ally: Water

Energetics: Violet is a sweet little friend. Her delightful delicacy teaches us to be curious, playful, and gentle. Perhaps a little shy, violets are mysterious and entrancing, promoting our sensual and sexual selves.

Caution: Avoid ingesting voilet in large doses.

Western Red Cedar—*Thuja plicata*

Actions: Cedar has a multitude of uses, including the use of its wood for house and boat building and for building wonderful, aromatic fires. Its leaves can be used as a smudge to purify and enliven the energy of a space. As a smudge, cedar has been used by the Native American peoples as a ceremonial tool for ritual purposes. Medicinally, its stimulating properties act as an antibiotic, cleansing the lungs and aura of impurities.

Planetary Allies: Venus, Neptune

Sign Ruler: Pisces

Elemental Ally: Water

Energetics: Cedar is a strong, wise force, magnificent in her beauty. She brings a calm, deliberate power to any situation. Cedar helps relax, strengthen, and nourish us at the deepest core level.

Caution: When ingested, many or all parts of this tree may be toxic.

Willow—*Salix* sp.

Actions: The bark of the willow tree is used as a curative for headaches and migraines.

Planetary Ally: Moon

Sign Ruler: Cancer

Elemental Ally: Water

Energetics: Willow is a strong and witchy wood. It can be a strong protective totem and confers ease and grace on those who connect with her spirit. Witches' brooms were often bound with willow. It is very helpful for moon magic.

Yarrow—*Achillea millefolium*

Actions: Yarrow has long been used as an external wound-healing agent. Yarrow is especially used as a remedy for fevers and as a skin cleanser. It helps move the blood when there is stagnancy.

Planetary Ally: Venus

Sign Ruler: Leo

Elemental Allies: Earth, fire

Energetics: Yarrow is a very hardy herb that often grows in waste areas. There is strong magic and beauty within its multidisected leaves and multiple flowers. Yarrow helps protect, strengthen, and erase fear. It is great for activists who need courage to go into battle.

Caution: Contact with yarrow may cause dermatitis. Avoid ingesting yarrow in large doses.

Elemental Associations with Herbs, Plants, and Trees

Fire	Basil, borage, burdock, calendula, cayenne, cinnamon, echinacea, elder, eyebright, fennel, garlic, gentian, ginger, ginseng, goldenseal, hawthorn, hops, hyssop, juniper, nettle, oak, peppermint, red clover, rosemary, St. John's wort, sunflower, thyme, tobacco, yarrow
Water	Aloe, catnip, western red cedar, feverfew, kelp, kinnickinick, lemon balm, licorice, madrona, marijuana, marshmallow, mugwort, raspberry, sage, sarsaparilla, valerian, violet, willow

Air   Borage, caraway, chamomile, dill, dock, eyebright, hops, lavender, lobelia, maple, mullein, oats, parsley, pine, red clover, sage, skullcap, valerian

Earth   Cascara, chicory, coltsfoot, comfrey, dandelion, dock, ginseng, horsetail, mullein, mugwort, oak, Oregon grape, plantain, vervain, yarrow

Planetary Associations with Herbs, Plants, and Trees

Sun   Calendula, chamomile, cinnamon, eyebright, goldenseal, hawthorn, rosemary, St. John's wort, sunflower

Moon   Aloe, lemon balm, marshmallow, willow

Mercury   Caraway, coltsfoot, dill, elder, fennel, lavender, oats, parsley, peppermint, red clover, valerian

Venus   Burdock, catnip, western red cedar, elder, feverfew, licorice, mugwort, raspberry, rose, thyme, vervain, violet, yarrow

Mars   Basil, cayenne, garlic, gentian, ginger, ginseng, hops, juniper, nettle, pine, sarsaparilla, tobacco

Jupiter   Borage, cascara sagrada, chicory, dandelion, dock, echinacea, hyssop, lemon balm, maple, oak, Oregon grape, rosemary, sage

Saturn   Comfrey, horsetail, mullein, plantain, slippery elm

Uranus   Fennel, lavender, lobelia, skullcap

Neptune   Aloe, western red cedar, hops, kelp, licorice, marijuana, sage

Pluto   Garlic, kinnickinick, madrona

Associations of Plants, Herbs, and Trees with the Signs

Aries Cayenne, cinnamon, dock, feverfew, garlic, ginger, goldenseal, juniper, thyme

Taurus Coltsfoot, sage, slippery elm

Gemini Mullein, peppermint, vervain

Cancer Aloe, caraway, dill, hyssop, lemon balm, marshmallow, mugwort, willow

Leo Borage, burdock, calendula, catnip, chamomile, hawthorn, red clover, St. John's wort, sunflower, yarrow

Virgo Cascara sagrada, catnip, chicory, fennel, oats, Oregon grape

Libra Dandelion, licorice, parsley, rose, tobacco, violet

Scorpio Basil, kinnikinick, madrona, raspberry, sarsaparilla, valerian

Sagittarius Echinacea, elder, oak

Capricorn Comfrey, pine, plantain

Aquarius Lavender, lobelia, skullcap

Pisces Western red cedar, horsetail, kelp, marijuana

Nourishing the Elements with Herbs, Plants, and Trees

Fire
- To help stimulate the fire element in someone who lacks it, try herbs that are heating such as basil, cayenne, cinnamon, garlic, and ginger.
- For people who want to strengthen their fire element over the long term, try tonic herbs such as nettle and ginseng.

- Hawthorn is another wonderful and gentle fire herb that helps strengthen the heart and circulation.
- Dandelion, yellow dock, and Oregon grape are all helpful for cleansing and healing a damaged liver from an excessive lifestyle.

Water
- Elder, echinacea, and thyme all help strengthen the immune system.
- Coltsfoot and slippery elm help with expectoration due to excessive phlegm.
- Kinnikinick and parsley help with urinary infections.
- Raspberry and angelica help strengthen and heal the uterus.
- Marshmallow, slippery elm, and aloe all help soothe and relax the stomach when there is tension.

Air
- Valerian, skullcap, chamomile, and lemon balm all help calm the nerves.
- Mullein and coltsfoot are good for healing lung complaints.
- Aromatherapy in the form of sage, lavender, and rose oil is soothing to the nervous system.
- Licorice and ginseng are helpful for strengthening the kidneys and the adrenal system.

Earth
- Horsetail, comfrey, and nettle are all rich in nutrients and are helpful for strengthening the bones, muscles, and tendons.
- Culinary herbs in the form of thyme, rosemary, and basil all help strengthen the digestive tract and help it process food more easily.
- External lotions containing comfrey, lavender, and calendula help heal and vitalize the skin, giving it a natural, lustrous glow.

Nourishment of the Modalities with Herbs, Plants, and Trees

Cardinal
- Taking herbs that are more relaxing, like chamomile, lemon balm, and skullcap, can be helpful when stressed.
- It is also smart to take digestive herbs that help assimilate nutrients. These are herbs like basil, fennel, garlic, and gentian.

Fixed
- Fixed-energy folks need herbs that periodically cleanse them and also energize and motivate them to move when they are stuck physically and emotionally. Burdock, dandelion, and Oregon grape are all wonderful cleansers and liver tonics.
- Ginger and cayenne are great herbs for increasing heat and circulation.

Mutable
- Herbs that are soothing and nourishing, that tonify the entire system, are very important for this modality. Ginseng is a supreme tonic that strengthens the entire system. Licorice helps strengthen the adrenals and kidneys.
- Lavender and peppermint have the unusual ability to be both stimulating and relaxing at the same time.

Balancing and Nourishing the Signs and Planets with Herbs, Plants, and Trees

Aries/ Mars
- For headaches, try willow, chamomile, and feverfew.
- To clear excess heat and for liver problems, try dandelion, burdock, milk thistle, and yellow dock.
- To strengthen and purify the blood, or reduce inflammation and skin diseases, try nettles, red clover, and yarrow.
- To soothe and relax the body, try taking marshmallow and hops.
- To stimulate more heat and fire in the system, try cayenne, garlic, and ginger.

Taurus/
Venus

- For sore throats, try thyme to fight infections, and slippery elm and licorice to soothe the throat and strengthen the thyroid glands.
- For thyroid-gland regulation, try kelp to nourish an underactive thyroid and bugleweed to calm an overactive thyroid.
- For feelings of lethargy and "stuckness," add stimulating herbs such as cayenne, basil, and peppermint.
- To increase feelings of calmness and groundedness, take oats, nettle, and marshmallow.

Gemini/
Mercury

- For anxiety and nervousness, try valerian, skullcap, hops, and lemon balm.
- For lung complaints, try mullein, coltsfoot, and hyssop.

Cancer/
Moon

- To combat indigestion and calm an upset stomach, try thyme, fennel, caraway, peppermint, and oregano.
- For fatigue and low spirits, try licorice, Siberian ginseng, and lemon balm.

Leo/
Sun

- To regulate the heart, try hawthorn.
- To strengthen the circulation, try warming herbs such as clove, cinnamon, and ginger.
- For sadness and to help cheer the heart, try borage and St. John's wort.

Virgo/
Mercury

- For indigestion affecting the intestines, try rosemary, fennel, thyme, and peppermint.
- For anxiety and worry, try skullcap, valerian, hops, chamomile, and lavender.

Libra/
Venus

- To strengthen and nourish the kidneys, try licorice, ginseng, and nettles.
- To heal urinary-tract infections, try parsley and kinnikinick.

Scorpio/
Pluto and
Mars

- To strengthen the libido and sexual functions, try nettles, ginger, ginseng, and sarsaparilla.
- To strengthen the reproductive system in women, try angelica and raspberry leaf.
- To help offset constipation and to help with elimination, try cascara, aloe, rosemary, and garlic.

Sagittarius/
Jupiter

- To help cleanse and strengthen the liver, try dandelion, dock, and Oregon grape.
- To strengthen the fire element and cleanse the blood, try red clover, sarsaparilla, ginger, and garlic.

Capricorn/
Saturn

- To help build the strength of the bones, nails, and teeth, try horsetail, comfrey, and nettles.
- To reduce pain associated with arthritis and rheumatism, try sarsaparilla and willow.
- To offset melancholy, try borage, lemon balm, and St. John's wort.

**Aquarius/
Uranus**

- To help soothe frazzled nerves, try valerian, skullcap, and hops.

- To strengthen circulation, try cinnamon and cloves.

**Pisces/
Neptune**

- To help strengthen the immune system, try taking ginseng, licorice, and nettles.

- To help fight off colds, try a combination of echinacea and goldenseal.

- To increase psychic receptivity, try using mugwort in a dream pillow before going to sleep at night.

---

1. Albertus Magnus, *The Book of Secrets* (1550; reprint, York Beach, ME: Weiser, 1999).

2. Scott Cunningham, *Cunningham's Encyclopedia of Magical Herbs* (St. Paul, MN: Llewellyn Publications, 1999) 74.

8

The Energetics of Food

Food and diet play a controversial role in our society. At the beginning of the twenty-first century, there are six billion people on this planet and all of them need to be fed. Huge portions of the population are either malnourished or starving. Much of the rest of the world relies on gigantic agribusiness corporations to feed them. Though these corporations have allowed the world to grow and expand like never before, they have also caused tremendous damage in the form of damming, pesticide pollution, soil erosion, and water-quality damage. Cattle, pigs, and chickens are kept in massive factories where the quality of life for the animals is only minimally considered. Chemicals and hormones are fed to the livestock to help them fatten and produce more milk. Crops are grown with tremendous amounts of pesticides on vast farms and then are shipped and trucked to all corners of the globe to be sold in supermarkets to consumers.

Within this context, we buy our food and prepare our meals. Though it is not talked about often, this system of living directly affects our health and relationship to food and nature. The large majority of us are disconnected from the process of seeding, growing, and harvesting crops. We are often unaware of the toil and labor that goes into our meals. We take for granted the abundance of almost any type of food imaginable. Some food may come from exotic locations, yet it is readily available to the consumer with enough money to purchase it.

We also choose increasingly to eat on the run at fast-food restaurants or buy ourselves quick snack meals that are processed and packaged. This contributes to a further separation from our food and how it is gathered, made, and served. Because of the busy pace of our lives and our fast-paced society, it is often easiest to buy food that is ready made. Much of this food is of low quality and is not nutritious. It is also usually filled with chemicals and preservatives. There is little chi flowing through this food, and indeed it can feel almost lifeless and dead. Eaten in abundance, it starts to weigh us down, deadening our own internal energy and eventually causing illness and disease.

Food can, however, be our closest connection to nature throughout the day. When we eat, we have a chance to connect to food that is grown outside amid the four elements. Crops retain the energy of fire from the sun, the energy of earth through the soil, the energy of air through the sky, and the energy of water through the rain falling down upon them. When food is eaten, we are in turn taking part in the four elements. We are gathering that energy into our bodies to balance and nourish us. When chemicals, fertilizer, and pesticides are placed in crops, the life force and chi of the vegetables and grains become sapped and deadened. It is literally like putting a blockade between the food and the four elements. When we allow crops to grow and flourish naturally, they can gather that energy easily. Furthermore, the closer we are to the crops that are harvested and the sooner we eat the harvested food, the more energy we retain. Food acts as our greatest support mechanism and our greatest daily connection to nature when we are unable to live outdoors. Each meal is an opportunity to connect to the four elements, and is a chance to connect to the planets that the food is allied with and to connect to the limitless supply of chi generated in nature that can sustain and support us.

How we choose to prepare a meal is also vastly important. When done with care, love, and mindfulness, food retains its sweet, glowing nature. When treated as simply a meal that must be consumed rapidly, food becomes unhappy and lifeless, and fails to nourish us. When I eat my meals, I look at the quality of the food served in terms of chi. Chi is the Chinese term for the energetic essence of all of creation. If the meal is prepared well, then the food looks like it is truly glowing and is full of good chi. The vegetables look alive and fresh, almost dancing on my plate. This is what I call a high chi meal. When the food looks limp or soggy, dull and lifeless, this is what I call a low chi meal. This is an easy exercise to do and anyone can do it. Feel your food on all levels—does its smell pour off it and tantalize your stomach? Does it glow with aliveness, and taste fresh and crisp? It really is easy to tell. No matter how good the ingredients are or how healthy the meal should be, if the food is low in chi, then it will not nourish the body and its energetic currents well. Food that is lifeless or low chi is often found in prepared and packaged foods and processed and frozen meals.

Well-grown, harvested, and prepared food has a high chi content and therefore can augment our own level of chi and can bring us to a better energetic state. This is actually the basis of all healing—resonating with a better energetic state by taking in substances that will augment our energy. Food is one of the prime forces for healing and is capable of delivering a powerful level of heightened chi. Each vegetable and each grain has a story or mythology to impart. They tell stories of the quality of the soil, its richness, sandiness, or rockiness. Each tells a story of the sun and how it has shined on them. They tell a story of the moon and how they felt growing and unfurling underneath it. They tell a story of the way the wind blew over them, how the water felt being drunk through their roots. They tell a story of the humans who have grown and eaten them for thousands of years. The stories show the web of interlinking: one hand delivering the seed to the ground, nurturing growth, and then harvesting and bringing the food to the mouth to be eaten before excreting it back to the land where the cycle starts again. This powerful cycle mirrors all the circular cycles in nature and the solar system. Everything returns to where it began, draws deeper wisdom with each pass, and grows in power and depth with each turn.

With food, the freshest, cleanest, and closest to handpicked is the best, but the way it is chopped, cooked, and prepared is also vital. If we place a great deal of mindfulness into preparation—the onions are lovingly cut, the rice is cooked on not too high a flame, and the vegetables are gently sautéed—then a very high level of chi remains. So, too, with our home: if we take the time to lovingly clean it, open the windows to allow fresh air to circulate, and burn sage or incense to sweeten the smell, then the chi level of the home goes up. This in turn nourishes the chi of the inhabitants and makes them stronger. In the West, we like to cover up odors with perfume, give ourselves facelifts to make us look younger, and eat radical diets to slim ourselves. These things do nothing to improve our overall chi levels, our energetic equilibrium.

In the following compendium of food, I list the medicinal and nutritional value of a particular food and also describe its energetics. Our kitchens are the center of our household, the place where we cook and nourish ourselves. The kitchen can be the most magical place in the house, because it is the place where we act as sorcerers, melding different ingredients, selecting food, and chopping, grating, and cutting. We then use heat (the fire element) to cook the food (earth). The heat causes evaporation (water) and creates an aroma (air) that stimulates certain beneficial moods and feelings. The food then becomes magically transformed into sustenance, healing, and vitalizing nutrition for our mind, body, and soul. When we sit down to a meal, we partake in a daily ritual. That is why it is wonderful to give thanks and make a prayer before eating. We can make a prayer for the life-giving qualities of the food, for the farmers and shopkeepers who helped deliver it to our hands, and to the four elements and to the Spirit that is the basis of our meal.

Astrology and Nutrition

When choosing food for a meal, it is helpful to take into account our astrological chart to see where any strengths and weaknesses lie. People with a lot of fire in their chart may want to avoid heating foods and stick to more cooling foods. People with a lot of earth in their chart, who are feeling low and melancholy, may want to eat an orange and feel its uplifting, cheerful properties. People who are lacking strength and who have a debilitated Mars may want to eat more red foods like beets to fortify them.

I have compiled a partial list of vegetables, grains, dairy products, and meats with their energetics and planetary and elemental allies. At the end, I give some ideas for working with diet according to one's individual astrological chart. But first, here are some other ways of working with food:

Eat It!

Simply eating food will help us take in not only its medicinal qualities but its energetic qualities as well. Think of the difference between eating a bag of Doritos or a juicy apple right off the tree. Raw food tends to be more cooling and is often better in limited doses for fire types, while cooked food tends to be more warming and is often better for earth types.

Aromatherapy

Cooking food gives off pungent aromas that are very healing and stimulating to our emotional centers and that help us feel pleasure, relieve tension, and warm our spirits.

Gardening

Growing a little crop of organic foods in the backyard is supremely healing and nourishing. The process of being out in the elements, tending a vegetable until it is full grown, and then harvesting it, helps us have a direct relationship with the food we are eating. Food grown and eaten this way tends to be the juiciest and most succulent, and is much better than store-bought food!

Wildcrafting

Collecting food and herbs in their natural state is known as wildcrafting. Blueberries, blackberries, nuts, and roots can often be found growing nearby. These foods offer immense vitality because they are in their perfect natural environment. This type of food is supremely nourishing to the body and soul.

Use Food as an Offering

Placing a plum or an apple on an altar for a ritual is a wonderful way to channel some of the energy from food while working it into our prayers and spells. Take a look at the energetics of the food to understand its powers.

Compendium of Food

Almond

Actions: Almonds have a sweet and slightly bitter taste that helps strengthen and nourish the spleen and stomach as well as lubricate the lungs and relieve coughs and excessive phlegm conditions. It is smart to refrigerate almonds, for they can easily go rancid, causing numerous health problems.

Planetary Allies: Jupiter, Sun

Sign Ruler: Leo

Elemental Ally: Fire

Energetics: Almonds bring grounding sweetness to our lives. If we need fortitude, strength, and courage, we can work with almond. Almond is a small and dense nut packed with potential energy that helps us activate and stimulate our energy and directs us into action.

Apple

Actions: Apple has a sweet and sometimes sour taste, depending on the apple. The sourer apples act more to stimulate the liver and digestive system, while the sweeter apples are more nutritive. All are helpful in building up the body's energy.

Planetary Ally: Venus

Sign Ruler: Libra

Elemental Allies: Air, water

Energetics: Apples have a pleasing and refreshing energy. If we need to release anger and fear, especially when it comes to issues of love, apple helps promote transformation in these areas.

Asparagus

Actions: Asparagus reduces excess heat in the system and also regulates fluidity and mucus in the body, decreasing or increasing it as is appropriate.

Planetary Ally: Jupiter

Sign Ruler: Pisces

Elemental Ally: Water

Energetics: Asparagus has a primordial energy that conjures images of dinosaurs and large swamps. Her power lies in helping us move with less fear and with more fluidity and sureness.

Banana

Actions: Banana is a great source of mucilage and has a sweet, cooling, and moistening quality. It is great for people who are weak and in need of a little blood sugar.

Planetary Ally: Venus

Sign Ruler: Libra

Elemental Ally: Water

Energetics: Banana helps lighten and brighten the day, giving it a sweetness and natural joy.

Barley

Actions: Barley serves as a tonic for the blood, builds moistness and strength, soothes inflammation of the urinary tract, and reduces fever.

Planetary Ally: Saturn

Sign Ruler: Virgo

Elemental Ally: Earth

Energetics: Barley is a strong grain ally, an earth friend. Barley helps root and ground us and strengthen and nourish our essential divinity.

Beef

Actions: In moderation, beef helps strengthen and tonify the entire system and is great for building blood, bones, and muscles. The grazing of cattle to produce beef has caused untold damage to the environment from the cutting down of forests to make pasture land. The antibiotics and hormones in industrially raised beef is also incredibly harmful to our health. That is why it is important to eat beef rarely and to only buy free-range and organically fed beef.

Planetary Ally: Saturn

Sign Ruler: Capricorn

Elemental Ally: Earth

Energetics: If eaten in a sacred manner, beef helps strengthen and nourish us at a core level and also brings us greater stability and steadiness. When we are confused and cloudy and feel weak and powerless, beef gives us courage, vitality, and solidity.

Beet

Actions: Beet strengthens the heart and liver, purifies the blood of toxins, and aids in circulation.

Planetary Allies: Mars, Saturn

Sign Ruler: Aries

Elemental Ally: Fire

Energetics: Beet's blood-red color links it to our own blood and circulation, our heat, and the root functions of our body. Beet gives us warrior strength and stimulates us to action. Beet is an aphrodisiac and a heart opener.

Butter

Actions: Most butter eaten comes from cows, and it has a warming and sweet quality that helps enrich and moisten our bodies at a cellular level. Its fats strengthen the body to do physical work in the world. Eaten excessively, butter can weigh down and dampen the body, leading it to lethargy and heaviness. Again, it is important to buy organic butter, as factory-raised dairy cows are pumped full of hormones and antibiotics that are dulling and aggravating to our health.

Planetary Ally: Venus

Sign Ruler: Taurus

Elemental Ally: Earth

Energetics: Butter in the form of ghee is sacred to Indians, as it is the purified form that comes from cows. It is a powerful healing substance and is often used in rituals and medicines. Butter helps build and strengthen us and bring out a glow and a color to our spirit.

Cabbage

Actions: Cabbage is a great source of roughage, clearing out unwanted particles in the intestines through elimination. It strengthens the kidney and is a diuretic.

Planetary Ally: Moon

Sign Ruler: Cancer

Elemental Ally: Water

Energetics: Cabbage is a friendly and beneficent vegetable, helping clear and cleanse negative energy. Planting and growing it in our yard will help dispel bad influences. Cabbages bring a positive and receptive mindframe.

Carrot

Actions: Carrot has long been known to be good for the eyesight. It is also sweet and nourishing to the entire system, especially the lungs, digestive system, and liver.

Planetary Ally: Mercury

Sign Ruler: Gemini

Elemental Ally: Earth

Energetics: Carrot is a root vegetable and helps us get grounded and softens us. It helps us become a little sweeter, a little friendlier.

Celery

Actions: Celery cools the system and nourishes the liver and digestive system. It helps dry up excessively damp conditions (brought on by eating too much dairy, sugar, fats, and refined foods).

Planetary Allies: Uranus, Mercury

Sign Ruler: Aquarius

Elemental Ally: Air

Energetics: Celery brings us to a more detached, less impassioned place, which is important when we become overwhelmed and tend to veer between extremes.

Cheese

Actions: In small amounts, cheese is a tremendously nourishing food that helps tonify and moisten us. In the amounts often eaten today, cheese is a leading cause of weight gain, and also dampens and deadens our energy reserves. Many people are allergic to cheese, and it can cause a host of immune and allergenic problems. It is therefore best to eat cheese sparingly (but lovingly).

Planetary Allies: Venus, Saturn

Sign Ruler: Taurus

Elemental Ally: Earth

Energetics: Cheese that comes from cows will take on the energy of the cow it came from. That means that if the cheese is factory farmed, it could store much of the stress and discomfort the cow experienced. If gathered from a free-range cow that was not fed hormones and pesticide-laden food, cheese can be a source of tremendous power—a concentrated form of energy that gives us ease, pleasure, and strength.

Cherry

Actions: Cherries are sweet and nourishing. They are beneficial to the heart and circulation as well as tonifying to the whole system.

Planetary Ally: Venus

Sign Ruler: Aquarius

Elemental Allies: Air, fire

Energetics: Cherries ward off depression and fatigue and uplift us. They help move us away from negative-thinking cycles and into a more generous and free-flowing energy.

Chicken

Actions: If not factory farmed, chicken is a supreme tonic to the system, helping warm and build the entire system. If cooked well, chicken is great for debility and weakness, lack of energy, and poor blood.

Planetary Ally: Sun

Sign Ruler: Aries

Elemental Ally: Fire

Energetics: Factory-farmed chicken will take on the energy of its surroundings. Chickens in this environment are often living in atrocious conditions and are butchered and processed in horrible and often unclean ways. Chickens treated well in free-range environments are friendly and curious and bring those qualities to those who eat them.

Coffee

Actions: Primarily warming and stimulating, coffee has a diuretic and laxative effect on those who drink it. Because of its high caffeine content, coffee is one of the most highly consumed beverages in the world. Caffeine helps bolster and invigorate us, but can also produce a crash effect that is depleting and tiring after the effect of the caffeine has worn off. The acid in coffee destroys the stomach lining and leads to poor absorption of nutrients, thus causing vitamin and mineral deficiencies.

Planetary Ally: Mars

Sign Ruler: Aries

Elemental Ally: Fire

Energetics: Coffee in small doses can be a magical beverage, increasing mental and physical energy. In greater doses and over prolonged periods of time, it becomes a depleting and sapping beverage. Coffee can then become a symbol for empty energy, with little healing energy. Moderate consumption can stimulate conversation, connection, and interchange with the people around you.

Corn

Actions: Corn helps tonify the digestive system and especially the eliminative functions. It also helps relax and strengthen the heart and kidneys.

Planetary Allies: Sun, Venus

Sign Ruler: Taurus

Elemental Ally: Earth

Energetics: Corn comes from the New World and had not been used in Europe, Asia, and Australia until after the conquest of the Americas in the 1500s. Corn held tremendous power in indigenous societies like those of the Mayans and the Incas, who grew many different varieties of corn on their lands. It is a sad fact that today we mainly eat only one variety of corn, although there were hundreds in those earlier times. Corn is a sweet friend that takes on the radiance and power of the sun. It shines its energy through to those who eat her and enlivens our spirit to its fullest potential.

Cucumber

Actions: Cucumber is a cooling vegetable that moistens and purifies our system.

Planetary Ally: Moon

Sign Ruler: Cancer

Elemental Ally: Water

Energetics: Cucumber has a refreshing quality that clears away any negative impulses and leaves us clear-headed and relaxed. It lessens extremes.

Date

Actions: Dates are an extremely sweet fruit that make a great snack when we just have to have a little sugar. Dates tonify our stomach, blood, and whole system.

Planetary Ally: Venus

Sign Ruler: Libra

Elemental Ally: Air

Energetics: Date's beautiful sweetness adds sensuality, pleasure, and delight to any environment. They bring out the hedonist in all of us.

Eggplant

Actions: Eggplant has a cooling and sweet nature that reduces swelling and clears stagnant blood from the system.

Planetary Ally: Pluto

Sign Ruler: Scorpio

Elemental Ally: Earth

Energetics: Eggplant helps uncover and unturn; hidden emotions and deep feelings can be brought to the surface with eggplant.

Egg

Actions: Eggs have a strong building and warming quality, tonifying our blood, bones, tissues, and tendons. They are a great source of protein.

Planetary Allies: Moon, Venus

Sign Ruler: Cancer

Elemental Allies: Earth, water

Energetics: The word egg conjures up the notion of the original seed, an incredible potential stored in one small shell. Eggs have the ability to develop our core strength and help us unlock this inner potential.

Fish

Actions: Fish has a sweet and nourishing quality to it and can be tremendously healing to all the organs in the body. With a high content of omega-3 fatty acids, fish can help cleanse the circulatory system of cholesterol, fortify the nerves, and build tissue strength in the body.

Planetary Allies: White fish: Moon, Neptune

Red Fish: Sun, Mars, Neptune

Sign Ruler: Pisces

Elemental Ally: Water

Energetics: There are many different types of fish, each with their own energy and capability. Salmon are tremendously powerful and vigorous and have long been aligned with their native habitats by indigenous tribes. We can work with red fish like salmon to develop power, fortitude, and spiritual growth. White fish tend to be gentler and sweeter in disposition and are gently nourishing and replenish our strength.

Grape

Actions: Grapes are a wonderful blood and chi tonic. They strengthen the liver, kidneys, bones, and tissues.

Planetary Ally: Sun

Sign Ruler: Pisces

Elemental Ally: Air

Energetics: Grapes are restorative, cheerful, and strong in energy. Ripe and bursting from the vine, they promote courage and activity.

Honey

Actions: A great tonic for the blood and the chi, honey has a moistening quality that helps in dry conditions. It is great for lung, stomach, and liver disorders.

Planetary Allies: Sun, Venus

Sign Ruler: Leo

Elemental Ally: Fire

Energetics: The bee is a mystical creature. Living together in large colonies, bees have an almost telepathic sense of how to work, live, and operate. Honey carries great healing and protective energy if the bees are relaxed and well tended. Honey can moisten and relax our soul, bringing nourishment and ease at deep levels.

Kale

Actions: Kale is one of the most nutrient-rich vegetables and is a wonderful ally. Kale restores and rejuvenates, and benefits the lungs and stomach.

Planetary Ally: Saturn

Sign Ruler: Capricorn

Elemental Ally: Earth

Energetics: A winter crop, kale is a hearty friend, capable of remaining steadfast and loyal through the darkest times. It is good for working through emotions of fear, paralysis, and insecurity.

Kelp

Actions: Kelp has a strong moistening and nourishing effect and therefore benefits the kidneys and tonifies the blood through its high mineral content.

Planetary Ally: Neptune

Sign Ruler: Pisces

Elemental Ally: Water

Energetics: Kelp is Neptune's friend, a healer to all who are diminished physically and spiritually. Bathe in the gentle energy of kelp, surrender to your deepest emotions and let them pass over you, feeling everything as part of the web of life. Like a green, luminescent milk, allow kelp to nourish you at your core.

Kidney Bean

Actions: Kidney beans help clear excess heat in the system and strengthen the digestive system and the kidneys.

Planetary Ally: Pluto

Sign Ruler: Scorpio

Elemental Ally: Water

Energetics: Kidney beans allow us to move through our fears, especially those caused by nervousness and stress. They allow us to relax, rejuvenate, and get stronger.

Lemon

Actions: Lemon has a sour and stimulating quality that promotes liver bile and better digestion. Lemons have antibacterial properties that help fight off infections. Lemon juice also helps calm the nerves and reduce anxiety.

Planetary Ally: Sun

Sign Ruler: Leo

Elemental Ally: Fire

Energetics: Refreshing, curious, and relaxing, lemon helps move out tired and stagnant emotions to revitalize and renew us.

Lettuce

Actions: Lettuce cools and relaxes our nerves. It helps clear out excess toxins from the digestive system and dries any dampness in the system.

Planetary Ally: Moon

Sign Ruler: Leo

Elemental Ally: Water

Energetics: Lettuce is a sweet and lovely companion, helping us become gentler and more compassionate.

Milk

Actions: Milk has a tonifying quality, lubricating and moistening all parts of the body. Avoid milk when there is excess dampness. Some people are allergic to cow's milk. In general, milk should be consumed sparingly.

Planetary Ally: Moon

Sign Ruler: Cancer

Elemental Ally: Water

Energetics: Milk is a soothing and loving friend, nourishing our sweetest qualities and helping us glow.

Millet

Actions: Like all whole grains, millet is a strong chi nourisher, healing our kidneys and tonifying our blood, muscles, and tendons. It also has a cooling quality that reduces toxins in the system.

Planetary Ally: Venus

Sign Ruler: Virgo

Elemental Ally: Earth

Energetics: Millet is a wonderful grain that soothes, strengthens, and nourishes us on all levels.

Mushroom—Button

Actions: Button mushrooms remove heat from the system and are excellent for the lungs and digestive system.

Planetary Allies: Moon, Neptune, Pluto

Sign Ruler: Cancer

Elemental Allies: Earth, water

Energetics: Mushrooms have a very powerful and exotic energy. They grow in clumps, have supernatural and magical properties, and are to be called on to manifest and intend. Mushrooms are also good if we want to cool down our energies and strengthen our connection to the earth.

Mushroom—Shiitake

Actions: Shiitakes are a great blood and stomach tonifier. Immensely healing, shiitake mushrooms are capable of removing toxins and nourishing all parts of us, including our bones, teeth, eyes, and liver. Shiitakes are a good source of germanium, an element that improves our immunity and increases the transport of oxygen on a cellular level. Shiitakes have been used in the treatment of cancer.

Planetary Ally: Pluto

Sign Ruler: Scorpio

Elemental Allies: Earth, water

Energetics: Shiitakes have a deeper healing power than button mushrooms. Their deep, rich power draws up the medicine of the earth's rich humus and delivers it potently to those who eat them. Shiitakes are capable of bringing us through cathartic transformations.

Oat

Actions: Oats act as a wonderful nervine, relaxing our nerves as well as nourishing all our organs. They are a supreme rejuvenator for those who are convalescing.

Planetary Ally: Mercury

Sign Ruler: Virgo

Elemental Ally: Air

Energetics: Oats are a fundamental earth plant, storing tremendous energy and power in their small grains. Oats talk and weave a magic spell through their waving wands of grass, and are a sweet rejuvenator of life and gentle nourisher of the soul.

Olive

Actions: Olives have a sweet-and-sour taste that helps soothe and nourish our throats, lungs, and stomachs.

Planetary Allies: Sun, Jupiter

Sign Ruler: Cancer

Elemental Ally: Air

Energetics: Olives help balance our ability to be open with our ability to be firm and say no from time to time. They also help cleanse us of anger and bottled-up frustration. They can help build a sense of fortitude and reserve so that we can withstand negativity and stress.

Onion

Actions: Onions have a warm and pungent quality, helping clear mucus from the lungs and sweat out toxins. They also stimulate the appetite.

Planetary Ally: Mars

Sign Ruler: Aries

Elemental Ally: Fire

Energetics: Along with garlic, onion is a strong protector of any kitchen and home. Planting onions in a garden helps reduce infestations of crop-eating bugs. Onion's strong odor and powerful taste link it with Mars and other warrior herbs.

Orange

Actions: Oranges are sweet and cooling as well as moistening and lubricating, healing us from dry and overheated conditions. They are also generally helpful in case of poor digestion, and reduce inflammations associated with acidic diseases such as rheumatism and arthritis.

Planetary Ally: Sun

Sign Ruler: Leo

Elemental Ally: Fire

Energetics: Oranges bring happiness, prosperity, and friendship. They promote joy and help us radiate with love and service.

Papaya

Actions: Papaya has a wonderful tonifying effect on the stomach, helping nourish it and improve digestion. It also moistens and soothes the lungs when inflamed due to excessive dryness and coughing. Papaya is not good for damp conditions.

Planetary Allies: Moon, Venus

Sign Ruler: Cancer

Elemental Ally: Water

Energetics: Papaya has a strong connection to the night, the moon, and the stars. It is great for opening mystical awareness and expanding consciousness. It also helps promote romantic love.

Peach

Actions: Peach helps heal dry conditions of the lungs and is also easy to digest and therefore good for people with stomach and intestinal problems.

Planetary Ally: Venus

Sign Ruler: Cancer

Elemental Ally: Earth

Energetics: Peach has a sweet and friendly nature and serves as a strengthener and binder for all occasions of a romantic, business, or friendship nature.

Pea

Actions: Peas tonify the digestive system and the liver. They have a sweet and slightly relaxing, refreshing quality.

Planetary Ally: Mercury

Sign Ruler: Gemini

Elemental Ally: Air

Energetics: Peas teach us that we do not have to take the straight and narrow path. They wind and curve, gently easing themselves upward toward the sun. They are fluid and flexible, wrapping themselves around poles and fences to find the best avenue for growth. Peas teach us to be open and adaptable in our approach to life.

Pear

Actions: Pears help relieve and reduce excess heat in the body, especially in the lungs. Pears are great healers for throat complaints and are helpful in alleviating mild depression.

Planetary Ally: Venus

Sign Rulers: Libra, Cancer

Elemental Allies: Water, air

Energetics: Pears have a bell shape that makes us think of being prosperous, round, and fat, enjoying the sensual delights of life. Go on—you don't have to feel guilty—take a big, juicy bite!

Plum

Actions: Plums help heal any stagnancies and depletions in the liver area. They are slightly cooling and moistening.

Planetary Ally: Venus

Sign Ruler: Cancer

Elemental Allies: Water, air

Energetics: Plums help release stagnant emotional energy and repressed feelings. Liver is related to the emotion of anger in Chinese medicine. Plums can help release the buildup of suppressed anger and frustration.

Pork

Actions: Pork is a strengthener of the blood, bones, tissues, and chi in the system. It is very helpful for people who are weak and debilitated, strengthening the kidneys and digestive system.

Planetary Ally: Saturn

Sign Ruler: Capricorn

Elemental Ally: Earth

Energetics: Pigs are very intelligent and grounded beings. They are familiar with the soil, the grass, and the plants around them. They offer a strong protective force to those around them. They are very perceptive and can catch on to any bad vibes or odd sensations in the area. It is imperative that pork be secured from a free-range and hormone-free farm. This reduces the fear in the meat that's eaten. Pork helps reduce anxiety and brings us greater solidity and strength.

Potato

Actions: Potato is a tonic for the digestive system and for the chi; it is a very nourishing and rejuvenating tuber. Potatoes also help reduce inflammations such as rheumatism and arthritis.

Planetary Allies: Venus, Saturn

Sign Ruler: Taurus

Elemental Ally: Earth

Energetics: Potatoes improve our general sense of ease and relaxation, what is called the yin aspect of nature in Chinese philosophy. Potatoes help us be more calm, considerate, and nurturing.

Pumpkin

Actions: Pumpkin helps regulate the blood sugar in the body and relieves excess dampness, especially in the lungs and throat.

Planetary Allies: Moon, Pluto

Sign Ruler: Cancer

Elemental Allies: Earth, water

Energetics: Pumpkin is used at Halloween time in the form of jack-o'-lanterns. This holiday allows us to tap into our shadow side and externalize intense emotions in the form of a mask and costume. Pumpkins play a part in this role because they are harvested close to the time of Halloween. Pumpkins help us visit the darker elements and difficult emotions in our being and then to accept, transform, and release them.

Radish

Actions: Radish has a very pungent quality that detoxifies and eliminates dampness. It is not very nourishing, but it helps release stagnancy in the system.

Planetary Ally: Mars

Sign Ruler: Aries

Elemental Ally: Fire

Energetics: Radish stimulates and energizes us when we feel drained and stagnant. It also helps clear out toxic emotional energy and helps us express ourselves and direct our energy.

Rice

Actions: Rice is one of the supreme grains that lies at the core of a good diet. Rice helps nourish all aspects of the body, including the digestive system, the kidneys, and the lungs. It promotes a healthy nervous system and expels toxins from the system.

Planetary Allies: Venus, Sun

Sign Ruler: Virgo

Elemental Ally: Earth

Energetics: Rice is a deeply nourishing friend, capable of healing us at a basic level. It grounds us, warms us, and helps reduce negative thought patterns. Rice builds our energy and provides us with a core support system.

Rye

Actions: Rye has a healing effect on the liver and digestive system and also relieves dampness and tonifies and nourishes the body.

Planetary Allies: Saturn, Venus

Sign Ruler: Virgo

Elemental Ally: Earth

Energetics: Rye enjoys growing in dry, gravelly, and sandy soils and has a hardness and firmness that strengthens us when we work with her. She gives her heart generously and heals us from intractable emotional pain, allowing it to surface and then be released.

Seaweed

Actions: There are numerous edible seaweeds including hijike, kombu, dulse, wakame, and nori. (Kelp is listed separately.) All of these have different properties, but share certain characteristics. They are all tremendously healing and rejuvenative. They carry an enormous amount of nutrients and minerals and are capable of detoxifying and nourishing the entire system. They are also moistening, cleansing, and healing.

Planetary Ally: Neptune

Sign Ruler: Pisces

Elemental Ally: Water

Energetics: Swim with seaweeds for a while and we touch on their deepest capability: to heal fear. Their salty and moist nature brings us to our core and helps transform us and enables us to become stronger. They allow us to contact our emotional selves and experience our feelings deeply and powerfully, but not to drown in them.

Spinach

Actions: Because spinach carries a great deal of iron, this vegetable is a great blood builder. It also cleanses the blood and nourishes the tendons and bones. Spinach cools and moistens us.

Planetary Allies: Saturn, Mars

Sign Ruler: Capricorn

Elemental Ally: Earth

Energetics: Spinach is a formidable warrior, a fighter for just causes, and an ally to the sick and weak who need strength.

Squash

Actions: Squash is a wonderful tonifier of the digestive system and also strengthens and nourishes the tendons, muscles, and chi.

Planetary Allies: Moon, Venus

Sign Ruler: Cancer

Elemental Ally: Earth

Energetics: Squash helps us return to who we are, our sweet, slightly vulnerable human nature. Squash helps us remember that all of us are the same, that we are linked and therefore need to "do unto others what we would have them do unto us." When we are feeling ungrounded, aggravated, and edgy, working with squash returns us to our core.

Sugar

Actions: Refined sugar is one of the leading causes of health disturbances in our modern world. When sugar goes into the bloodstream, it shocks the stomach and pancreas and causes an acid reaction that destroys the body's natural store-house of minerals. Calcium is lost, which leads to bone and teeth illnesses. It also increases the likelihood of contracting diseases such as diabetes, heart disease, immune-system deficiencies, yeast infections, and cancer. A little sugar is fine, especially in the form of honey or maple syrup, but a lot of sugar will deplete and damage our health.

Planetary Allies: Jupiter, Venus

Sign Ruler: Libra

Elemental Ally: Air

Energetics: Sugar has a stimulating and unbalancing effect when taken in large amounts. At first it brings a sense of pleasure and mild euphoria and then quickly produces a crash-and-burn effect, leaving us feeling more tired, agitated, and depleted than before. Unrefined sugar brings an empty and destructive high. Sugar binges once in a while are fine, but a long-term sugar habit is ultimately self-defeating.

Strawberry

Actions: Strawberry is helpful to the digestive system and strengthens the tissues and ligaments. It is helpful in cooling and moistening the throat and lungs.

Planetary Ally: Venus

Sign Ruler: Libra

Elemental Allies: Water, earth, fire

Energetics: Strawberry is a delicious and friendly ally. She gives of her sweetness and delight, helping us find pleasure and joy in the simple things in life.

Tofu

Actions: Tofu is a compressed food made from soybeans. It is wonderfully strengthening and nourishing to the system. Tofu enables us to sustain energy longer and benefits our lungs. Tofu moistens us and removes toxins from the body.

Planetary Ally: Venus

Sign Ruler: Taurus

Elemental Allies: Water, earth

Energetics: Tofu is one of the strongest allies for vegetarians. Soybeans are at the core of a diet that is moving away from meat consumption. Soy asks us to think about living more simply, wisely, and mindfully. Tofu has a gentle and relaxing quality that helps strengthen and build our spirit.

Tomato

Actions: Tomato has a very cooling nature and also moistens any dryness in the system. It acts as a tonic to the digestive system and removes toxins. Any excess heat is also diminished in the body. Though tomato is cooling, I find that it can sometimes be enervating to the nervous system.

Planetary Ally: Jupiter

Sign Ruler: Cancer

Elemental Allies: Water, fire

Energetics: Growing ripe on the vine in the hot sun, tomato offers herself to help cool us from this summer sun. When we are overheated and overly concerned, or caught up in the trivial, tomato cools us down and lets us see things more dispassionately. It is good for people with excessive fire.

Walnut

Actions: Walnuts are a wonderful tonic for the kidney/urogenital system, helping lubricate and fortify it.

Planetary Ally: Sun

Sign Rulers: Leo, Gemini

Elemental Allies: Fire, air

Energetics: Walnuts soothe and calm us in times of fear. They act as a friendly reminder that nothing has to be hurried or rushed. We can relax and ease into our
rhythm, confident that we will be carried through any obstacle.

Watermelon

Actions: Watermelon cools and moistens us. It is especially good for the kidneys
and inflammations of the urogenital system.

Planetary Ally: Jupiter

Sign Rulers: Pisces, Sagittarius

Elemental Allies: Water, fire

Energetics: Watermelon is often seen at picnics and serves as a friendly, fun fruit
that brings us together with shared laughter. It helps temper our anger and brings
out our jovial side.

Wheat

Actions: Wheat is a very helpful grain to clear heat and strengthen the kidney and
heart. Wheat calms our nervous system and builds and regenerates chi. Many
people are allergic to wheat, and its glutenous properties can sometimes drag us
down and weaken our energy if we are susceptible to its negative effects.

Planetary Ally: Venus

Sign Rulers: Taurus, Virgo

Elemental Ally: Earth

Energetics: Wheat has a long history of use as a main ingredient in bread. In
Christian mythology, bread is called the "staff of life" and is used in rituals where
bread is transformed into the body of Christ. It has an even older relationship to
the pagan "Old Religion" as a symbol of the Goddess and is used in Wiccan rites
as a reminder of the Goddess in her many forms. Bread is often at the core of
our diet, helping us become strong, sufficient, and well nourished.

Yam

Actions: Yam strengthens the digestive system, especially the tendons, muscles, and chi. It regenerates the kidneys and promotes lactation in nursing mothers.

Planetary Allies: Venus, Saturn

Sign Ruler: Taurus

Elemental Ally: Earth

Energetics: Yams help us feel strong and nourished and become more compassionate to others. Its beautiful, rich energy brings us calmness, stability, and gentle strength. When we need to reduce stress and feel peace and centeredness, a good cooked yam can be tremendously helpful.

Associations of the Elements with Food

Fire	Almonds, beets, cherries, chicken, coffee, honey, lemons, onions, oranges, radishes, strawberry, watermelon
Water	Apples, banana, cabbage, cucumber, eggs, fish, kelp, kidney beans, lettuce, milk, mushrooms, papayas, pears, plums, pumpkins, shiitake mushrooms, seaweeds, strawberries, tofu, tomatoes, watermelons
Air	Apples, celery, dates, grapes, oats, olives, pears, peas, plums, sugar, walnuts
Earth	Barley, beef, butter, carrots, cheese, corn, eggplant, eggs, kale, millet, mushrooms, peaches, pork, potatoes, pumpkins, rice, rye, spinach, squash, strawberries, tofu, wheat, yams

Associations of the Modalities with Food

Cardinal	Apples, bananas, beef, beets, cabbages, chicken, coffee, cucumber, date, eggs, kale, lettuce, milk, mushrooms, olives, onions, papayas, peaches, pears, plum, pork, pumpkins, radishes, spinach, squash, sugar, strawberries, tofu, tomatoes

Fixed   Almonds, butter, celery, cheese, cherries, corn, eggplant, honey, kidney beans, lemons, oranges, potatoes, shiitake mushrooms, walnut, yams

Mutable   Asparagus, barley, carrots, fish, grapes, kelp, millet, oats, peas, rice, rye, seaweed, watermelon, wheat

Associations of the Planets with Food

Sun   Almonds, chicken, corn, grapes, honey, lemons, olives, oranges, red fish, rice, walnuts

Moon   Cabbages, cucumber, eggs, lettuce, milk, mushrooms, papayas, pumpkins, squash, white fish

Mercury   Carrots, celery, oats

Venus   Apple, bananas, butter, cheese, cherries, corn, dates, eggs, honey, millet, papayas, peaches, pears, plums, potatoes, rice, rye, squash, sugar, strawberry, tofu, wheat, yams

Mars   Beets, coffee, onions, radishes, red fish, spinach

Jupiter   Almonds, asparagus, olives, sugar, tomatoes, watermelon

Saturn   Barley, beef, beets, cheese, kale, pork, potatoes, rye, spinach, yams

Uranus   Celery

Neptune   Fish, kelp, mushrooms, seaweed

Pluto   Eggplant, kidney beans, mushrooms, pumpkins

Associations of the Signs with Food

Aries   Beets, chicken, coffee, onions, radishes

Taurus   Butter, cheese, corn, potatoes, wheat, yams

Gemini   Carrots, peas

Cancer   Cabbages, cucumbers, eggs, lettuce, milk, mushrooms, olives, papayas, peaches, pears, plums, pumpkins, squash, tomatoes

Leo   Almond, honey, lemon, orange, walnut

Virgo   Barley, millet, oats, rice, rye, wheat

Libra   Apples, bananas, dates, pears, sugar, strawberries, tofu, walnuts

Scorpio   Eggplant, kidney beans, shiitake mushrooms

Sagittarius Watermelon

Capricorn   Beef, kale, pork, spinach

Aquarius   Celery, cherries

Pisces   Asparagus, fish, grapes, kelp, seaweeds, watermelon

Elemental Nourishment Through Diet

Fire   *To warm the system gently:* Cook nourishing meals such as soups, stirfries, and casseroles. Grains and tubers help gently stoke the fires without damaging it, like caffeine and white sugar tend to do. A few stimulating and hot herbs such as cayenne, ginger, and garlic will add heat and fire to a meal. When excessive use of drugs and a lack of rest and sleep have hurt the fire element, it's helpful to eat slowly and at similar times each day (8:00, 12:00, 3:00, and 6:00).

To decrease fire: Eat more raw and cold foods like salads and fruits.

Water   *To moisten the body:* Drink plenty of healthy fluids like water and herbal teas. Eat tubers like sweet potatoes and yams as well as squashes to lubricate the entire system. Soups are a wonderful way to moisten and add the water element to the diet. Avoid excessively hot and spicy foods, which dry out the body.

To decrease the water element: Avoid excessive sugars and starches and mucus-inducing foods. Increase astringent and heating herbs.

Air   *To augment the air element in the body:* Try eating less and cleansing the body to purify the system of excess heaviness. Eat salads and fruits, which lighten and rarify the energy. Be careful not to do this for too long, as too much raw and cool food will unbalance the system.

If there is too much air: Add more grounding and weighting foods like grains, potatoes, and squashes to bring down the energy.

Earth   *To increase the earth element:* Eat more grains, vegetables, and tubers, and add salt to the diet. Meat and dairy also bring solidity and help ground our energies. Eat slowly and surely, digesting each mouthful. Avoid caffeine, sugar, and processed foods, which unground and destabilize the system.

To decrease the earth element: Increase consumption of fruits and salads, which lighten the body. Try a few heating and moving herbs like cayenne, pepper, and vinegar, and also eat less and avoid eating late at night. Avoid a heavy starch and sugar diet, as well as dairy and excessive meat consumption.

Nourishment of the Modalities through Diet

Cardinal   Cardinal people need to eat food that relaxes and soothes the system while providing vital nourishment for the heavy workload that they often have. For those who eat meat, a good basic diet of whole grains and vegetables with limited amounts of fish and meat to nourish the blood and bones is the optimal diet. For non-meat eaters, it's important to find a good source of nourishment in tofu, beans, and nuts, along with whole grains and vegetables. Cardinal people tend to overwork, stress, and crash, and need to avoid taxing foods like sugar, caffeine, and drugs. A little alcohol in the form of beer or wine is fine for cardinal people, as it relaxes them.

Fixed   Fixed people need to eat food that gets the energy moving. Spicy and a slightly hot food will generate heat and activity if these folks get lethargic. Warming foods tend to be a better idea, as they help generate nourishing and gentle energy. Avoid excessive starchy, greasy, and heavy foods, which can stagnate in the body, including excessive starches and dairy. Add cleansing foods like leafy greens, broccoli, lettuce, and lemons. Root vegetables like potatoes and squash are good in moderation.

Mutable   Mutable people should watch out for food that is overstimulating to the nervous system. Caffeine, sugar, and tobacco are often consumed by these people to provide quick energy, but this can quickly burn out their adrenals. It is important to avoid these foods and to enjoy meals made primarily with whole grains and tubers. These foods help ground and relax those with a mutable emphasis. Fish and a little meat is especially good at nourishing, strengthening, and tonifying the system.

Planetary Nourishment Through Diet

Sun   Solar foods are ones that increase our light and luminescence, make us feel more confident, and strengthen our aura. Oranges, grapes, and honey all tend to lift the mood. Red fish, almonds, and walnuts provide sustaining energy and give a lustrous glow to the skin so that we can shine like the sun.

Moon   Lunar foods are ones that increase our receptivity, gentleness, and psychic nature. Eggs, milk, and white fish all nourish our core and help ease stressed-out emotions. Papayas and squash soothe the stomach, and cucumbers and lettuce cool us down if we have been overheated and anxious.

Mercury   Foods that increase our communicative function and our interactivity and brain capacity are Mercurial foods. Raw carrots and celery encourage a light and airy mood. Oats help decrease nervousness and anxiety often associated with Mercurial people.

Venus   Grains, potatoes, and dairy are primarily Venusian foods. These increase a sense of comfort and well-being. Fruits like apples, peaches, pears, and plums contain sugar, which is associated with Venus and helps elevate and brighten the mood.

Mars   Foods that are energizing and stimulating are Martian. Beets and radishes are both red (the color associated with Mars) and are invigorating to the system. Red fish and spinach are tremendously building and fortify the blood, tendons, tissues, and muscles.

Jupiter   Jupiterian foods increase a sense of expansiveness, generosity, and wisdom. They also tend to be large, like watermelon and asparagus. Sugar is also expansive, but eating it leads to a crash and is not healthy unless it is in a natural form in small amounts.

Saturn   Foods that strengthen the bones, teeth, and nails are strong Saturnian foods. Meat in the form of beef and pork is tremendously strengthening and building for the system. Leafy greens in the form of kale and spinach are wonderful for tonifying the body. Barley, potatoes, and yams are wonderful grains and tubers for fortifying all aspects of the constitution.

Uranus   Light foods that increase mental stimulation and affect the nervous system are Uranian foods. Caffeine and stimulants increase Uranian energy, but at a cost. Celery gently lifts and lightens the energy.

Neptune   Neptunian foods help lubricate and moisten the system. Fish, kelp, and seaweed all increase the moistness in the body and also strengthen the immune system, which is linked to Neptune in medical astrology.

Pluto   Plutonic food is deep and rich and helps detoxify and release stored, damaging chemicals in our bodies. These foods include kidney beans, shiitake mushrooms, and pumpkins.

Nourishment of the Signs Through Food

Aries   Foods that strengthen the muscles, tendons, and the blood are all wonderful for Ariens. Leafy greens, beets, and most kinds of meat accomplish this function. Aries people need to avoid eating food that is too stimulating and hot, which can overtax their system and lead to adrenal burnout. They need to nourish their generally strong and vital energy with regular organic meals and lots of clean water. It would help if they slow down when eating meals, so they can assimilate the full nourishment from the food before rushing on to the next project.

Taurus   Although tubers, dairy, and wheat are often favorite foods of Taureans, it is important to guard against excessive consumption of these items, as they can lead to stagnation and weight gain. Add a few stimulating foods such as radishes and beets in order to cleanse and move the energy. Taureans need to eat slowly and surely so that they don't upset their calm, steady disposition.

Gemini   Geminis need to eat a diet that promotes clarity, good humor, and brightness, while decreasing nervousness and tension. They should try to eat warm meals filled with whole grains and vegetables and avoid caffeine, sugar, and alcohol, which will destabilize them. Their fast metabolism usually enables Geminis to handle a little more dairy, meat, and fats in their diet, and these are good for grounding them.

Cancer   Cancers need to be careful to avoid too much heavy and stagnating food like dairy, beef, and fatty starches. These foods have a tendency to weigh them down, increase mucus, and deaden their emotions. Cancers should try to eat in a relaxed, pleasant atmosphere, as their stomachs are sensitive and can be easily upset. One of the best foods for Cancers is fish. Filled with essential nutrients, fish helps strengthen the digestion as well as the nervous system.

Leo   These solar beings have a pretty strong digestion and can usually handle a lot of different kinds of food. Their weakness is their heart, and over time fatty and greasy foods, dairy, and red meats can place an undue burden on this organ. They should try to strengthen the heart with periodic cleansing food in the form of roughage and fiber. Citrus fruits like oranges and grapefruit will also cleanse and enliven the body.

Virgo   Like Cancers, Virgos also need to watch out for a nervous stomach, and benefit from eating in a gentle and relaxed way. The more they can eat at home and cook their own meals slowly and mindfully, the better. A little meat in their diet will help build and strengthen their blood and nerves. Whole grains like brown rice, oats, and rye are wonderfully strengthening for Virgos. They should make sure to add culinary herbs that will help the stomach digest food well.

Libra   Because their kidneys are at risk, it is important for Libras to flush their systems of toxins periodically with salads, radishes, and citrus fruits. They also should avoid junk foods and beverages, as these need to be processed by the kidneys and will eventually weaken and debilitate them. Food that is elegantly prepared and pleasing to look at will help stimulate their digestion and strengthen their health.

Scorpio   Scorpios tend to store and carry the energy of the food they eat and can have a difficult time eliminating toxins from the body. That is why it is especially important for Scorpios to eat a diet that is not too extreme or unbalancing. A steady diet of whole grains and vegetables, soups, and casseroles will go a long way toward ensuring the emotional stability of Scorpio. They should definitely avoid unbalancing processed and junk foods and make sure to drink plenty of water throughout the day to eliminate toxins. A little lean meat is fine, but they should avoid greasy and fatty foods and too much dairy as that will increase mucus and decrease the libido.

Sagittarius   Known for their love of life, Sagittarians usually have a very strong constitution and can handle a lot of different kinds of food. Eventually, heavy meat, dairy, and alcohol consumption will tax the liver and increase feelings of stagnation and anger. To offset this, Sagittarians need to clean themselves periodically by eating raw, fibrous foods like salads, carrots, radishes, and cucumbers. They should try to avoid excessive use of heating spices, caffeine, and sugar, as they can be overly stimulating and eventually damaging to the liver and to the overall health.

Capricorn   Capricorns need to relax and enjoy their meals. How they eat is almost more important than what they eat. If eaten in a hurry, the food will not be able to strengthen and nourish the system properly. When they relax with their meal, Capricorns can reduce the stress and tension from the day and make sure their bodies can handle the stress of life better. They should be sure to add building and stabilizing foods to their diet like whole grains, kale, broccoli, carrots, and tubers. A little meat is wonderful for strengthening and building Capricorns, but they should watch out for excessively heavy foods, which will increase feelings of lethargy and melancholy.

Aquarius   Aquarians need to watch out for their nervous system. Like Capricorns, these folks need to avoid hurrying through their meals. They can add warming spices to help improve their circulation and would do well to eat some grounding foods such as dairy, whole grains, a little meat, and tubers. Aquarians should avoid processed and junk foods, which damage the nervous system and leave them more confused and fearful. Stimulants such as coffee and sugar are the most dangerous for this sign.

Pisces   People with this sensitive sign often are prone to colds, flus, and mucous conditions. They would do well to avoid white starches and sugars as these injure the immune system. Seaweeds like kelp and dulce are some of the best foods for Pisceans, as they strengthen the immune system, decrease toxins, and nourish the body at a cellular level. Pisceans tend to take on the energy of the food they eat, so they need to make sure the food is not processed and is free of pesticides. Pisceans would do well to eat a few spicy and warming foods like onions, garlic, and radishes to help stimulate and direct the energy. Drinking lots of water and eating three meals a day at the same time each day will help strengthen this sign as well.

9
Animals and Other Creatures

In the summertime I like to take off into the Olympic Mountains and hike along the long streambeds and valleys up into the hills and low mountains. The tremendous amount of rainfall helps create one of the most magnificent temperate rainforests in the world. Lush moss circles tall cedars and hemlocks where beds of trillium, wild lily of the valley, and Oregon grape grow below. As I walk the hills, I can see kingfishers swooping along rivers, brown bears foraging for grass and berries, and elk proudly but cautiously walking along well-worn paths through the woods. The Olympics are an incredible environment for a diverse array of animal life to grow and thrive in. These animals teach me many lessons as I walk with them. The bear teaches me to be slower and more attentive. The eagle teaches me to be stronger and to see with clear vision. Each animal carries itself in a certain way that enlightens and heals me when I pay attention.

These animals can act as powerful allies and healers of our soul if we take the time to watch them and take their spirit into our hearts. Many indigenous tribal peoples have a long history of viewing animals as powerful spiritual entities with much to teach. North American Plains Indians work with buffalo as a totem animal and honor its spirit in ceremony and ritual. I once witnessed a Quichua Indian shaman from Ecuador taking on the attributes of a jaguar while doing healing work. Coastal Native Americans have had profound reverence for whales for thousands of years. The whale is not only a source of food and fuel, but also a form of spiritual sustenance for the entire tribe.

Animals and Astrology

When I take the time to observe these animals' habits, I notice their natural affinity to the various elements and planets we study in astrology. Birds have a strong connection to the air element, and seals and whales have an association with the water element. But when we study the animals a little more deeply, we can see how their characteristics attune to different planets as well. Though dolphins may have a basic affinity to the water element, their playfulness and communicative style links them to the planet Mercury. And though great blue herons are connected to air, their graceful majesty and large stature show their Jupiterian nature.

Each environment produces its own diversity of animal life, and its climate will help attune animals to a certain disposition. A dry, sunny region like the canyons of southern Utah will naturally have more fiery animals like lizards and reptiles. Windswept plains and tall, gusty crags will have creatures that are connected to the air element such as ravens, hawks, and eagles.

Animals as Medicine

We can learn what animals have to teach us by studying, watching, and reading about them. Perhaps the lesson is about steadfastness and perseverance (buffalo), or perhaps the lesson is about agility and speed (hummingbird). In each case, when we study these animals, we can start to learn their skills and emulate their abilities so that we may grow stronger and wiser ourselves. Often it is helpful to work with an animal that connects with our astrological chart. If we have a predominance of planets in fire signs, we may want to work with a fiery animal to learn how to better access our own innate energy. We may also want to work with an animal that balances our chart and strengthens an element that we are missing. If we have a lot of fire, we may want to work with a water creature like whale or otter. If we have a lot of air in our chart, we might want to work with an earthy creature like elk or buffalo.

There are numerous ways to work with animal totems, some of which we have already talked about in previous chapters. Here are a few suggestions:

Observation

The best way to learn and take on animal attributes is by watching and observing animals in their natural terrain. This helps build an understanding of their characteristics and nature. These skills can then be emulated in everyday life.

Studying and Drawing

Once you have spent time watching animals in the wild, you can get to know these creatures more deeply by reading about them in natural history books and by drawing them in a special notebook. This will enhance your ability to understand their powers and characteristics and decide which planets and signs they would best be associated with.

Gathering Totem Material

Bones, teeth, fur, and claws are powerful physical and emotional symbols of the animal you are working with. It is best to find these objects in an animal that has already passed away, but if you are a hunter, sacred materials can also be gathered after a kill if this is carried out in a sacred manner and with reverence.

Wearing and Displaying

Totem objects can be worn or placed in sacred places like an altar to strengthen the connection to an animal's medicine. Necklaces, pendants, and clothing made from animals are powerful ways to display and take in the energy and beauty of an animal. Again, it is essential to be reverential when making jewelry and apparel. Too often our society uses animal parts in poor and destructive ways.

Shamanic Journeying

As I described in chapter 6, we can connect to animal totems through shamanic methods. By connecting to these creatures through nonordinary perception, we can gain insights that are powerful and make connections and friendships with these beings. Remember to pick a good Moon time to connect with these wise beings.

Shapechanging

As I also wrote in chapter 6, we can use tools such as drumming and dancing to change our perceptions and take on the characteristics and personality of the animals we are interested in. When we do this, we make a connection at a fundamental level. We learn the powerful ways that these animals move, walk, communicate, and see life.

Animal Medicine

Badger

Properties: This animal is a small creature, but fights with great tenacity when attacked. Badgers are nocturnal creatures that burrow into holes where they often stay inside. They are fast diggers and are also omnivores, eating a variety of foods including mice, berries, grass, and fungus.

Planetary Ally: Mars

Sign Ruler: Aries

Elemental Ally: Earth

Energetics: Badger is a great totem for people who need to defend themselves from psychic, emotional, or physical attack. It is also good for those who are in hermit mode, needing time and space to reflect.

Bat

Properties: Bats like to live in dark homes, preferably in caves, underhangings, old barns, and tree snags. They use echolocation (like radar) to single in on their prey and to prevent bumping into walls and each other. They usually hunt for food (mainly insects) at twilight. This is the only mammal that has mastered how to fly.

Planetary Allies: Pluto, Moon

Sign Ruler: Scorpio

Elemental Ally: Air

Energetics: Bats are associated with darkness, the underworld, and vampirism. In truth, bats are not as dangerous as myth makes them out to be, but they can be feisty if their space is invaded. They can be called on to work sorcery and magic during powerful and intense times. Bats help us transform our natures and release unwanted fear. They are not to be worked with lightly.

Bear

Properties: Bears are known for their slow and lumbering presence. They are often found grazing on grasses and berries, hunting for fish, or sipping water at a river's edge. When a bear becomes aroused, it can use its immense strength and agility to move at lightning speed to escape, defend, or attack. Bears lack good eyesight, but have a tremendous sense of smell. They hibernate during the winter months and then come out hungry and ready to find food.

Planetary Allies: Mars, Neptune

Sign Ruler: Taurus

Elemental Allies: Earth, water

Energetics: There are a number of different kinds of bears, each with their own magic. In general, they are seen as powerful and forceful creatures who are gentle on one level, but have strength and intensity when required. Linked to dreams, they help us tap into our reservoirs of subconscious imagination and creativity. Bear is also a good animal for developing strength, courage, surety, and confidence.

Beaver

Properties: This industrious creature lives near rivers or by ponds created through their own dam building. Beavers are best known for their dam-making abilities, using nearby twigs and branches to construct these edifices. The dams help create a spot where fish, birds, and plants dwell and where beavers can have a ready source of food to eat.

Planetary Ally: Saturn

Sign Ruler: Capricorn

Elemental Allies: Earth, water

Energetics: Beaver is a great totem to increase earth energy. This is a strong totem for Capricorns, as beavers are builders and shapers. It is a helpful ally to call on to increase security, wealth, and a good home.

Buffalo

Properties: At one time, buffaloes roamed in huge herds over North America, but they were hunted nearly to extinction. Buffaloes were a strong source of food, medicine, ritual, and clothing to Native American plains tribes.

Planetary Ally: Saturn

Sign Ruler: Aquarius

Elemental Ally: Earth

Energetics: Buffalo has a serene and steady disposition, gently grazing on grasses in open lands. Buffaloes migrate and live in herds of their kin, heading south in the winter and north in the summer. Buffalo is a wise and benevolent ally, teaching skills of slow and steady movement toward our goals.

Bull

Properties: The bull stands alone in the field, strong, steady, and sure. Only when threatened or tormented does the bull come alive, snorting his nostrils and directing his full weight to bear down on his victim. Their powerful strength and pointed horns make bulls a fearful animal to tangle with.

Planetary Ally: Mars

Sign Ruler: Taurus

Elemental Ally: Earth

Energetics: Strong and silent or enraged and devastatingly threatening, these creatures are a force of supreme strength and resiliency. Bull can be called on to develop skills of steadfastness, perseverance, power, and strength.

Coyote

Properties: Coyotes can be heard out on lonely prairies or on hilly landscapes, howling their familiar call. They often hunt alone or with one other and are not as fearsome as their reputation. They usually have a diet of mice, voles, and rabbits, and rarely kill large animals like cows or pigs.

Planetary Ally: Mercury

Sign Ruler: Gemini

Elemental Allies: Earth, air

Energetics: Coyote has been known as the "trickster" to Native Americans. This title refers to the mythology woven around Coyote as the one who plays games, turns things upside down, and shows us another take on reality. Often Coyote uses humor to do this in stories about him. Coyote helps develop our sense of play as well as our ideas of light and dark and duality. He also helps strengthen our communicative function and increases our intelligence.

Cow

Properties: Cows are now domesticated and are a source of beef and milk. They stand or lie down docilely in the fields, gently grazing and placidly watching the day go by. They are shy creatures who don't enjoy being startled or stressed-out by too much activity and noise.

Planetary Allies: Venus, Moon

Sign Ruler: Taurus

Elemental Ally: Earth

Energetics: Cows are revered as sacred in India and are very much protected there. Here we treat them with disdain, often placing them in huge factory farms, injecting them with growth hormones and demanding milk production. The true nature of Cow, though, is sweet, slow, and serene—a great Taurus totem. They help us retain a gentle and simple attitude toward life.

Crab

Properties: There are numerous varieties of crab, but it is best known as having a hard shell (exoskeleton) and outstretched pincers that it can extend and retract to attack, defend, and gather food. Occasionally, the shell will be cast off (molted) and replaced by a larger one. Crabs live on shorelines, in tidepools, and under rocks.

Planetary Allies: Moon, Saturn

Sign Ruler: Cancer

Elemental Ally: Water

Energetics: Crabs have the ability to be curious and probing, but also defensive and fierce if threatened. Crabs help us explore our emotions, especially issues such as fear, insecurity, courage, and anger. They help put us in touch with the watery realm of our deepest feelings. These are strong and feisty creatures that can be strong and protective allies.

Crocodile

Properties: Crocodiles live and sleep on banks of lakes and streams, sunning themselves in reptile fashion for long periods of time. Then they gently slither into the water to swim, hunt, and play. These beings are fearsome with their jagged teeth and are capable of killing large creatures with their swiftness and deadly force. They are one of the few animals that humans fear, along with sharks and bears.

Planetary Allies: Mars, Pluto

Sign Ruler: Scorpio

Elemental Ally: Water

Energetics: Crocodiles are strong and powerful beasts. They have been seen as descendants of the dinosaurs and carry an ancient earth wisdom about them. Crocodiles are great allies when working magic of transformation, stealth, strength, and courage.

Deer

Properties: Watch the careful, light steps the deer makes, cautious and with good intent. It uses its strong sense of smell to sense its surroundings and guard against danger. If something is amiss, it can dart out from where it stands and bound over shrubs and branches with leaps and hops, quick and sure.

Planetary Allies: Venus, Mercury

Sign Ruler: Libra

Elemental Ally: Earth

Energetics: Deer promotes agility, swiftness, and heightened senses. Instead of using force, we can call on Deer for grace, perceptiveness, and caution in achieving goals.

Dog

Properties: This fellow is usually found in someone's home, completely domesticated and comfortable near its guardian's chair or bed. Dogs also exist in the wild, where they are a much different breed, desperately scrounging for food, hunting in packs, and often dangerous to humans and other creatures. Dogs have long been bred for their companionship and their tracking and hunting skills, and are also a lovely ally to blind people.

Planetary Ally: Jupiter

Sign Ruler: Sagittarius

Elemental Ally: Earth

Energetics: Our relationship to dogs can be a magical one, for they can help us flow more with the moment. Dogs often like nothing better then to be played with, petted, and given affection. This unbridaled loyalty and enthusiasm for giving and receiving affection helps us open our hearts and shine our love out. Dogs can act as our guard, our friend, and our familiar.

Dolphin

Properties: Dolphins are supreme swimmers of the underwater ocean. Dolphins are family oriented and will often swim with their kin and in groups. Dolphins have a strong sense of hearing and often chatter among each other. They tend to eat fish and shrimp.

Planetary Allies: Uranus, Neptune, Venus

Sign Rulers: Pisces, Aquarius

Elemental Ally: Water

Energetics: Dolphins have an inquisitiveness and friendliness about them that is magical. Some of my friends have had the chance to swim out among a group of dolphins, and their openness to humans is truly amazing. Call on dolphins to increase playfulness, intelligence, and group interactivity.

Elephant

Properties: These huge creatures are the largest land mammal and are mainly found in India and Africa. They have poor eyesight, but a keen sense of smell. This is obvious when looking at the elephant's elongated trunk. Female elephants live in separate herds, with male bulls only joining them for mating season.

Planetary Allies: Jupiter, Neptune

Sign Ruler: Sagittarius

Elemental Ally: Earth

Energetics: These powerful creatures are majestic and royal in stature. They strengthen our sense of inner pride and confidence. Elephants are also playful and tender with their families and comrades. They help strengthen our healing nature, our fertility, and our family connections. They also have a prophetic nature and can help us with divination.

Elk

Properties: Elks can be up to ten feet long and five feet tall and are found in mountain forests and valleys. In the fall, male elks (bulls) emit a loud bugling call to signify the start of the mating season. Elk has tremendous strength and stamina and can maintain a fast trot for extended periods of time (usually to escape predators). Elk eat mainly grasses and vegetation.

Planetary Ally: Mars

Sign Ruler: Leo

Elemental Ally: Earth

Energetics: Elk can be called on for their tremendous power and strength. Their long antlers signify libido and yang force. This is a helpful ally for working through problems of impotence and infertility. They also help increase endurance and stamina.

Fox

Properties: Foxes are quick and elusive, able to dart between trees and holes with rapidity. They are usually nocturnal, preferring to hunt for game or scavenge a meal in the dark of night. Foxes communicate through a type of barking, but also yelp and scream to attract attention.

Planetary Ally: Mercury

Sign Ruler: Gemini

Elemental Ally: Fire

Energetics: Foxes can be called on for their agility and quick intelligence. Foxes can be sly and secretive with a dash of humor. Foxes help us become camouflaged and invisible when we need to. When we need slyness, spontaneity, and laughter, we can call on Fox.

Frog

Properties: Frogs are famous for their unified croaking chorus that returns in the spring. These beings begin their lives underwater as tadpoles and then slowly progress into above-land creatures who are capable of swimming and searching above the water's surface for insects to eat.

Planetary Allies: Moon, Neptune

Sign Ruler: Cancer

Elemental Ally: Water

Energetics: Frog is a great ally for birthing and is an ancient totem for fertility. Frogs add a sense of wonder and mystery to our experience. They also help us touch the deepest core of resonance, the universal OM that resides under the surface.

Goat

Properties: Mountain goats live high up in alpine areas and tend to roam in flocks. Their sure-footedness and agility allow them to jump and step nimbly between crags and rocks. If startled, they will bound away with amazing speed and purpose. They are often seen perched on high boulders, startlingly close to the edge and perched over long precipices.

Planetary Ally: Saturn

Sign Ruler: Capricorn

Elemental Allies: Earth, air

Energetics: Goats have a strength and surety and a love of hills and mountains that make them the totem of Capricorns. Their ability to be directed, sure, and persevering, and to climb tall hills and mountains makes them a friend and ally to all Saturnian types. Their love of rugged landscapes, out on distant windswept hills, also makes them a friend to the air element.

Horse

Properties: Strong, sure, and fast, horses live in herds when found in the wild. The horse has been domesticated for thousands of years and has been used as a pack animal, for sport, as a means of transportation, and as a tool in warfare. They possess a natural intelligence that allows them to make quick decisions, and they have tremendous endurance that enables them to travel hundreds of miles at a stretch.

Planetary Ally: Jupiter

Sign Ruler: Sagittarius

Elemental Allies: Earth, fire

Energetics: Horse can be called on for regal surety and for its proud and noble disposition. Horse helps us build strength, confidence, and intelligence.

Lion

Properties: The lion and her feline allies move with graceful sleekness, always watchful for prey to hunt or an attack from an opponent. Lions can be very quiet as they gently walk on their tender paws, but then can become dangerously violent, springing and attacking with sharp, outstretched claws and razor-sharp teeth. This animal is feared by most wildlife, as Lion can hunt and kill with ease.

Planetary Allies: Sun, Mars

Sign Ruler: Leo

Elemental Ally: Fire

Energetics: Lion is a totem of Leo and can be called on for protection, strength, warrior energy, and regal confidence.

Lizard

Properties: The lizard can often be found baking out in the hot sun, its head outstretched to catch the full rays of light. This primordial creature eats plants and insects as its main source of nutrition. Lizards have scales and lay eggs when giving birth.

Planetary Allies: Pluto, Sun

Sign Ruler: Scorpio

Elemental Ally: Fire

Energetics: Lizards are totems of transformation. They have a very mystical and psychic quality to them and can be called on for scrying, prophesy, and psychic work.

Mouse

Properties: This tiny creature is known throughout most of the world. Mice often are found living in holes and cracks in the wall and in small openings out in the woods. They are resourceful and enduring beings, usually giving birth to large litters and living off scraps and crumbs of human waste, insects, and plant life.

Planetary Ally: Mercury

Sign Ruler: Virgo

Elemental Ally: Air

Energetics: Mice are agile and quick creatures we can call on to get through difficult situations with deft swiftness and intelligence. Their natural communicativeness and ability to breeze through any difficulty make them a strong ally.

Otter

Properties: Otters are creatures of the rivers and lakes. Their sleek coat helps them navigate waters with ease. They are amazing swimmers, alternately diving, propelling forward, and then making a swift somersault to swim in another direction. They feed on fish, birds, frogs, and other creatures for nourishment.

Planetary Allies: Neptune, Mercury

Sign Ruler: Pisces

Elemental Ally: Water

Energetics: Otters are very playful, jovial creatures and have a wonderful sense of humor. Otter is a great totem for swimmers and for those attracted to water. Otters can be called on for their ability to move and glide through any situation, avoid any obstacle, and still maintain a playful joyfulness.

Porcupine

Properties: This smallish creature roams the forest and resembles a prickly guinea pig. Porcupines do not actually shoot out their quills when attacked, but their quills do become loosened and imbed themselves in their enemy. The quills then tend to drive themselves in deeper over time, penetrating further into the flesh.

Planetary Allies: Mars, Saturn

Sign Rulers: Taurus, Aries

Elemental Ally: Earth

Energetics: Porcupines are a symbol of defense and protection. When we need security and to ward off any negative influences, Porcupine is a good creature to make friends with and call on.

Rabbit

Properties: These fleet-footed beings display a natural speed and agility that allows them to move swiftly and adeptly through many different kinds of terrain. Their oversized legs and feet allow them to hop as well as run at lightning speed. This is fortunate because rabbits have many natural predators that enjoy rabbit as a tasty meal. Rabbits also breed and proliferate in high numbers and are nocturnal. They have large ears that give them a keen sense of hearing.

Planetary Allies: Mercury, Moon, Uranus

Sign Ruler: Libra

Elemental Ally: Air

Energetics: Their speed and acute hearing make rabbits natural allies to Mercury. Their nocturnal behavior gives them a relationship to the Moon. Rabbit has an ancient relationship to passion, fertility, and childbirth. Rabbit is a wonderful totem for an expectant mother or for young lovers desiring pregnancy.

Raccoon

Properties: Many of us have seen raccoons in our backyards, pressing their noses against the garbage cans and scavenging for scraps. These nocturnal creatures tend to live near water or in the woods, enjoying an omniverous diet and having few predators (humans being their greatest threat).

Planetary Ally: Moon

Sign Ruler: Pisces

Elemental Ally: Earth

Energetics: Raccoons tend to be curious, forthright, and smart. They help us explore life with stealth and invisibility.

Rat

Properties: Feared and detested since antiquity by humans, rats are an intelligent and prolific species. They have been noted as carriers of disease; vermin were carriers of the Black Plague that wiped out one-third of the population of Europe in the fourteenth century. Rats can eat almost anything and often travel in packs.

Planetary Ally: Pluto

Sign Ruler: Aries

Elemental Ally: Earth

Energetics: Rats are symbols of survival, proliferation, and tenacity. They can overcome many obstacles and can thrive even under very difficult circumstances.

Salmon

Properties: Salmon are very quickly becoming endangered in many rivers and ocean areas due to having been overharvested and to soil erosion caused by overforesting. Salmon spawn high up in riverbeds and then swim down to the ocean, only to return again, swimming upstream in maturity. This is a proud and regal fish that has been a main food source and totem for many coastal Native American tribes.

Planetary Allies: Neptune, Mars

Sign Ruler: Pisces

Elemental Ally: Water

Energetics: Salmon is a tremendously powerful ally that connects with Goddess worship as it has a direct connection with seasonal cycles. Salmon help us understand the interconnectedness of all beings, the land, the sky, and water. Its precarious position today shows our lack of respect for the natural cycles of life and our need to honor them again in order to stay healthy and in tune with our environment. Salmon can be called on for strength, determination, will, and service to Spirit.

Seal

Properties: Seals were designed and built to swim the waters; their sleek and oily coats help them glide, dive, and surface easily and rapidly. Seals carry a tremendous heft, which enables them to survive in cold climates. They live both in the water, where they hunt and eat, and on the land, where they breed and give birth to their young. Seals have been hunted by humans in such great numbers that today we are seeing a significant reduction in their numbers.

Planetary Allies: Jupiter, Neptune

Sign Ruler: Pisces

Elemental Ally: Water

Energetics: Seals live gracefully in difficult climates and can be a symbol of gliding through hard times and places. When we need assistance to live and thrive well in frugal or demanding circumstances, we can call on Seal. Seals embody a natural wisdom and majesty that can be called on when we feel weak, confused, or frail.

Shark

Properties: Feared and abhorred by many humans, sharks are one of the few creatures that will attack and kill humans without provocation. We have all heard of surfers or swimmers becoming targets of shark attacks. The lucky ones escape, but many have been injured or killed by the attacking shark. The internal skeleton of the shark is made up of cartilage, and they are carnivores, spending much of their time hunting prey. Their skin is rough like sandpaper.

Planetary Ally: Mars

Sign Ruler: Aries

Elemental Ally: Water

Energetics: Sharks are fearsome creatures that can be a very protective ally. They can also help us act as warriors when we need to defend land from being clearcut, water from being polluted, or people from being discriminated against. Sharks help us feel empowered and safe, and help us make swift and firm decisions.

Snake

Properties: Snakes have long, slithering bodies with skin made up of overlapping scales. They have large mouths to swallow food and forked or notched tongues. There are a wide variety of snakes, some relatively docile while others can be extremely dangerous and poisonous.

Planetary Allies: Mars, Pluto

Sign Ruler: Scorpio

Elemental Allies: Fire, water

Energetics: Snakes are capable of transformation through shedding their skin. This type of physical change demonstrates why they symbolize metamorphosis. Snakes have also been ancient symbols for healing and growth. When we have gone through great sorrow, travail, and even death, Snake helps guide us back. This is a powerful totem and not to be worked with lightly. Some snakes have a poisonous bite if not treated with respect.

Squirrel

Properties: Squirrels are a type of rodent, although they are deemed cuter and more loveable than most rodents. They live in a variety of habitats and have a quickness and agility about them. We find them scurrying from place to place, busily searching for food or nesting materials. They are resourceful and cautious, avoiding contact, as they have many predators.

Planetary Ally: Mercury

Sign Ruler: Virgo

Elemental Ally: Air

Energetics: Squirrels have quick and adaptable energy—their beautiful, bushy tails give them balance and grace amid the landscape. They increase our energy and our sense of pleasure in the world through their inquisitiveness and curiosity. They also gather food and store it well in the lean months and can help us develop habits of frugality and prudence.

Turtle

Properties: The turtle is a slow and unusual-looking creature. Its hard, oval shell masks a soft interior. The turtle sticks its arms and head through holes in its shell and retracts them when danger lurks nearby. The turtle is content to swim gently through the water or dry itself on the banks of a river or lake. This reptile has ancient roots that tie it to both land and water.

Planetary Allies: Saturn, Moon

Sign Ruler: Cancer

Elemental Allies: Water, earth

Energetics: Turtle can be called on when disciplined and careful work needs to be carried out. It is also a helpful totem for safety, protection, and security. This is a grounded and stable being.

Whale

Properties: There are many different kinds of whales, but the one most of us are familiar with is the image of a massive body of blubber swimming gracefully through the oceans. This mammal sings, snorts, emits noises, and communicates with its pod with clarity and emotion. Having been overhunted, the number of whales diminished rapidly in the nineteenth and twentieth centuries. Today, whales are slowly being taken off the endangered species list, but are not out of danger yet.

Planetary Allies: Neptune, Jupiter

Sign Ruler: Pisces

Elemental Ally: Water

Energetics: Whale is a great totem from the ocean. Its undeniable size gives it tremendous power. It is the largest mammal on earth. When we tap into this being, we find a fountain of spiritual strength, wisdom, and knowingness. These creatures are incredibly sensitive and carry with them the spirit of the ocean with its vast, interconnected web of life. Call on Whale for spiritual serenity and strength, or to open up emotions and the heart.

Wolf

Properties: This four-legged predecessor to the dog has been feared and reviled in many sections of the world as a voracious predator of farm livestock. Though Wolf has been known to do this, his reputation in this area far exceeds his misdeeds. Wolves usually live in packs of up to twenty or so kin. When in groups, they hunt, using periodic howls and yelps to signal to one another. They usually dine on rabbits and rodents; they also mate for life.

Planetary Allies: Mars, Moon, Uranus

Sign Ruler: Aries

Elemental Allies: Earth, air

Energetics: The wolf is an intelligent, enduring hunter, capable of working well in groups and communicating important information to members of its clan through a variety of different ways. Wolf can be called on to gather vision, awareness, strength, confidence, and leadership ability.

Association of Animal Allies with the Elements

Fire	Fox, horse, lion, lizard, snake
Water	Bear, crab, crocodile, dolphin, frog, otter, salmon, seal, shark, snake, turtle, whale
Air	Bat, coyote, goat, mouse, rabbit, squirrel, wolf
Earth	Badger, bear, beaver, buffalo, bull, coyote, cow, deer, dog, elephant, elk, goat, horse, pig, porcupine, raccoon, rat, turtle, wolf

Association of Animal Allies with the Modalities

Cardinal	Badger, beaver, crab, elk, goat, porcupine, rabbit, rat, shark, turtle, wolf

Fixed	Bat, bear, buffalo, bull, cow, crocodile, lion, lizard, pig, porcupine, raccoon, snake, turtle, whale
Mutable	Coyote, deer, dog, dolphin, elephant, fox, horse, mouse, otter, raccoon, salmon, seal, squirrel

Association of Animal Allies with the Planets

Sun	Lion, lizard
Moon	Bat, cow, crab, frog, rabbit, raccoon, turtle
Mercury	Coyote, deer, fox, mouse, otter, rabbit, squirrel, wolf
Venus	Cow, deer, dolphin
Mars	Badger, bear, bull, crocodile, elk, lion, porcupine, shark, snake, wolf
Jupiter	Dog, elephant, horse, seal
Saturn	Beaver, buffalo, crab, goat, pig, porcupine, turtle
Uranus	Dolphin, rabbit, wolf
Neptune	Bear, dolphin, frog, otter, pig, salmon, seal, whale
Pluto	Bat, crocodile, lizard, rat, snake

Association of Animal Allies with the Signs

Aries	Badger, porcupine, rat, shark, wolf
Taurus	Bear, bull, cow, pig, porcupine

Gemini	Coyote, fox
Cancer	Crab, frog, turtle
Leo	Elk, lion
Virgo	Mouse, squirrel
Libra	Deer, rabbit
Scorpio	Bat, crocodile, lizard, snake
Sagittarius	Dog, elephant, horse
Capricorn	Beaver, goat
Aquarius	Buffalo, dolphin
Pisces	Dolphin, otter, raccoon, salmon, seal, whale

Nourishment of the Elements with Animal Allies

Fire
- Work with Lion to promote courage, strength, and nobility.
- Work with Fox to develop spontaneity and humor.
- Work with Horse and Snake for speed and power.

Water
- Work with Seal and Whale to learn flexibility and grace.
- Work with Dolphin, Frog, and Whale to develop psychic abilities.
- Work with Snake and Frog to explore emotional realms.
- Work with Salmon and Crab to develop sensitivity.
- Work with Snake and Crocodile to help in transformation.

Air
- Work with Coyote and Dolphin to develop playfulness.
- Work with Rabbit and Mouse to nurture communicativeness.

- Work with Wolf and Goat to develop poise and equilibrium.
- Work with Dolphin and Mouse to stimulate the mind.

Earth
- Work with Buffalo, Elk, Turtle, and Goat to promote grounding and centeredness.
- Work with Porcupine and Wolf to establish boundaries.
- Work with Beaver, Buffalo, Elk, and Goat to accomplish goals and activities.

Nourishment of the Modalities with Animal Allies

Cardinal
- Work with Beaver, Buffalo, Elk, and Goat to accomplish goals.
- Work with Beaver for focused bursts of energy.
- Work with Buffalo and Elk for longer, more demanding work over a period of time.
- Work with Goat for scaling tough obstacles.

Fixed
- Work with Cow, Elephant, Whale, and Seal to remain solid and firmly rooted.
- Work with Bull, Bear, Porcupine, and Snake to establish boundaries.
- Work with Buffalo and Whale to draw others in and be magnetic.

Mutable
- Work with Mouse and Otter to be organized and fastidious.
- Work with Coyote, Dolphin, Fox, and Rabbit to be adaptable and playful.
- Work with Dolphin, Mouse, and Rabbit to be communicative.
- Work with Deer and Otter to be graceful and poised.

Nourishment of the Signs and Planets with Animal Allies

Aries/

Mars
- Work with Bear, Porcupine, Rat, and Shark to develop strength and warrior power.
- Work with Shark and Wolf to become a leader.

Taurus/

Venus
- Work with Bear and Cow to remain rooted, solid, and calm.
- Work with Bear and Bull to strengthen self-confidence.
- Work with Cow and Pig to promote gentleness.
- Work with Cow and Porcupine to be slow and sure.

Gemini/

Mercury
- Work with Coyote and Fox to develop humor and playfulness.
- Work with Coyote and Dolphin to promote communication and the interchange of ideas.

Cancer/

Moon
- Work with Turtle to promote peacefulness and security.
- Work with Frog to explore emotional realms.
- Work with Crab to defend and create boundaries.

Leo/

Sun
- Work with Elk and Lion to promote nobility, majesty, and authority.
- Work with Horse and Lion to develop strength, courage, and will.
- Work with Lizard to develop serenity and joy in the moment.

Virgo/
Mercury
- Work with Squirrel and Mouse to develop fastidiousness and organizational ability.
- Work with Dolphin and Otter to develop skill, speed, and precision.
- Work with Deer and Otter to develop efficiency and ease in movement.

Libra/
Venus
- Work with Deer to develop grace and poise.
- Work with Dolphin and Rabbit to develop social skills.

Scorpio/
Pluto
- Work with Snake and Bat to help in transformational work.
- Work with Crocodile to develop warrior skills.
- Work with Bat, Lizard, and Snake to visit intense emotional places for healing.

Sagittarius/
Jupiter
- Work with Horse to develop an expansive attitude and playful attributes.
- Work with Dog for friendliness of disposition.
- Work with Elephant and Horse for travels and exploration.

Capricorn/
Saturn
- Work with Beaver and Goat to help build and develop strength and foundations.
- Work with Elk and Buffalo for stamina and endurance.
- Work with Elk and Wolf to develop leadership skills.

Aquarius/
Uranus

- Work with Dolphin and Buffalo to help in communication skills and "group mind."

- Work with Porcupine to be the rebel in the group.

- Work with Dolphin and Rabbit to develop lightning-quick ideas.

Pisces/
Neptune

- Work with Seal and Whale to yield and surrender to the flow of life.

- Work with Salmon, Seal, and Whale for grace, effortlessness, and agility.

- Work with Seal and Whale to develop the psychic and mystical self.

- Work with Bear, Crocodile, and Whale to develop visualization and dreaming skills.

10

Birds and Other Winged Creatures

Birds have a special relationship to the air element as they all fly, hunt, dance, and play in the wind. With their beautiful feathers and plumage, they carry a powerful magic that we can call on to help us. Though all birds are associated with the air element, each also has a relationship to a specific planet. Some birds are related to other elements as well. For example, ducks and herons are related to the water element as well as the air element. Birds that live in sunnier climates have a special relationship to the fire element. These birds can act as our totems, our guides, and can give us strength and wisdom. When we honor and respect them, they each individually have something to teach.

When we observe these avians in our environment, we immediately recognize their connection to the wind currents and to the air. They swoop, dive, and hover in the skies and show us the power of their sight, sharp instincts, and multifaceted talents of hunting, guarding, communicating, and nurturing. Birds come in all shapes and sizes, with different characteristics individual to each one. A cardinal's beautiful red coloring reminds us of the creative and dynamic principles in nature and reminds us of blood and the planet Mars. A sweet yellow meadowlark sings its beautiful song and reminds us of gentle and cheerful energy as well as the planet Venus. Birds can be categorized according to their coloring, size, expression, and inherent nature. When we work with bird medicine, we work with a symbolic force and we work with a transformational energy made manifest in the physical plane. As potent symbolic forms, they can help us nourish our own internal strengths and also balance parts of our nature that are lacking or weak. Just as a bodybuilder lifts weights to strengthen muscles, we can work with the wisdom and power of bird medicine to lift up our souls and strengthen our sense of clarity and balance.

Although each bird has different attributes and is connected to different planets, all are useful for connecting us with the element of air. Watch the graceful motion of a great blue heron as it alights from tall reed grasses, or watch bald eagles circle high up in the clouds. Each has the ability to shape and guide its feathers for maximum efficiency and allow the strength of its wings to carry it off the ground. When we feel weighed down and tied up in the confusions of everyday life, we can look to birds for the inspiration to lift ourselves up and to leave the mundane world behind. Birds give us a sense of transcendence, of power and magic, because they can navigate the earthly and airy planes.

Since ancient times, birds have been revered and associated with deities. One primary myth is that of the phoenix. In Greek mythology, the phoenix was a powerful bird that rose from the ashes after being burnt in sacrifice. The phoenix gives us a sense of the power of birds to overcome obstacles and rise up from difficult circumstances. In much of Western religious lore, angels are seen as having wings. There is an ancient connection between the sky realm and heaven. Angels are heavenly messengers sent from above. We often associate the heavens with harp-playing angels up in the clouds. These connections give us a sense that the sky world is sacred and more pure and holy than the mundane, earthly realm. Birds are our link to this heavenly world because they can soar to the heavens.

The air realm is connected to breath and oxygen. Breath is vital to our health and maintenance, and without it we quickly die. When we take the time to breathe slowly and draw in chi to all parts of our being, we are enlivened and relaxed. Birds can remind us to slow down to truly draw in the air element. They remind us that deep, slow breathing adds immense enjoyment and peace of mind and deepens our quality of life. When we do chi gong or yoga exercises, we can truly experience a slice of heaven here on earth. The breath reminds us to live simply and enjoy every moment of our life. If we are lacking in air in our chart, it can be vital to connect with the realm of the birds. There are a number of ways to connect powerfully with bird medicine. Here are a few:

Observation

One way to connect with birds is to spend time observing their habits and go bird watching. Birds have very particular habits and routines, and examining them can be marvelously entertaining. They can help augment our skills of patience, observation, and simple delight at the wonders of the universe. Even with binoculars, you need a keen sense of sight to see all the colorings and markings in birds. Observing them in the wild will help hone this sense.

Studying and Drawing

Once you have spent time watching birds in the wild, you can get to know these creatures better by reading about them in natural history books and by drawing them in a special notebook. This will enhance your ability to understand their powers and characteristics and what planets and signs they would most be associated with.

Feather Medicine

If you can, gather a feather from the bird you are attracted to. This will help solidify your connection to that particular bird. Make sure that you find the feather or that it is given to you. Some feathers, like those of the eagle, are actually illegal to own, so be careful what you collect. Feathers carry the energetic properties of the bird. Their coloring, size, and shape all help discern which kind of bird it belongs to. When you place the feather on an altar or a sacred place, you can allow it to remind you of the bird's medicine. Use the feather in rituals, and when you make prayers, honor the energy of the bird. Speak aloud its attributes and strengths until you feel the bird's energy completely in your soul. Make offerings to the spirit of this creature. Light candles and thank the spirit of the bird from time to time. Cleansing and bringing your feathers outside in the air and sunshine is another way to honor the bird. Offering tobacco, hair, or special herbs is yet another way to give something back for the teachings and lessons you are receiving.

Journeying and Shapechanging

On a deeper level, you can contact the spirit of the bird you admire through trance or on a shamanic level. Use the techniques I discussed in chapter 6 for contacting the spirit of the bird. Through the power of chanting, drumming, and dancing, you can communicate and take on the medicine of the bird on a soul level. This is best done during a Full Moon or during an air Moon time. When you transform into the spirit of a bird, you metamorphose into another creature, another entity. This is an intense experience and it may be wise to have friends and guides to assist you with the process. During this experience, you are embodying another life force and working with it in your own heart, so it is important to have a strong and grounded sense of yourself before undertaking shapechanging work.

Compendium of Birds and Other Winged Creatures

Bee

Properties: With two pairs of wings, these tiny, beautiful insects gather pollen from flowers to make honeycomb nests where the queen bee lives. With their sharp stingers, bees can be dangerous, but they also create one of the sweetest foods found in nature.

Planetary Allies: Mercury, Venus, Uranus, Neptune

Sign Ruler: Virgo

Elemental Ally: Air

Energetics: Go near a bee hive and hear the droning, unified body of bees doing their work to build and stabilize a nest. Bees help us find the sweet nectar in life and help us work in unison with our community. With their stingers, they are protective allies as well. Bees teach us to communicate at subtle and telepathic levels with each other. They also teach us to serve (in their case, the queen) and work for the common good.

Butterfly

Properties: Like other insects, butterflies have three pairs of legs, but the front pair is usually reduced in size. Before butterflies can fly, they must warm their bodies to at least 81° F. To do this, they hold their wings in characteristic positions so they can bask in sunlight and heat themselves up. Certain butterflies, like swallowtails, mimic their surroundings or give off an unpleasant odor to avoid predation. Butterflies are formed when caterpillars spin silk cocoons and metamorphose into these beautiful, winged beings.

Planetary Allies: Mercury, Pluto

Sign Rulers: Gemini, Scorpio

Elemental Ally: Air

Energetics: Butterflies are light, delicate creatures and symbolize the ability to transform from one form to another. They are often marvelously colored and bring magic, play, and joy into our lives. When we need to open our hearts and move out of a difficult and dead place in our lives, we can call on the medicine of Butterfly.

Canada Goose

Properties: This large bird lives in large groups and is the most common of all geese. They tend to live near the water's edge, but some live on rock ledges in cliffs and in abandoned tree nests. Geese mate for life, and both the male and the female share in the raising of the young. They also migrate in V formations and have a keen sense of sight.

Planetary Ally: Jupiter

Sign Ruler: Sagittarius

Elemental Ally: Air

Energetics: Canada geese are powerful totems for group activities. These geese easily arrange and rearrange themselves in flight to help the whole flock fly better when they migrate. They also help increase our sense of vision and our sense of commitment in relationships.

Cardinal

Properties: With a rich, red coating, cardinals are easy to spot. They also have a distinct whistle that is usually repeated several times. They are often found in open woods, forest edges, thickets, and parks. They usually lay three to four eggs at a time, which then go on to hatch twelve days later.

Planetary Ally: Mars

Sign Ruler: Aries

Elemental Allies: Air, fire

Energetics: Cardinals brighten and enliven their environment. They are warm and intelligent creatures with a playful spirit. They help renew our vitality and vigor.

Chickadee

Properties: With its distinctive black cap and striped, white features, the chickadee is fairly recognizable. The chickadee is one of the first birds to return and call out its whistle in the spring. Chickadees can be found in forests and parks.

Planetary Ally: Mercury

Sign Ruler: Gemini

Elemental Ally: Air

Energetics: Their painted head symbolizes the thinking function, and along with their quick and lively movements, chickadees are strong indicators of intelligence and the mind. We can call on chickadees to become more quick-witted, swift, and expressive.

Crow

Properties: This highly intelligent bird is found throughout the world and has a well-developed social structure and hierarchy. These watchful and observant creatures will work together as a group to scavenge food and ward off predators. Crows have an intricate communication system and have been known to learn to count when they have been domesticated.

Planetary Allies: Moon, Saturn, Pluto

Sign Rulers: Capricorn, Scorpio

Elemental Allies: Water, earth, air

Energetics: This smart bird is associated with magic and the occult and can be a powerful totem for exploring the deeper mysteries of life. Its black color signifies the wisdom of the night and the moon. Crows are also associated with death and transformation, and also teach us observational and communication skills.

Dove

Properties: The dove originally came from Europe and Asia and can sometimes be found nesting in human buildings. Doves breed several times a year, and both the male and the female tend to their young. They feed off a mixture of seeds from the ground.

Planetary Ally: Venus

Sign Ruler: Libra

Elemental Ally: Air

Energetics: Known as the dove of peace, doves help put us in touch with gentle, soothing energy. Their cooing reminds us of a mother with an infant, making soft, loving sounds. It is a gentle bird associated with fertility, grace, and femininity. It is also a lovely totem for women wishing to heal their relationship to their sexuality.

Dragonfly

Properties: With a long, slender body, two pairs of wings, and often brightly colored, dragonflies sparkle and dazzle the eye as they dart by. These hunters catch mosquitoes and other insects by making a basketlike trap with their legs. Pairs often fly together, with the male flying in front of the female and grasping her with an appendage on his abdomen.

Planetary Allies: Mercury, Neptune

Sign Ruler: Gemini

Elemental Allies: Fire, air

Energetics: These beautiful little creatures help quicken our tempo and give us life and vitality when we call on them. They help us shine and move and act with precision and directness when we need to. Dragonflies bring out our adventurous, fun-loving side. There is also an aura of mystery about them, and they can be good totems for doing psychic and trance work.

Duck

Properties: The most common of waterfowl, there are many different kinds of ducks, including the mallard, the teal, the merganser, and the goldeneye. Each of these ducks spend much of their time on or near water. They can dive down deep into the waters to search for prey and usually lay eight to fifteen eggs for incubation.

Planetary Ally: Venus

Sign Ruler: Cancer

Elemental Allies: Water, air

Energetics: These birds show a special affinity to water and are a wonderful totem for those needing assistance in the emotional realms. They help us be more open and receptive and dive down into the quieter and more hidden aspects of ourselves. Ducks are generally a serene and gentle totem to have.

Eagle

Properties: This magnificent creature is one of the largest of the birds, and the bald eagle is known for its distinct white head. As a bird of prey, it takes aim and swoops down on carrion, waterfowl, or fish for its meal. Eagles hunt with precision and spend hours soaring high up in the air or perched in tall crags and trees.

Planetary Allies: Jupiter, Mars

Sign Ruler: Aries

Elemental Allies: Air, fire

Energetics: The eagle is a powerful totem for people needing vision, insight, a sharp mind, and the ability to make quick, accurate decisions. Eagles also help us aim for our goals and achieve them. Eagles are large creatures and help us develop confidence and surety in our path. They bring out the warrior in all of us.

Great Blue Heron

Properties: With long legs and long, thick necks, these water birds fly with grace and majesty across lakes and river beds. With their long legs, they spend time wading in waters, searching for fish to prey on. Their sharp beak enables them to spear fish easily, killing them before enjoying them as a meal.

Planetary Allies: Neptune, Jupiter

Sign Ruler: Pisces

Elemental Allies: Water, air

Energetics: Great blue herons are important totems for people needing more grace, beauty, and poise in their lives. They symbolize a dichotomy of delicacy with power and can strengthen our sense of stability and innate wisdom.

Hawk, Red-Tailed

Properties: Soaring high above the ground, the red-tailed hawk preys on small animals and makes its home in nests found in tall trees. The female lays two to three eggs, which take three-and-a-half weeks to incubate. The hawk likes to perch in crags and utility posts. It has a powerful sense of sight.

Planetary Allies: Mars, Sun

Sign Ruler: Aries

Elemental Allies: Air, fire

Energetics: The red-tailed hawk helps develop our sight and vision and can bring us a sense of soaring strength with a grounded stability. Hawks are sharp and precise—they know what their aim is and go for it. The red tail symbolizes a Martian warrior strength located at their base or root. This root power can be harnessed for positive growth and evolution.

Hummingbird

Properties: This delicate and intensely swift bird likes to feed on the nectar of flowers and can be seen zipping madly from one flower to another. Its wing speed is unbelievably quick and its ability to hover and move backward and forward is awe-inspiring. Hummingbirds usually lay two eggs and will migrate across immense distances (up to 2,500 miles or more).

Planetary Allies: Mercury, Uranus

Sign Ruler: Aquarius

Elemental Ally: Air

Energetics: This little miracle bird is capable of finding the sweet nectar in life. If we are lacking in joy, cheer, and playfulness, the hummingbird can help draw it out of us. It is also helpful for working with flower medicine and for increasing our vibratory level. If we are feeling dull and lethargic, Hummingbird medicine can energize and vitalize us.

Kestrel

Properties: This falcon prefers to perch atop treetops, poles, and telephone wires and is best known for its ability to hover in midair like a helicopter. As the smallest bird of prey, the kestrel dives and glides when it hunts, usually for insects and small mammals.

Planetary Ally: Mars

Sign Ruler: Aries

Elemental Allies: Air, fire

Energetics: With its incredible precision and grace, kestrels can be called on if we are feeling cloudy, confused, or out of sorts. The kestrel will bring back pinpoint accuracy, an observant and watchful mind, and the ability to be quick and patient at the same time.

Kingfisher

Properties: I usually spot these creatures zipping just above waterways, making their distinctive rattling call. Kingfishers have a shaggy crest with a blue-gray head and breast band. They live in nests in holes along waterbanks and lay six to eight eggs.

Planetary Ally: Jupiter

Sign Ruler: Cancer

Elemental Allies: Air, water

Energetics: These wonderful, small birds can teach us to move with accuracy and precision and to express ourselves without fear or reservation. They help us be more regal, knowing, and confident. When we need to draw something up or find something, we can call on the power of the kingfisher.

Meadowlark

Properties: With its distinctive, sweet singing voice, the meadowlark is easily recognizable with its bright yellow breast. The meadowlark usually stays along the ground, walking and feeding off small insects. The meadowlark lives in prairies, meadows, and open areas and has a playful motion when it flies.

Planetary Ally: Sun

Sign Ruler: Leo

Elemental Allies: Air, fire

Energetics: As a playful bird and with a sweet song, the meadowlark helps our soul shine and soar, and lifts any melancholy from our spirit. It also helps us regain a sense of play and silliness in the world. When we act silly, we can't take ourselves too seriously. Meadowlark brings the light in.

Nuthatch

Properties: If you've ever heard this bird's call, you will never forget it. It has a distinct *yna, yna, yna, yna* that rises in pitch each time. This bird likes to live in natural cavities and old woodpecker holes. This is an active bird, scurrying from tree to tree looking for insects and insect eggs to feed on.

Planetary Ally: Mars

Sign Ruler: Aquarius

Elemental Allies: Air, earth

Energetics: With its almost mocking call, the nuthatch seems to test us, to question us. Do you have your head in the clouds? Are you too "out there"? Nuthatch wants to remind us to ground and center and to remember to laugh (a good sign of being grounded). Ultimately, Nuthatch tries to remind us of the simple things in life, learning faith and trust when we become scattered and confused.

Owl

Properties: There are many different kinds of owls, including the great horned owl, the barn owl, and the screech owl. All share the same nocturnal habits, the same deep-set eyes, and the ability to swivel the head almost completely around.

With their incredible sense of sight and hearing, they make great hunters, swooping and gliding down silently so as to surprise their prey.

Planetary Ally: Moon

Sign Ruler: Scorpio

Elemental Allies: Air, water

Energetics: These powerful aviators have long been associated with the moon, the night, and the dark mysteries. When we want to explore the deeper realms of our unconscious, or study arcane lore such as tarot, astrology, or the kabbalah, Owl can be a wonderful guide. Owl is also wonderful for moon magic. It can be an ally for doing rituals under the light of the moon. It is also associated with death and transformation and is a powerful totem for healers and shamans. Owl will help you be silent, watchful, invisible, precise, wise, and powerful.

Red-Winged Blackbird

Properties: As it calls out *Con-Ka-Ree*, the blackbird seems to claim victory over the winter. With a distinct red wing and yellow trim on its shoulder, this blackbird likes to live in marshes and farmlands.

Planetary Ally: Pluto

Sign Ruler: Aries

Elemental Allies: Fire, air

Energetics: The splash of red emitting from the black plumage of red-winged blackbirds reminds us of the birth of light after a long night. It is a sign of hope and optimism as well as deep wisdom from the exploration of the darker mysteries. It helps ally us with the red creative forces of our root chakra. We can utilize this red energy for strengthening and nourishing our vitality. Red-winged blackbirds help us renew our strength after dark and difficult times.

Robin

Properties: A member of the thrush family, robins are one of the most common birds, easily found in backyards, parks, farmlands, or open forests. They will often build their nest on a branch of a tree or on a ledge of a porch. They confidently hunt for earthworms under the lawn and will also feed on insects and fruit.

Planetary Ally: Sun

Sign Ruler: Leo

Elemental Allies: Air, fire

Energetics: With their red breast and cheerful song, robins herald one of the first signs of spring. Their confident manner allies them with the sun and with those needing to express and assert themselves. They are clear and direct, unhidden and unmasked. For people needing to walk onstage, present themselves fully, and shake off any old and guarded baggage, this bird is a wonderful totem.

Starling

Properties: These birds were introduced into North America in 1890 from Europe and have now spread across this hemisphere. Starlings have a long, pointed bill and a short, square tail with black feathering. Moving in flocks, starlings have a tendency to bully other birds to assert their superiority and their sense of territory. They are also amazing imitators, able to take on the vocalizations of many other types of birds.

Planetary Allies: Mars, Neptune

Sign Ruler: Aries

Elemental Ally: Air

Energetics: With their power to grow and multiply easily as well as imitate and overwhelm other bird populations, this bird is a totem for those working with boundary issues. Starlings help us assert ourselves and push others away if they are applying a negative influence. They can also help us imitate, mutate, and merge with others. By merging with others, we learn new skills and gain new attributes that help us become stronger and more powerful.

Swallow

Properties: Swallows build their nests out of mud in culverts, under bridges, and in garages and tree snags. They feed on insects and are known for their swooping, graceful flight. They can be seen darting down to just above the surface of a pond, splashing themselves from time to time.

Planetary Allies: Sun, Mercury

Sign Ruler: Libra

Elemental Ally: Air

Energetics: This playful bird loves to dance in the air, swooping in circles and gracefully diving and rising with the currents of the air. We can call on this playful friend when we need a dash of summer in the wintertime, when we need to lift our spirits if we are feeling melancholy. We can also work with this bird when we want to increase our playfulness, our sociability, and our communicativeness.

Swan

Properties: Feeding on aquatic plants and insects, swans build their nests in the reeds and the shallow parts of the water. With long and graceful necks, swans lay up to twelve eggs a year and have powerful wings. They are known for their all-white bodies and their large and stately, yet delicate, stature.

Planetary Ally: Venus

Sign Ruler: Libra

Elemental Allies: Water, air

Energetics: Swans help us get in touch with the gentle emotional realms. Like looking in a reflection in a pond, swans help us take a deep look at ourselves and discover the grace, poise, and inner beauty we all have. They also help us see the fragility and tenderness of life and the need for an open and vulnerable heart. For people who have become hardened, world-weary, and insensitive, Swan will help soften the expression and bring forth an inner peace and tranquility.

Vulture

Properties: Known for feeding off carrion, vultures are powerful and majestic birds, capable of soaring to great heights. With a wingspan of up to six feet, these raptors do not primarily hunt and kill prey (their claws are too short), but will act as scavengers for leftover morsels of meat. The more common vulture is the turkey vulture, a large, black bird with a bare red head and a long tail.

Planetary Ally: Pluto

Sign Ruler: Scorpio

Elemental Allies: Air, water

Energetics: Long associated with death, vultures provide a powerful service by protecting other birds and animals from the diseases of dead carcasses. Their medicine comes from recycling and regenerating what has passed away. When we need to transform and let old parts of ourselves die away, we can call on Vulture. We can also call on this bird to take us to powerful heights and help us rise above and transcend the pain of dying and transmute it into the joy of living.

Woodpecker

Properties: All the various species of woodpeckers share the ability to bore holes in wood and feed off the insect and larval life hiding in tree snags. Their claws have a tenacious strength that allows them to climb up and down trees. Woodpeckers can often be heard in the woods making their rhythmic tapping and knocking sounds as they work industriously to feed themselves.

Planetary Allies: Saturn, Mars

Sign Rulers: Taurus, Capricorn

Elemental Allies: Earth, air

Energetics: With their incredibly strong bills, woodpeckers are an ally for those who need to work hard and endure and be patient for success. They help strengthen our will, drive, and purpose, and move us toward our goals. They also have an innate sense of rhythm and timing and will help us regain a steady beat in life if we have become erratic. Their direct approach is helpful to those who feel shy and unconfident.

Wren

Properties: Wrens are bouncy and bubbly creatures, easily flitting from branch to branch with their distinct upturned tails and inquisitive eyes. Wrens often have a white stripe above their eyepatch and a stocky appearance, and have a darting and assertive manner.

Planetary Ally: Mars

Sign Ruler: Taurus

Elemental Allies: Air, earth

Energetics: Wrens are helpful for gathering our talents and resources and directing them for a purpose. When we need help establishing our intent and purpose,
we can call on the wren with its sharp and wise eyes. Wren will tell us the truth
plain and simple. He will brush off any attack from the outside and will act as a
protective influence in our life.

Association of Elements with Bird Allies

Fire   Cardinal, dragonfly, eagle, red-tailed hawk, kestrel, meadowlark,
            red-winged blackbird, robin

Water   Crow, duck, great blue heron, kingfisher, owl, swan, vulture

Air   All birds

Earth   Crow, nuthatch, woodpecker, wren

Association of Modalities with Bird Allies

Cardinal Cardinal, crow, eagle, hawk, kestrel, kingfisher, red-winged
            blackbird, starling, swallow, swan, woodpecker

Fixed   Crow, dove, duck, great blue heron, meadowlark, nuthatch, owl,
            robin, vulture, wren

Mutable   Bee, butterfly, canada goose, chickadee, dragonfly, great blue
            heron, hummingbird, swallow

Association of Planets with Bird Allies

Sun   Red-tailed hawk, meadowlark, robin, swallow

Moon   Crow, owl

Mercury	Butterfly, chickadee, dragonfly, hummingbird
Venus	Bee, dove, duck, swan
Mars	Cardinal, eagle, red-tailed hawk, kestrel, nuthatch, starling, woodpecker, wren
Jupiter	Canada goose, eagle, great blue heron, kingfisher
Saturn	Crow, woodpecker
Uranus	Bee, hummingbird
Neptune	Bee, dragonfly, great blue heron, starling
Pluto	Butterfly, crow, vulture, red-winged blackbird

Association of the Signs with Bird Allies

Aries	Cardinal, eagle, red-tailed hawk, kestrel, red-winged blackbird
Taurus	Woodpecker, wren
Gemini	Butterfly, chickadee, dragonfly
Cancer	Duck, kingfisher
Leo	Meadowlark, robin
Virgo	Bee
Libra	Dove, swallow, swan
Scorpio	Crow, owl, vulture
Sagittarius	Canada goose

Capricorn Crow, woodpecker

Aquarius Hummingbird, nuthatch

Pisces Great blue heron

Nourishment of Elements with Bird Allies

Fire
- For joy and playfulness, call on Robin and Meadowlark.
- For vitality and strength, call on Cardinal, Eagle, Hawk, and Kestrel.
- To draw in warm, healing energy, call on Cardinal and Red-Winged Blackbird.
- To transform depression, call on Dragonfly.

Water
- To explore the mysteries and do psychic work, call on Crow and Owl.
- To work with issues of dying and death, work with Vulture.
- To draw forth sweet, nourishing, and gentle energy, call on Duck and Swan.
- To gain balance, poise, grace, and beauty, call on Great Blue Heron.

Air
- Work with Bee and Hummingbird for communication skills and to raise the energy.
- Work with Canada Goose, Swallow, and Starling to improve group skills.
- Work with Nuthatch to be unusual and different.
- Work with Dove, Swallow, and Swan for grace and poise.

Earth
- Work with Wren and Woodpecker for help in building, making, and accomplishing goals.
- Work with Wren and Crow to be simple, practical, and "down to earth."
- Work with Bee to be industrious and work easily with the community.

Nourishment of Modalities with Bird Allies

Cardinal
- Call on Cardinal, Eagle, Hawk, and Woodpecker to direct your intent and accomplish your purpose.
- Call on Kingfisher and Red-Winged Blackbird to generate energy and move through difficult emotions.
- Call on Swan to be direct, but gentle, in your approach.

Fixed
- Call on Great Blue Heron and Owl for immovable and solid energy.
- Call on Meadowlark and Robin to remain joyous, magnetic, and attractive.
- Call on Nuthatch and Vulture to do things "your way" and to trust in the outcome.

Mutable
- Call on Butterfly, Chickadee, and Swallow to adapt to new circumstances.
- Call on Butterfly, Hummingbird, and Swallow for playfulness and to avoid taking life too seriously.

Nourishment of Signs and Planets with Bird Allies

Aries/
Mars

- Develop leadership and strength of will with Eagle and Hawk.
- Develop purpose and intent with Cardinal, Eagle, and Hawk.
- Strengthen fiery vitality with Cardinal, Hawk, and Red-Winged Blackbird.
- Strengthen warrior strength and intensity with Eagle, Hawk, Kestrel, and Woodpecker.

Taurus/
Venus

- Strengthen gentle, sensual beauty with Dove.
- Strengthen stable, calm feelings with Duck and Swan.
- Stay simple and practical with Woodpecker and Wren.
- Find the sweetness in life with Bee.

Gemini/
Mercury

- Chickadee helps us communicate, connect, and increase our intelligence.
- Butterfly and Hummingbird help enliven and brighten our spirits.
- Dragonfly helps us be analytical and precise.

Cancer/
Moon

- Draw up emotions and deep-seated feelings with Kingfisher.
- Increase wisdom, psychic abilities, and your connection to the moon and the night with Crow and Owl.
- Increase security and gentleness with Duck.

Leo/
Sun

- Develop joy and playfulness with Meadowlark, Robin, and Swallow.
- Be majestic and regal with Hawk and Eagle.
- For romance, call on Robin and Swallow.

Virgo/
Mercury

- To be precise and orderly, call on Chickadee and Dragonfly.

- To work hard and be efficient, call on Bee.

- To enjoy the moment and live simply and beautifully, call on Butterfly.

Libra/
Venus

- For grace, poise, and simple beauty, call on Dove and Swan.

- For playful communication in groups, call on Swallow.

- To gather the beautiful and sweet things in life, call on Bee.

Scorpio/
Pluto

- To explore the mysteries and do psychic work, call on Crow and Owl.

- To transform pain and darkness into light, call on Butterfly and Red-Winged Blackbird.

- To work through issues of death and dying, call on Owl and Vulture.

Sagittarius/
Jupiter

- To develop an adventuresome nature, call on Kingfisher and Eagle.

- For play, generosity, and an appetite for life, work with Canada Goose.

- To develop magnanimity and wisdom, and for teachers, work with Great Blue Heron.

Capricorn/
Saturn

- To develop industriousness, drive, and ambition, call on Wood-pecker.

- To develop serious intent and will, work with Crow.

Aquarius/
Uranus

- Develop a quick and agile mind and the ability to gather insights and wisdom with Hummingbird.

- Work with Nuthatch to develop a quirky and rebellious spirit.

- Work with Bee to strengthen "group mind" and communication abilities.

Pisces/
Neptune

- Work with Great Blue Heron to develop wisdom, grace, and inner beauty.

- Work with Bee and Dragonfly to develop mystical and psychic energy.

- Work with Starling to tap into "mass consciousness."

- Work with Bee to be of service to the greater good.

11

The Magic of Stones and Metals

As I traveled through Mexico in 1995, I went walking through a market bazaar when I happened upon a stall where people were selling stones. As I looked through the lovely array of turquoise, tiger's eye, and jade, my eyes fell upon a beautiful necklace of red amber. The necklace fit perfectly as a choker around my throat and I decided to buy it. Over the years I have seen it not only as a gorgeous piece of jewelry, but as a wonderful healing amulet. At the time, I was having a great deal of difficulty with my communication and my general energy levels. Over the years as I have worn this necklace, both of these areas have healed to a great degree. Of course, there were many other things that I did to help restore myself, but the amber acted as a symbol and actual potent tool for healing in my life.

Stones have a long history of being used for their healing and curative powers. From ancient times, practitioners of astrology noted the relationship of the stars to metals and gems. Each stone has a different character and personality that can be easily classified in terms of astrology. Amber's rich red and yellow colors link it to the fire element and to the Sun. Opal's soft milkiness links it to the water element as well as the Moon. Stones that are darker and green or black are often connected to the earth element. Stones with a light and often yellow or pale-green color are linked to the air element.

The Healing Power of Stones

When we wear stones, display them in the house or garden, or use them in ritual, we can access their healing powers. We can pick stones to heal us on a number of levels. One of the best ways is to pick a stone that will augment an element that is lacking in our chart, or will balance and fortify an element that predominates in our chart. For example, if there is a lack of fire in the chart, there may be problems periodically with energy levels, passion, creativity, and "get up and go." Certain fire stones can help strengthen the weak fire element and give it a natural boost. Another example is people with a lot of fire in their chart who may be overly exuberant, flirtatious, dominating, and have difficulty sitting still and remaining grounded. In this case, they may decide to pick an antidote stone (perhaps a stone of water or earth to offset the fire) or pick a fire stone that is naturally in harmony. A fire stone will provide a balanced and healthy expression of fire, and will temper the extremes of a fiery personality.

Stones and metals have the ability to absorb and take on the energies of the people and environment around them. This can be good or bad depending on who or what is near them. This is why it is especially important to clear and purify stones before using and wearing them. There are a number of different ways to do this. We can simply bathe the stones in water that has some good unrefined salt in it. We can smudge them with sage, cedar, or other herbs. We can also bury them in the earth for a short while to help them reconnect to the ground from which they came. Sunlight and clean air also help refresh their energies and augment their powers. It is important to be aware where we buy or get a stone. The energy of where it came from, how it was mined, or who helped produce the stone may taint the energy and ruin the positive influence we had hoped for.

Once a stone has been purified, it can help magically transform our lives. Used in ritual and in magic, stones have the ability to concentrate energies and commit our will and power to our intent, drawing the energy of the earth for good purposes. We need to be careful how we work with the stones, as they can truly solidify intention. If that intention is malefic or is tainted with darker emotions, the outcome can be disastrous. We need to be careful and respectful with these entities.

Another thing to mention is that stones are mined from the earth and are often done so in a highly industrial and sometimes rapacious manner. We are very quickly using all the resources of the earth to the point where they are becoming depleted and damaged. When we harvest stones from the mountains and hills, we can truly damage the environment. We need to be watchful and aware of how many stones we are collecting or buying. Is it necessary? Do we have too many? Stones should not be hoarded and overaccumulated. They can add tremendous magic and beauty to our lives, but only when used with care and consideration.

Empowering Stones for Four Element Work

Stones can be magical allies for healing our emotions and spirit. When we work with them, it is helpful to make an alliance with their essential energy. Spending time with them, cleaning them, displaying them, and working with them in a ritual setting are all powerful ways to access their power and magic. If you can, visit with them in their natural setting. If that is not possible, experience them in a quiet and natural setting. Their characteristics and properties will become apparent more readily. If you desire, you can use shamanic methods for contacting their essential nature. Use the steps I outlined in chapter 6 to do this.

The essential method for empowering and charging stones and metals you work with is to bring them into your ritual setting. When you are setting up an altar, lay the stones in the direction you feel they are most associated with—moonstone with water, ruby with fire, etc. In the context of the ritual that you make, charge them by smudging them with incense and calling out their powers and abilities and how you want to work with the stone in the near future. This work creates a relationship between you and the stone and helps develop the power of the stone itself.

Once you have created a relationship with the stone you are working with and have charged it with ritual energy, there are a number of ways to work further with the stone. Here are a few:

Wearing as a Pendant or Necklace

This is a common and powerful way to work with stones, as they affect our heart and throat areas in this manner. Our throat is connected to communication and our heart is connected to our joy, self-expression, and ability to connect and love. Necklaces and pendants hanging over the throat and heart are especially powerful for these themes.

Wearing as a Ring

Rings are another way to transport a stone and feel its effects in everyday life. Hands and fingers are extensions of our will and intent. When we wear magical stones, we are actively calling on their energy to transform our lives and direct that energy out into the outer world. We write, work, and meet people with our hands. Rings are not easily hidden and are apparent to the outside world. This affects our relationship to the community and how we behave and act.

Displaying on an Altar or in a Sacred Place

Stones have a powerful environmental effect akin to a houseplant or a pet animal. They generate energy and express it into their immediate environment in subtle yet powerful ways. They can have a truly harmonious and nourishing quality and be protective as well. Their effect is more diffuse when it is placed in a particular part of a room. They can be healing for anyone in that space, or be aggravating if their energy reacts poorly to someone in that space.

Working with Them in a Ritual Setting

Stones can augment our prayers and the energy of our rituals when we display them in a ceremonial setting. They help compound the intentions of those in the ritual and compound the powerful effect of other ritual objects in the setting.

Spellcasting and Talismans

Stones can be used in both spellcasting and for talismans as physical representations of the symbolic desire. For example, if we need more energy and vitality, we may pick a stone like ruby or garnet and bundle it with other fiery objects in a spell or in the making of a talisman. A talisman can then be worn as a pendant or carried in our pocket for the desired purpose.

Gem Essences

Like flower essences, stones have also been infused into essences that capture their essential qualities. By taking these essences, we can gather the essential properties of the gem into our lives. Gem essences can often be purchased in the same places where flower essences are sold.

These are but a few ways to work with stones in the four element tradition. In this next section, I list a number of the most commonly used stones.

Compendium of Stone and Metal Medicine

Agate

Properties: Agate is formed when the gasses from volcanic lava escape into the air. Agate comes in many different colors.

Planetary Ruler: Mercury

Sign Rulers: All

Elemental Allies: All

Properties: Because there are many different kinds of agates with different colors, there are many different kinds of properties to the agate. Generally speaking, agates promote confidence and solidity in actions. They also increase the health and aura in the wearer. For example, blue lace agate is connected to the water element and is a gentle, restorative stone. Red agate is connected to the fire element and is protective. Green agate is connected to the earth element and augments health and radiance to the wearer.

Amber

Properties: Amber is actually not a stone at all, but fossilized resin from the sap of coniferous trees. We can sometimes find it with insects still imbedded inside. This is among the more rare and special varieties of amber. Amber usually has a gold to reddish color.

Planetary Ally: Sun

Sign Ruler: Leo

Elemental Ally: Fire

Energetics: Amber has a very special quality to it, imparting gentle nourishment to those who wear it. Amber increases the overall radiance of the wearer and increases confidence and magnetism. It is a very healing stone and has protective powers as well.

Amethyst

Properties: This variety of quartz crystal is a beautiful and magnetic-looking stone. Amethyst has a purple color that makes it immediately attractive. Crystals in general come in many shapes and forms including clusters, single, and double-terminated rods.

Planetary Allies: Jupiter, Neptune

Sign Ruler: Sagittarius

Elemental Ally: Fire

Energetics: Amethyst is a very healing crystal and has a potent but not overwhelming energy. It can help enliven us, bring us courage and peace of mind, and help our aura shine. It is very good for mental anxiety and worry, as it helps relieve stress. Amethyst can also be used for spiritual and psychic work.

Aquamarine

Properties: This stone is a member of the beryl family of stones, which includes emerald and morganite. Aquamarine is made of beryllium aluminum silicate, along with other minerals.

Planetary Allies: Moon, Neptune

Sign Ruler: Pisces

Elemental Ally: Water

Energetics: This is the stone of the fall, of sunset, of the dying times when psychic awareness becomes more clear. It helps us remember, divine, and gain prophesy. It also helps us relax and melt, letting go of anxiety.

Bloodstone

Properties: Bloodstone is a member of the chalcedony family of stones, which includes carnelian and agate. Chalcedony is a type of quartz crystal. Bloodstone gets its name from the appearance of dots and dapples of blood color on a green stone.

Planetary Ally: Mars

Sign Ruler: Aries

Elemental Ally: Fire

Energetics: Bloodstone has a strong and dense energy that gives nourishment and core vitality to the wearer. It helps strengthen our tissues and blood and also gives us solidity and courage.

Carnelian

Properties: Carnelian is a chalcedony stone. It is made of a combination of silicate dioxide and quartz. It comes in many colors, including red, brown, blue, and black.

Planetary Allies: Sun, Mars

Sign Ruler: Sagittarius

Elemental Ally: Fire

Energetics: Carnelian lifts our spirits when we feel discouraged, angry, or envious, and also helps ground and secure our energy. It promotes sexual energy as well.

Citrine

Properties: Citrine is a quartz crystal with a yellowish tint.

Planetary Ally: Sun

Sign Ruler: Leo

Elemental Allies: Fire, air

Energetics: Citrine has a wonderfully cheerful and warming quality. It helps dispel fear and anxiety in those who work with it.

Copper

Properties: This metal has an orange to reddish hue and is able to conduct electricity. We use copper as the base form of electrical transference throughout much of the world. It is thus the linking web, or thread, that unites the planet through information and electricity.

Planetary Ally: Venus

Sign Ruler: Taurus

Elemental Ally: Earth

Energetics: Copper is associated with the goddess Venus and therefore is related to her passions: love, wealth, and beauty. Copper is used for healing and balancing the energetic polarities in the body.

Coral

Properties: Coral is not a stone at all, but the skeleton of a sea creature.

Planetary Allies: Venus, Saturn

Sign Ruler: Pisces

Elemental Ally: Water

Energetics: Coral is a wonderful totem of the sea and of the Mother Goddess. Coral helps dispel fear and brings peace and serenity. It also has a special relationship to bones and calcium, so it can be a totem for Capricorns and Saturnian types.

Diamond

Properties: Diamond is one of the hardest stones available. It is highly valued and is often extremely expensive. Diamond's strength and durability make it one of the foremost stones to give for a marriage engagement.

Planetary Allies: Sun, Saturn

Sign Ruler: Capricorn

Elemental Allies: Fire, earth

Energetics: Diamond increases strength, endurance, concentration, and clarity. It helps strengthen and nourish our core energy. Diamond has also been associated with shamanism and ecstatic rituals. It is a strong stone for commitment ceremonies of any type.

Emerald

Properties: This beautiful stone has been revered for millennia and, like diamonds, is used extensively in cosmetic jewelry. Its luxurious green color makes it very attractive to the eye.

Planetary Ally: Venus

Sign Ruler: Cancer

Elemental Ally: Earth

Energetics: Emerald's green hue makes it a lovely talisman of nature, prosperity, fertility, and love. With emerald, we increase abundance in our lives and can call forth healing, especially of the heart and throat chakras. Emerald has also been revered as a strongly protective stone since antiquity.

Garnet

Properties: Garnet is generally a dark-red stone, but it comes in other colors as well. Garnet is made up of aluminum silicates and calcium silicates.

Planetary Ally: Mars

Sign Rulers: Aquarius, Aries

Elemental Ally: Fire

Energetics: Garnet improves health in the fire realm, including improving circulation, steadiness of heartbeat, and the strength of the blood, veins, and arteries. It also improves courage, determination, and confidence. It is a protective stone as well.

Gold

Properties: Gold is known to all of us as a shiny, yellowish metal that is pliable and is often made into wedding bands and many other types of jewelry.

Planetary Ally: Sun

Sign Ruler: Leo

Elemental Ally: Fire

Energetics: This "soft" metal has been revered since antiquity for its ability to draw forth divine energy and to increase health and radiance. It is a powerful metal for healing and generating strength, courage, and security.

Iron

Properties: When humans first "discovered" iron as a metal usable for tools, an entire new world was born as soldiers began battling one another with iron swords and lances. Iron weapons helped nations conquer other nations and build empires.

Planetary Ally: Mars

Sign Ruler: Aries

Elemental Allies: Fire, earth

Energetics: Iron is a protective metal and is connected to the planet Mars. Iron helps ground and defend us against intrusion. It is seldom used in magical or ceremonial practice as it seems to offset a clear flow.

Jade

Properties: Jade has a long history of magical and ceremonial use among a number of cultures including the Aztecs, the Egyptians, and the Chinese. We know jade primarily as a green stone, but it can also be yellow to whitish in color.

Planetary Allies: Venus, Neptune

Sign Rulers: Libra, Virgo

Elemental Allies: Earth, water

Energetics: This beautiful and receptive stone helps heal us, especially the kidneys, throat, and heart systems. It also helps us draw good energy in the form of love or money.

Jasper

Properties: Jasper is an opaque form of chalcedony and usually has a red, yellow, green, or brownish color.

Planetary Allies: Jupiter, Mars

Sign Ruler: Scorpio

Elemental Allies: Red: Fire; Green: Earth; Yellow: Air

Energetics: Red jasper is primarily a protective amulet. Yellow jasper helps clear and focus the mental functions. Green jasper helps with healing rituals and spells.

Labradorite

Properties: This green stone has an iridescent quality that includes shades of blue within it. Labradorite is found in Norway, Labrador, and Russia.

Planetary Allies: Moon, Neptune

Sign Ruler: Pisces

Elemental Ally: Water

Energetics: This beautiful stone brings harmony and gentleness to the wearer. Labradorite helps expand our consciousness and encourages prophetic vision. It helps dispel anxiety and nervousness and develops inner beauty.

Lapis Lazuli

Properties: Lapis lazuli is a beautiful, deep-bluish stone with flecks of pyrite and calcite in it. It originates primarily from central Asia and Afghanistan.

Planetary Allies: Moon, Venus, Neptune

Sign Ruler: Cancer

Elemental Ally: Water

Energetics: This powerful healing stone helps calm, tranquilize, and strengthen the wearer. It helps move us through states of depression and sadness into rebirth and renewal. It also helps us concentrate and become more meditative and psychic.

Lead

Properties: Lead is a heavy metal that is very dangerous and toxic if ingested.

Planetary Ally: Saturn

Sign Ruler: Capricorn

Elemental Ally: Earth

Energetics: Lead is primarily a metal of Saturn and can be used in ritual and spell-work to augment this planet's strength. Lead is protective and secures energy. If something needs to be hidden or enshrouded, it is best to place the object in a lead box.

Malachite

Properties: Malachite is a wonderful green stone with striated bands encircling it. Malachite contains a basic copper core.

Planetary Ally: Venus

Sign Rulers: Taurus, Virgo

Elemental Ally: Earth

Energetics: Malachite is a refreshing and pleasing stone, bringing joy, luck, and money to the wearer. It also helps lift our spirits, increases feelings of love and compassion, and also protects us from negative influences.

Moonstone

Properties: Moonstone is a luminescent, whitish-blue stone that is from the feldspar family.

Planetary Ally: Moon

Sign Ruler: Cancer

Elemental Ally: Water

Energetics: Moonstone helps us become more receptive and emotionally sensitive. It augments our psychic perception and allows us to become more gentle and fluid.

Obsidian

Properties: Obsidian is created when lava cools rapidly and becomes glass. It generally has a black color.

Planetary Allies: Pluto, Saturn

Sign Ruler: Scorpio

Elemental Allies: Fire, water, earth

Energetics: This stone has an intense strength and magnetism about it, as it is black and is born of fire. It has the power to attract strong energy, both negative and positive. Obsidian is a transformative stone, since it was once a liquid heated by fire and transformed into stone. Because it is transformative, it helps us in our transition from life to death and through the powerful changes that take place in our lives.

Onyx

Properties: Onyx is a black-colored form of chalcedony.

Planetary Allies: Saturn, Mars

Sign Ruler: Capricorn

Elemental Ally: Earth

Energetics: Onyx is a powerful aid for grounding and centering our energy. Onyx helps us concentrate, direct, and intend our will. It helps us be present and stable in the moment and repel negative forces.

Opal

Properties: Opals come in many different colors. The stone is easily cracked and broken, as it is relatively fragile.

Planetary Ally: Moon

Sign Ruler: Pisces

Elemental Ally: Water

Energetics: Opal has the ability to represent all the planets and elements and is a very adaptable and mutable stone. Its fragility makes it a difficult stone to wear, but it can be used for ritual and magical purposes. Opals help us when working in the spirit worlds, dealing with discarnate entities, ghosts, and the astral realm. It also helps increase our magnetism, beauty, and psychic powers when used wisely.

Pearl

Properties: Pearls are made when sand rubs the inside of oysters over a long period of time to make a round, calcified deposit.

Planetary Allies: Moon, Neptune

Sign Ruler: Pisces

Elemental Ally: Water

Energetics: Pearls are pleasing, beautiful stones often worn in strings as necklaces. Their simple roundness and origin from water reminds us of Goddess energy. Pearls increase receptivity, charm, grace, and elegance. They draw love and affection and are good in moon magic. Worn on a Full Moon (especially when the Moon is in a water sign), we can magically draw what we need. Pearls help heal the rhythms of menstrual cycles and help us through emotional transformations.

Peridot

Properties: This stone has a green and yellowish cast and is translucent. Olivine is a close relative.

Planetary Allies: Venus, Sun, Pluto, Uranus

Sign Rulers: Taurus, Leo, Scorpio, Aquarius

Elemental Allies: All

Energetics: Peridot works quite well with the fixed signs. It is a beautiful green stone that links it with Venus. It has long been associated with the Sun and the sign Leo. It carries a strong transmitting force and is capable of sending both positive and negative energies, which links it to Pluto and Scorpio. Peridot is also wonderful as a healing stone and helps calm and center us, especially if there is nervous dysfunction, thus linking it to Uranus and Aquarius.

Quartz

Properties: There are many different kinds of quartz crystals, but by this heading I mean the clear, colorless, and transparent type often found in necklaces and used in magical work. This type is made of silicon dioxide, which forms the hexagonal crystal shape that most of us are familiar with.

Planetary Allies: Mercury, Uranus

Sign Ruler: Aquarius

Elemental Ally: Air

Energetics: This commonly used stone is tremendously popular because it is a wonderful stone to work with. Quartz helps direct and send energy and helps solidify and ground our intent toward its manifestation. We can find it in wands and often on altars for just this purpose. Quartz crystals are transmitters of energy and can be used for cleansing and healing rituals.

Rose Quartz

Properties: This beautiful, pinkish stone is a member of the quartz family of stones.

Planetary Ally: Venus

Sign Ruler: Libra

Elemental Allies: Fire, air

Energetics: This is a very gentle stone that seems to emanate a positive, loving feeling to those around it. It is very helpful for healing conditions of the heart, especially excessive grief, pain, and remorse. It lightens and brightens the day with simple joy and love.

Ruby

Properties: Rubies have been highly regarded since antiquity. They have a beautiful, deep-reddish hue. Ruby is part of a set of stones known as corundum that includes sapphire.

Planetary Allies: Sun, Mars

Sign Ruler: Leo

Elemental Ally: Fire

Energetics: Rubies increase strength and power to the wearer, allowing us to lead and direct with a strong will. It helps protect the wearer from negative influences. Ruby helps strengthen our blood, muscles, and adrenals.

Sapphire

Properties: Sapphire is another stone of the corundum family and has dazzled people for millennia. It carries a dark to translucent bluish color.

Planetary Allies: Jupiter, Moon

Sign Ruler: Pisces

Elemental Ally: Water

Energetics: This beautiful stone is tremendously powerful and peaceful. It carries the ability to increase psychic awareness and meditative concentration. It helps cure nervous and depressive disorders and protects the wearer from negative influences.

Silver

Properties: Because it is somewhat rare, silver has been hunted and mined since ancient times and has been used in various kinds of personal adornments, jewelry, and currency.

Planetary Ally: Moon

Sign Ruler: Cancer

Elemental Ally: Water

Energetics: Silver is connected with lunar and receptive energies. It draws power from the deepest well and restores the wearer's confidence and grace. It also helps increase sweet and gentle energy, increases psychic awareness, and helps protect the wearer from undue negative influences.

Smoky Quartz

Properties: This is another type of quartz crystal that bears a darkish, somewhat blackish hue.

Planetary Allies: Pluto, Saturn

Sign Ruler: Scorpio

Elemental Ally: Earth

Energetics: This powerful stone is primarily protective, as it absorbs and dispels negative energies. It is also helpful as a healing stone in transformative processes where dark and difficult times must be visited. That is why it is helpful for those who are suffering from a deep illness or are dealing with the death of a loved one or their own dying process.

Tiger's Eye
Properties: This is another type of quartz with a brownish, mottled appearance.

Planetary Ally: Sun

Sign Ruler: Leo

Elemental Ally: Fire

Energetics: Tiger's eye is a wonderfully grounding and strengthening stone. It draws strong, warm energy from the environment to help protect and add life force to the wearer. When we need courage and willpower, we can call on the power of tiger's eye.

Topaz
Properties: Topaz is usually a yellow-orange stone, and sometimes green and bluish in color.

Planetary Ally: Sun

Sign Ruler: Gemini

Elemental Ally: Fire

Energetics: This stone engenders a warm flow in the system and increases positive emotions, dispelling fear and negativity from the wearer. It augments strength and radiance, boosts the immune system, and increases overall health.

Turquoise
Properties: This beautiful stone is characterized by an aqua-blue color and is usually associated with the southwestern states and with Mexico, where it is found and mined. It has been revered as a sacred stone by indigenous tribes in these parts. It is also found in Tibet and France.

Planetary Allies: Venus, Neptune, Moon

Sign Ruler: Pisces

Elemental Ally: Water

Energetics: Turquoise embodies a beautiful magic that increases harmony and spiritual peacefulness, and helps heal and center the wearer. It is a very protective stone (especially against spiritual and energetic attack).

Association of the Elements with Stones and Metals

Fire	Amber, amethyst, bloodstone, carnelian, citrine, diamond, garnet, gold, iron, jasper, obsidian, peridot, rose quartz, ruby, tiger's eye, topaz
Water	Aquamarine, coral, jade, labradorite, lapis lazuli, moonstone, obsidian, opal, pearl, peridot, sapphire, silver, turquoise
Air	Agate, citrine, jasper (yellow), peridot, quartz, rose quartz
Earth	Copper, diamond, emerald, iron, jade, jasper, lead, malachite, obsidian, onyx, peridot, smoky quartz

Association of the Modalities with Stones and Metals

Cardinal	Bloodstone, diamond, emerald, iron, jade, lapis lazuli, lead, onyx, rose quartz
Fixed	Amber, citrine, copper, gold, jasper, malachite, obsidian, peridot, quartz, ruby, smoky quartz, tiger's eye
Mutable	Amethyst, aquamarine, carnelian, coral, labradorite, opal, pearl, sapphire, turquoise

Association of the Planets with Stones and Metals

Sun	Amber, carnelian, citrine, diamond, gold, peridot, ruby, tiger's eye, topaz
Moon	Aquamarine, labradorite, lapis lazuli, moonstone, opal, pearl, sapphire, silver
Mercury	Agate, quartz
Venus	Copper, coral, emerald, jade, malachite, peridot, turquoise
Mars	Bloodstone, carnelian, garnet, iron, jasper, onyx, ruby
Jupiter	Amethyst, jasper, sapphire
Saturn	Coral, diamond, lead, obsidian, onyx, smoky quartz
Uranus	Peridot, quartz crystal
Neptune	Amethyst, aquamarine, jade, labradorite, lapis lazuli, pearl, turquoise
Pluto	Obsidian, peridot, smoky quartz

Associations of the Signs with Stones and Metals

Aries	Garnet, iron
Taurus	Copper, malachite, peridot
Gemini	Agate, topaz
Cancer	Emerald, lapis lazuli, moonstone, silver
Leo	Amber, citrine, gold, peridot, ruby, tiger's eye
Virgo	Jade, malachite

Libra	Jade, rose quartz
Scorpio	Jasper, obsidian, peridot, smoky quartz
Sagittarius	Amethyst, carnelian
Capricorn	Diamond, lead, onyx
Aquarius	Garnet, peridot
Pisces	Aquamarine, coral, labradorite, opal, pearl, sapphire, turquoise

Nourishment of the Elements with Stones and Metals

Fire
- Strengthen courage, confidence, and vitality with amber, bloodstone, carnelian, garnet, and ruby.
- Encourage creativity and playfulness with citrine, rose quartz, and peridot.
- Strengthen the heart, warmth, and the ability to love with rose quartz, citrine, and amber.

Water
- Encourage psychic receptivity with moonstone, labradorite, lapis lazuli, opal, and sapphire.
- Work with deeply intense emotions with obsidian and labradorite.
- Strengthen grace, adaptability, and poise with coral, lapis lazuli, silver, and turquoise.
- Relax, reduce stress, and feel at ease with aquamarine, lapis lazuli, and pearl.

Air
- Increase mental capacity and agility with agate and citrine.
- Develop sociability and playfulness with citrine and rose quartz.
- Stimulate your senses and your mind with peridot and agate.

Earth
- Ground and center yourself with malachite, onyx, and smoky quartz.
- Develop wealth, prosperity, and joy in the moment with copper, emerald, jade, and malachite.
- Slow down and increase patience and serenity with emerald, green jasper, and onyx.
- Develop will and concentration with onyx and smoky quartz.

Nourishment of the Modalities with Stones and Metals

Cardinal
- Strengthen will, purpose, and directed intent with diamond, garnet, iron, and onyx.
- Stimulate energy with bloodstone, diamond, garnet, and rose quartz.

Fixed
- Center and ground with amber, ruby, and smoky quartz.
- Be magnetic and strong with gold, ruby, and tiger's eye.

Mutable
- Adapt and flow with labradorite, opal, and pearl.
- Increase communicativeness and interactivity with agate, amethyst, and sapphire.

Nourishment of the Planets and Signs with Stones and Metals

Aries/
Mars
- Strengthen your leadership skills with garnet and ruby.
- Develop your strength, will, and power with bloodstone, iron, and ruby.

Taurus/
Venus
- Remain grounded, centered, and calm with emerald and malachite.
- Develop your sense of aesthetics and beauty with emerald, rose quartz, and turquoise.
- Bring prosperity and wealth with emerald, jade, malachite, and turquoise.

Gemini/
Mercury

- Stimulate your mind and your intelligence with agate and peridot.

- Develop your communication skills with citrine and topaz.

Cancer/
Moon

- Be gentle, receptive, and emotionally aware with moonstone, opal, and pearl.

- Develop your psychic skills with aquamarine, labradorite, lapis lazuli, opal, and sapphire.

- Be warm, nourishing, and compassionate with emerald, moonstone, and pearl.

Leo/
Sun

- Develop your confidence and magnetism with amber, carnelian, ruby, and tiger's eye.

- Strengthen your playfulness and humor with citrine and peridot.

- Develop your regal leadership skills with diamond, gold, and ruby.

Virgo/
Mercury

- Strengthen your mental agility and intelligence with agate and peridot.

- Strengthen your ability to be connected to the earth, be prosperous, and enjoy the moment with emerald, malachite, and jade.

Libra/
Venus

- Develop your sense of grace, poise, and beauty with jade and rose quartz.

- Strengthen your social graces and interaction with the community through citrine, coral, and rose quartz.

Scorpio/
Pluto

- Transform intense emotions with obsidian and smoky quartz.
- Develop power, will, and strength with obsidian and peridot.

Sagittarius/
Jupiter

- Become buoyant, playful, and expressive with carnelian.
- Gain wisdom and skills as a teacher with amethyst and sapphire.

Capricorn/
Saturn

- Build, strengthen, and develop grounding and steadiness with coral, diamond, and onyx.
- Strengthen gravity and seriousness with lead, obsidian, and smoky quartz.
- Develop will and purpose with diamond, onyx, and smoky quartz.

Aquarius/
Uranus

- Increase community social skills with quartz and peridot.
- Strengthen your ability to be different and unique with opal.

Pisces/
Neptune

- Develop psychic and receptive skills with amethyst, aquamarine, labradorite, and lapis lazuli.
- Develop a compassionate heart and the ability to serve the community with coral, jade, and turquoise.
- Strengthen artistic and creative skills with amethyst, coral, opal, and sapphire.

12
Lifestyle Choices and Conclusion

One of the most fundamental ways of helping ourselves heal and nourish our mind, body, and soul is to make lifestyle choices that are healthy and positive. Lifestyle choices constitute what we eat and drink, how we decorate our house, what music we play on the stereo, which friends we spend time with, and how we move, walk, talk, and breathe. All of the small choices that we make every day become the patterns that dominate our entire lives. When we neglect the cleanliness of our house or the clothes we are wearing, our psychic and emotional health can weaken and eventually our physical health is affected.

By looking at our elemental, modal, planetary, and sign strengths and weaknesses, we can work to nourish the parts of ourselves that are lacking in strength and balance the parts of ourselves that are emphasized. For example, if we have a strong emphasis on Cancer and the Moon, we may find ourselves more suited to quieter, nourishing activities with a few friends and family in the comfort of the home and hearth. These are sympathetic lifestyle choices, sympathetic to the natural qualities of the chart. While this can be positive, the emphasis on Cancerian, lunar activities can become excessively dampening and introverted. There may be a need for more balance through solar, Leonine activities that help draw us out and bring more expressiveness and dynamism to our life. Perhaps we need to spend more time in the sun, exercise outdoors, and have companions that help us laugh and be playful. Balancing and nourishing are the two key components in strengthening health and well-being.

In this section, I list some suggestions for nourishing the basic astrological qualities. We can use balancing methods as well for healing, regenerating, and increasing vitality.

Nourishing the Elements

Fire   Building and tending a fire, aerobic exercise, kundalini yoga, sauna and sweat, sunbathing (beware of sunburn), living in a sunny climate, making love, wearing red and orange colors, loud and expressive music.

Water   Taking baths, swimming, snorkeling, fishing, sauna and sweat, drinking water and herbal tea, tai chi, living in a rainy climate, wearing blue and sea-green colors, playing soothing and entrancing music.

Air   Climbing and walking in the open air, breath meditation and yoga, chi gong, flying, skydiving, kite flying, living in a windy or open environment, bird watching, wearing yellow and white colors, playing harmonious and uplifting music.

Earth   Hiking, mountain climbing, spelunking, meditating, sitting and lying down, abdominal breathing, yoga, gardening, living in the wilderness, wearing forest-green, brown, and black colors, playing steady, grounding music with a drum beat.

Nourishing the Modalities

Cardinal Directing, leading, martial arts, vigorous aerobic exercise, disciplined work, building, making, doing, driving, hiking, mountain climbing.

Fixed   Meditating, napping, yoga, gardening, sunbathing, listening to music, lifting weights, bird watching, cooking, drawing, painting, bathing, getting a massage.

Mutable   Talking and visiting, debating, travel, adventures, stimulating activities, hang gliding, skating, surfing, snowboarding and skiing, swimming, telephones and computers.

Nourishing the Planets

Sun   Sunbathing, moving to a sunny climate, letting light into the house and the workplace, using solar energy, the colors red and gold, uplifting music, playfulness, laughter, sex, outdoor exercise.

Moon   Moonlight walks, cleaning the home, calling mom and dad, curling up by the fire, a long bath, the color silver, psychic work, cooking.

Mercury   Deep breathing, meditation and yoga, reading books, conversation, intellectual studies, fixing things.

Venus   Shopping, decorating, putting on nice clothes, making love, aromatherapy, a long massage, baking cookies.

Mars   Aerobic exercise, boxing, racquetball, sports, race car driving, debates, the color red.

Jupiter   Going out to a bar, partying, giving gifts, buying presents, teaching, philosophizing, gambling, riding horses.

Saturn   Building, holing up like a hermit, deep study, meditative retreat, going inward, doing yoga (for the spine and bones), working, being disciplined.

Uranus   Astral travel, working on a computer, hanging out in groups, doing a daredevil stunt, being creative, wacky, and original.

Neptune   Swimming, bathing, sailing, dreaming, psychic work, Tarot, flower essences, energy work.

Pluto   Dancing, holotropic breathing, breath work, psychotherapy, tantra.

Nourishing the Signs

Aries   Starting and leading projects, being creative through making art, music, and writing, physical exercise in the form of martial arts, aerobics, kickboxing, and running.

Taurus   Deep massage, meditating, lifting weights, gardening, shopping, building, making love.

Gemini   Socializing, writing, e-mailing, phoning, activities with hands including fixing things, sewing and drumming, working on the computer, breathing fresh air, meditating.

Cancer   Long baths, drinking tea, swimming, water aerobics, walks on the beach, home improvement, family gatherings, scuba diving.

Leo   Romance, flirting, dancing, seeing a comedy act, laughing, sunbathing, charity work, acting, making music, being creative.

Virgo   Sewing, knitting, baking bread, cleaning, cooking meals, organizing the house, service work in the community, healing, health-related activities like yoga, eating health foods, and walking in the fresh air and sunlight.

Libra   Going out on dates or spending time with a partner, dressing up, balancing exercise like tai chi and other martial arts, breath meditation, socializing with friends and in the community.

Scorpio Making love, intimate conversations, healing work, the occult, transformational work in the form of seminars and workshops, holotropic breathing, rebirthing, cleansing diets, bathing, night swimming, yoga, tantra.

Sagittarius Travel, adventures, higher education, teaching, dance, play, laughter and meals with friends, philosophical conversations, horseback riding, outdoor exercise like biking and tennis, art, creativity, drinking a beer.

Capricorn Starting, building, and managing projects, focusing exercises, gardening, hiking, mountain climbing, yoga, weightlifting, carpentry, massages, sensual touch, making love.

Aquarius Community projects and gatherings, unusual enterprises, technology and sciences, breathing exercises, windy areas, tai chi, talking and connecting with friends, revolutionary and radical ideas, being progressive, eccentric, and eclectic.

Pisces Bathing, swimming, scuba diving, drinking lots of water, psychic and occult work, dreams, visions, channeling, making and playing music, meditation, prayer and spiritual work, service and charity, sensual connections with partners, watching movies, dressing up.

Conclusion

One day, I went hiking through the forest to a giant, 150-feet-tall waterfall that emptied itself into a small river below. The trail allowed me to hike right up close and watch and listen from some caverns behind the falls. Around me, majestic maples draped in moss stretched up toward the sky. Sorrel and wild ginger dotted the landscape below, mixed in with salal, Oregon grape, and salmonberry. Chickadees, wrens, and woodpeckers darted throughout the canopies of tall hemlocks and douglas firs. The majesty of the landscape entranced me and I felt at ease and content.

The rhythm of the woods asked me to slow down and become more observant and contemplative. Each rock, tree, and herb that I examined spun a tale that I could understand if I took the time to watch and listen. The lily of the valley beckoned me with her gentle, moist, lovely leaves, reminding me of the feminine beauty associated with Venus. Strong shoots of nettle pointed straight up to the sky, steady, powerful, and resilient, reminding me of the powerful force associated with Mars. A web of interactions and stories blanketed the forest environment and drew me in closer to its mysteries.

Sitting there, watching the waterfall, I made a prayer that the waterfall would still stand there hundreds, if not thousands, of years from now. I prayed that we would not tamper with the flow of the river so much that we would destroy its precious beauty. In our world today, an increasing number of species are going extinct. Logging, mining, and resource extraction along with petroleum fuel pollution has led to global environmental destruction on a catastrophic level. The relationship we have with the earth is one of slave owner to slave, demanding more and more work and effort until finally the slave dies from exhaustion.

The modern, industrialized-world perception of life has been one of linear growth toward more exploration, expansion, and control of the world. This model eventually has an endpoint, when there are no more resources left to extract, when the oil has run out and the land is barren from excessive farming with pesticides. Ultimately, our worldview has been shortsighted, and in the end, tremendously destructive to the health and well-being of the planet, not to mention the majority of people who live in it.

Nourishing and strengthening our health does not just mean taking the right herbs and eating well. It means changing how we perceive and interact with the world as a whole. We may be able to cure ourselves with healing modalities, but systemically we still live in a world out of balance that challenges our health and peace of mind wherever we go. Astrology does not just describe a system of understanding personality, it describes a system for understanding our relationship with the environment and the cosmos itself. Astrology points toward a rhythmic, cyclical way of viewing life, one in which there are natural periods of growth and decay, expansion and retraction. Astrology also points to a holistic view of the world around us, one in which everything is alive and vital, one in which all of creation expresses an important message and story. In astrological philosophy, every aspect of creation is connected and interrelated into one vast web.

Astrology mirrors the belief system of most indigenous peoples, the belief in a living, breathing universe infused with spirit. In this way, astrology points to animistic, shamanistic, and spiritual truths that have long been divorced from the modern, scientific analysis of life. In essence, there has been a split between these rationalist and holistic mindframes that goes back to at least the Age of Enlightenment. On our present track, we are left hurtling toward a chaotic and increasingly destructive future unless we reassess how we are viewing and living life.

Traditional Western medicine practitioners have long seen the relationship between humans, nature, and the stars. From the time of Hippocrates and Galen through the time of the Renaissance healers Paracelsus and Culpeper, the Western world was oriented toward the study of the stars to determine health and wellness. It is only in the past few hundred years that we have lost this ancient art. By reestablishing our roots in this age-old practice, we not only connect to a lineage of wise physicians and healers, but we also connect to the power and tremendous beauty of the natural world. Modern allopathic medicine only offers some of the answers in health and healing. Traditional-medicine forms help align us with our essential nature and bring us into closer contact with the natural forces that can strengthen and cure us. By bridging the gap toward a deeper relationship with the natural world, we can gain some of the deep wisdom that is held there. In essence, traditional Western medicine helps repair the massive rift that has developed between humans and the natural world and strengthens bonds that have been damaged or broken.

The word medicine often implies taking a drug or an herb as a curative measure to counteract illness. Perhaps in the future we can use the word medicine to encompass a much greater scope. Medicine could be as simple as wearing an amulet filled with chamomile, doing a ritual on a Full Moon, wearing the color red to offset melancholy, or practicing deep breathing to calm the nerves. Medicine could be a walk in the woods or stargazing at night. It could describe any activity that brings us into greater harmony and greater communion with the path we're walking on, the people we're connected to, and the environment around us. Medicine could be a word to describe our growth in awareness, like a fiddlehead fern unfurling its leaves toward the sky. Instead of being a word to describe curing illness, medicine could be a word to describe a path of wisdom, a path of meaning, a path of beauty.

Appendix
Practicing Four Element Medicine

Putting everything together to practice the ancient art of four element medicine can be difficult to figure out. Each of us manifests our chart in different ways. It is important not only to take a close look at the chart, but also to take a look at how those factors are expressed in everyday life. One person with a lot of Aries in his or her chart may express an exuberant and expressive personality, while another may be battling feelings of frustration and anger. These two people will need different healing modalities to balance and nourish their temperaments. To help understand four element medicine, it is helpful to look at a few examples of famous people and their charts.

Bill Clinton

Let's take a look at one of the most well-known Americans of the late twentieth century, ex-President Bill Clinton. This is a man we've watched for many years, and we have seen him go through many ups and downs. He is one of the most televised personalities ever in our history. By using the calculations from chapter 2, we can break down his chart into key components.

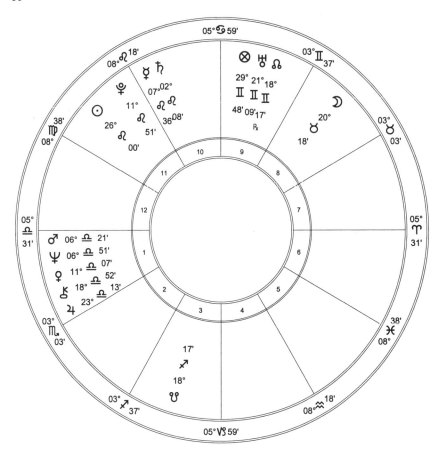

Sun in Leo
Moon in Taurus
Ascendant in Libra
Mercury in Leo
Venus in Libra
Mars in Libra

Jupiter in Libra
Saturn in Leo
Uranus in Gemini
Neptune in Libra
Pluto in Leo

Elements:	Fire	Water	Air	Earth
Planets in Elements:	Sun, Mercury, Saturn, Pluto	Nothing	Ascendant, Venus, Mars, Jupiter, Uranus, Neptune	Moon
	4+3+2+1	0	4+3+3+2+1+1	4
Total Point Value:	**10**	**0**	**14**	**4**

Modalities:	Cardinal	Fixed	Mutable
Planets in Modalities:	Ascendant, Venus, Mars, Jupiter, Neptune	Sun, Moon, Mercury, Saturn, Pluto	Uranus
	4+3+3+2+1	4+4+3+2+1	1
Total Point Value:	**13**	**14**	**1**

These simple calculations can be made to analyze any chart and determine which elements and modalities are strong or weak. In Clinton's chart, it is clear that he is strongly fiery and airy with weak earth and nonexistent water. He is also strongly cardinal and fixed, while almost completely lacking in mutable energy.

The next step in analyzing this chart is determining which signs and planets stand out. It is incredibly clear in this chart that the Leo and Libra myths dominate Clinton's personality. The ruling planets of these signs are the Sun and Venus, and therefore these planets play a crucial role in Clinton's health. Not only is Venus the ruler of the chart and the depositor of four planets, but it also sits very near the Ascendant and is in its own sign of Libra. Venus is therefore very powerful. Any planets that sit near the Ascendant (the closer, the more powerful) are very strong and color the whole chart. Therefore, Mars and Neptune are also strong planets and should be examined in terms of Clinton's health.

Next we look at the sixth house and see that it is empty. If there are planets here, they should be taken into account, as this house rules health and daily rhythm. If the house is empty, we can look to the planet ruling this house. In this case, Pisces rules the sixth house, and the modern ruler of this sign is Neptune. Neptune becomes key in understanding Clinton's health patterns and emotional and psychological vulnerabilities. This is even more so the case because Neptune is strong in the chart (conjunct the Ascendant).

Finally we look to see if there are any strong aspects that might affect the chart. Conjunctions, squares, and oppositions usually imply a degree of intensity that could show health characteristics. I have found that the outer planets, including Saturn and Jupiter, have the effect of strongly coloring the inner planets, meaning that in a conjunction of Mars and Pluto, the energy of Mars becomes much more deep, penetrating, intense, and sometimes violent. Outer planets also affect and magnify the energy of Saturn and Jupiter. On a health level, these aspects can work to hold a lot of stored power in the body that can become damaging if not harnessed well. This means that we could develop illness and disease if strong emotions and passions are not channeled to some degree, as in art, music, or therapy.

In Clinton's case, there is a strong conjunction of Mars, Venus, and Neptune with the Ascendant. While Mars might increase Clinton's assertiveness and leadership skills, Neptune would make him prone to deception, but also carry authority with mass audiences. Venus would help him appear attractive and have a very sweet and friendly disposition. While Mars would increase Clinton's constitutional strength a great deal, Neptune's influence might have the effect of weakening his immune system and making him prone to toxins, poisons, and the effects of drugs and alcohol. Venus would help Clinton feel at ease and be relaxed, but might upset his sugar balance and his relationship to the sensual pleasures of food, sex, alcohol, and drugs.

There is also a strong conjunction of Pluto, Mercury, and Saturn. Clinton's Mercurial functions of communication, intelligence, and thinking would all be strongly affected by Pluto and Saturn. He loves to talk for hours at a time (Saturn) and to probe deeply into the minutiae of every issue (Pluto) He has also gotten into trouble for hiding sexual transgressions and outwardly obfuscating the issues (Pluto). This very intense conjunction could indicate health issues surrounding Clinton's Mercurial functions, including his throat, lungs, and hands. His Saturnian functions could also be affected, including his bones, teeth, and nails. After this initial analysis, we have discovered some basic things about Bill Clinton:

Elements Predominating: Fire and air (water and earth lacking)

Modalities Predominating: Cardinal and fixed (lacking mutable energy)

Signs Predominating: Leo and Libra

Most Powerful Planets: Venus, Neptune, Mars, Sun

From this information, we can move on to a plan for aiding and nourishing his system optimally.

Diet

Many of us have heard the stories of Clinton's voracious eating habits and his love of junk food, probably increased by the stress and demands of his job. To protect his heart (Leo) and kidneys (Libra), Clinton should try to cut out these habits and also avoid excessively sugary foods (Venus). Clinton would also do well to drink plenty of water to flush out toxins that damage his kidneys. Caffeine, smoking, and excessive consumption of red meat are all hard on the heart (Leo) and should be ingested sparingly. Because of the predominance of fire and air in the chart, there is a tendency to burn the candle at both ends and to have difficulty being grounded and slowing down. Whole grains and root vegetables would help balance and offset this tendency. Warm meals eaten at regular intervals also would help increase earth and water energy.

Herbs

Clinton will need assistance on a number of levels. His dominating fire and air energy will tend to burn him out, and at times he could feel despondent and listless. His adrenals, heart, and overall circulation will feel taxed and he will need periods of deep rest. To assist the adrenals, Clinton could try regularly drinking licorice, chamomile, and ginseng teas. For his heart, Clinton could take herbs like hawthorn and borage.

Lifestyle

Now that Clinton is out of office, he would be wise to spend significant amounts of time sleeping, resting, and relaxing. The demands of the job of president are enormous and can lead to adrenal exhaustion, depression, anxiety, and confusion. Spas, warm baths, early nights, and massages would all help restore the balance that Clinton most likely has lost. Clinton probably will never be satisfied with just lying around and will soon embark on another project. Hopefully, this one will be less stressful and will offer him plenty of downtime as well. To offset all his air and fire, Clinton would do well to practice deep breathing and stretching (yoga) or to take up tai chi or chi gong as a way of relaxing and centering him.

Stones

Certain stones would help augment his good fortune. An emerald ring would help nourish his Venusian and Neptunian energies, bring him prosperity, and help him with matters of the heart (his marriage). Emerald is also grounding and earthy and would balance the excessive fire and air in his chart. A rose quartz stone could be placed in his house in a special place to help bring good fortune and increase love and care within his family. Amethyst is a stone of Neptune and provides clarity and truthfulness where there has been deception and cloudiness. It brings clarity and protection.

Animals and Birds

Because of all of his planets in Leo and the regal characteristics he has acquired from being president, I think Lion would be a good animal ally for Clinton. Its characteristics of grace, poise, and elegance would help strengthen Clinton's nature. The bird Robin fits Clinton's personal charm and robustness, while Swallow emphasizes his sweet, adaptable, and playful nature. It might be smart, however, to pick both birds and animals that are more grounding and that balance his strongly fire/air temperament. Porcupine would be a wonderful totem to help with his boundary (Neptune) problems. Both Elk and Turtle would help him slow down and regain a natural and not reckless rhythm. Simple, practical birds like Crow and Wren would help him become more stable, down-to-earth, and not so easily distracted by the needs and wishes of all the people around him.

Hillary Clinton

Though her husband has been a tremendous star on the political stage, Hillary Clinton has also been in the spotlight and has secured herself a spot in the Senate for at least six years. Her strong will and ability to withstand attack and tremendous problems and tenaciously survive are apparent in this Scorpio's chart.

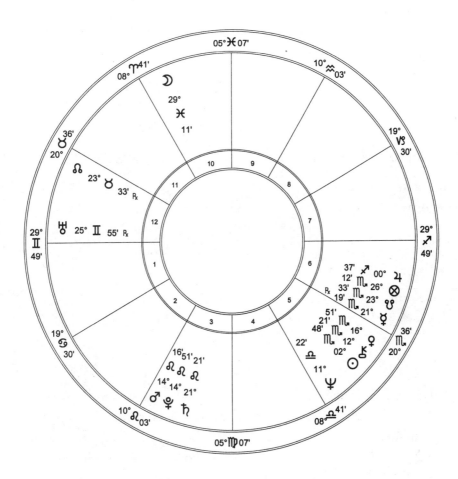

Sun in Scorpio	Jupiter in Sagittarius
Moon in Pisces	Saturn in Leo
Ascendant in Gemini	Uranus in Gemini
Mercury in Scorpio	Neptune in Libra
Venus in Scorpio	Pluto in Leo
Mars in Leo	

Elements:	Fire	Water	Air	Earth
Planets in Elements:	Mars, Jupiter, Saturn, Pluto	Moon, Mercury, Venus	Ascendant, Uranus	Nothing
	3+2+2+1	4+3+3	4+1	0
Total Point Value:	8	10	5	0

Modalities:	Cardinal	Fixed	Mutable
Planets in Modalities:	Neptune	Sun, Mercury, Venus, Mars, Saturn, Pluto	Ascendant, Moon, Jupiter, Uranus
	1	4+3+3+3+2+1	4+4+2+1
Total Point Value:	1	16	11

In Hillary's case, it is apparent that she is strongly watery and fiery and lacking earth, and also strongly fixed and mutable, while lacking cardinal energy. Her chart describes an interesting balance to Bill's chart. She provides much of the emotional (water) sustenance to offset his lack. They are both very fixed, which often shows up in powerful, magnetic people. Their fixed energy ultimately leads to problems in both charts as they can get stuck in habits that are very difficult to break and then can become incredibly damaging character flaws. Both charts are very unbalanced, showing huge emphases in one area of the chart (Leo and Libra for Bill, Scorpio and Leo for Hillary) that can allow them to be very prominent, powerful people, but can also show a tendency toward extremes. The Leo emphasis in particular often shows up in people who are charismatic, attractive, exuberant, and fun, but can also be found in those who are selfish, self-centered, and megalomaniacs. A touch of both exist in these two.

In terms of Hillary's chart, certain planets are stronger than others. The ruling planet of Scorpio is Pluto. Pluto happens to be in a very powerful conjunction with Mars and squares both Venus and Mercury by aspect. Pluto is also the ruler of the sixth house, the house of health in medical astrology. Uranus is strong because it almost exactly conjoins the Ascendant. Because Uranus rules an air sign, this strengthens the airy nature of her Gemini Ascendant. Mars is strong because it conjoins Pluto, is strong in Leo, and is the traditional ruling planet of Scorpio. The Sun is emphasized because it rules the sign of Leo. Hillary's Sun also sits in the fifth house, traditionally associated with the sign of Leo. So let's look at what we've discovered:

Elements Predominating: Water and fire (lacking earth)

Modalities Predominating: Fixed and mutable (lacking cardinal)

Signs Predominating: Scorpio and Leo

Planets Predominating: Pluto, Uranus, Mars, Sun

The strong Plutonic feature can help create deep-seated tension and intensity in Hillary's chart and show up as ulcers, rashes, boils, or even cancer. Scorpio and Pluto are connected to sexual dysfunction and there is a high likelihood of issues there. Issues of power and control can create tension in this area. Her husband's regular infidelity plays a role in exacerbating these issues. The emphasis on water and fire can describe someone who is very impassioned and intense, feels things strongly, and can sometimes be extreme in action and reaction. The Uranian features show that she could sometimes be unpredictable and unusual in her approach and won't follow the status quo. (Hillary is the first First Lady who has gone on to be a senator after her husband ended his term.) Uranus and the Gemini Ascendant can bring a degree of nervous energy and anxiety along with a good dollop of intelligence and maybe even brilliance. Hillary's strong water element points to possible emotional problems surfacing from time to time, an intense sensitivity, and occasional difficulties with boundaries. In terms of health, it could also cause increased difficulty with the immune system. Let's look at some ways to balance and nourish Hillary in terms of her horoscope:

Diet

Hillary would be smart to cleanse herself periodically, as her strongly fixed, Scorpionic chart shows a proclivity to holding on to anything that comes into her system. Illnesses and problems could become chronic in her case, and she needs to flush out toxins with regular, pure-water consumption. She should watch out for food and drink that is too extreme, as these foods will exacerbate her already intense disposition. She should also guard against excessive use of stimulants such as sugar and caffeine, as they will increase her nervousness. Grounding foods in the form of whole grains, squashes, yams, and potatoes will help nourish the earth element that is lacking in her chart. Warm, well-cooked meals eaten slowly and at regular intervals will also help ground and "earth" her.

Herbs

There are a number of herbs that will help relax Hillary and release stress. Teas of chamomile, lemon balm, skullcap, and valerian are all tremendously gentle and soothing. Taking long baths with essential oils of lavender and rose oil will help soothe her and put her in touch with her Scorpio Sun and Pisces Moon. These relaxing practices will also help alleviate any tension and frustration she may feel from having a strong Mars. Herbs that strengthen the immune system, such as nettles, licorice, and ginseng, would be very beneficial for Hillary and help balance her strong water energy. These herbs also can be potent rebuilders for sexual dysfunction.

Lifestyle

The most essential task Hillary faces is to learn to relax in the face of tremendous pressure. Because she tends to store and bottle her emotions, she needs to find release valves. She could take short vacations to get away from the tremendous pressures of her lifestyle. Having friends that help her laugh and put her at ease will be very helpful. Long walks in verdant forests, gardening, yoga, and meditation are all wonderful practices for relieving stress and revitalizing the spirit. Warm baths will help complement her water energy, while swimming and scuba diving might also be very helpful nourishing practices. Any form of relaxation she practices should be minimally competitive and adversarial.

Stones

Hillary would do well to wear stones that nourish her essential watery, magnetic energy. Obsidian would add a touch of fire that would complement her Leonine side. Onyx would also be lovely for her to wear or have near her. A fire stone such as amber or ruby would help bring out her fun, playful side. She essentially needs to balance her chart with earthy, grounding stones that will balance any nervous tension and rising anger she may feel. Obsidian and onyx are definitely grounding, but it may be helpful to add a stone like jade or malachite—lucky green stones that would strengthen her foundations and give her a sense of increased ease.

Animals and Birds

With Scorpio as Hillary's chart ruler, I like to think of several creatures as being suited to her. Salmon describes her tenacity and perseverance. Wolf describes her leadership abilities and her incredible power and stamina. Dolphin describes her light and playful, chattering side. Again, it may be helpful to choose to work with an animal that balances her chart and nourishes her lacking earth element. Turtle is one of the best examples of a slow and steady creature who can defend itself from any intense attack coming from the outside world, so this may be a good creature for Hillary to work with. For birds, Hillary is aligned with raptors like Hawk and Eagle with their Martian characteristics. She may want to choose a bird that is gentler and more at ease like Swan or Dove. These would help her feel more at peace with her surroundings.

Bibliography

Introduction

Ficino, Marsilio. *The Book of Life*. Translated by Charles Boer. 1489. Reprint, Irving, TX: Spring Publications, Inc., 1980.

Tobyn, Graeme. *Culpeper's Medicine: A Practice of Western Holistic Medicine*. Rockport, MA: Element Books, Inc., 1997.

Chapter 1

Aveni, Anthony. *Conversing with the Planets: How Science and Myth Invented the Cosmos*. New York: Kodansha America, Inc., 1992.

Brooke, Elizabeth. *An Astrological Herbal for Women*. Freedom, CA: The Crossing Press, 1992.

Culpeper, Nicholas. *Culpeper's Complete Herbal*. 1652.

———. *The English Physitian*. 1652.

Daath, Heinrich. *Medical Astrology*. Santa Fe, NM: Sun Publishing Co., 1992.

Ficino, Marsilio. *The Book of Life*. Translated by Charles Boer. Irving, TX: Spring Publications, Inc., 1980.

Guttman, Ariel, and Kenneth Johnson. *Mythic Astrology: Archetypal Powers of the Horoscope*. St. Paul, MN: Llewellyn Publications, 1993.

Jung, Carl. *Psychological Types*. New York and London: Bollingen Series, 1923.

———. *Synchronicity*. New York and London: Bollingen Series, 1927.

Loudon, Irvine. *Western Medicine*. New York: Oxford University Press, 1997.

McCoy, Edain. *The Sabbats*. St. Paul, MN: Llewellyn Publications, 1999.

Pachter, Henry M. *Paracelsus: Magic into Science*. New York: Henry Schuman, Inc., 1951.

Rhyner, Hans. *Ayurveda: The Gentle Health System*. New York: Sterling Publishing Co., Inc., 1994.

Rudhyar, Dane. *The Pulses of Life*. Berkeley, CA: Shambhala Publications, Inc., 1970.

Tester, Jim. *A History of Western Astrology*. New York: Balantine Books, 1987.

Tobyn, Graeme. *Culpeper's Medicine: A Practice of Western Holistic Medicine*. Rockport, MA: Element Books, Inc., 1997.

Van Helden, Albert, trans. *Siderius Nuncius, or, The Sidereal Messenger*, by Galileo Galilei. Chicago: University of Chicago Press, 1990.

Zolar. *The History of Astrology*. New York: Arco Publishing, Inc., 1872.

Chapter 2

Tobyn, Graeme. *Culpeper's Medicine: A Practice of Western Holistic Medicine*. Rockport, MA: Element Books, Inc., 1997.

Warren-Davis, Dylan. *Astrology and Health*. Coventry, England: Hodder and Stoughton, 1998.

Chapter 3

Arroyo, Stephen. *Astrology, Psychology, and the Four Elements*. Reno, NV: CRCS Publishing Co., 1975.

Mabey, Richard. *The New Age Herbalist*. New York: Macmillan Publishing Co., 1988.

Rhyner, Hans. *Ayurveda: The Gentle Health System*. New York: Sterling Publishing Co., 1994.

Chapter 4

Arroyo, Stephen. *Astrology, Karma and Transformation*. Sebastapol, CA: CRCS Publications, 1978.

Burt, Kathleen. *Archetypes of the Zodiac*. St. Paul, MN: Llewellyn Publications, 1993.

Greene, Liz, and Howard Sasportas. *The Inner Planets*. York Beach, ME: Weiser, 1993.

George, Llewellyn. *The New A to Z Horoscope Maker and Delineator*. St. Paul, MN: Llewellyn Publications, 2002.

Guttman, Ariel, and Kenneth Johnson. *Mythic Astrology: Archetypal Powers of the Horoscope*. St. Paul, MN: Llewellyn Publications, 1993.

Oken, Alan. *Soul Centered Astrology*. New York: Bantam Books, 1990.

Theroux, Michael, and Brian Butler, eds. *The Astrological Body Types: Face, Form and Expression*. Illustrated by Judith A. Hill. Bayside, CA: Borderland Sciences Research Foundation, 1993.

Chapter 5

Cunningham, Scott. *Magical Aromatherapy*. St. Paul, MN: Llewellyn Publications, 1989.

———. *Wicca*. St. Paul, MN: Llewellyn Publications, 1988.

Galenorn, Yasmine. *Embracing the Moon*. St. Paul, MN: Llewellyn Publications, 1988.

McCoy, Edain. *Making Magick*. St. Paul, MN: Llewellyn Publications, 1997.

———. *The Sabbats: A New Approach to Living the Old Ways*. St. Paul, MN: Llewellyn Publications, 1999.

Medici, Marina. *Good Magic*. New York: Simon and Schuster, 1988.

Chapter 6

Alexander, Skye. *Magickal Astrology*. Franklin Lakes, NJ: Career Press, 2000.

Conway, D. J. *By Oak, Ash and Thorn*. St. Paul, MN: Llewellyn Publications, 1995.

Cruden, Loren. *Compass of the Heart*. Rochester, VT: Destiny Books, 1996.

Dander, Donald. *Navaho Symbols of Healing*. Rochester, VT: Healing Arts Press, 1979.

Doore, Gary. *Shaman's Path*. Boston, MA: Shambhala Publications, Inc., 1988.

Eliade, Mircea. *The Sacred and the Profane*. Orlando, FL: Harcourt Brace and Co., 1957.

Harner, Michael. *The Way of the Shaman*. New York: Harper and Row, 1980.

Logan, Jo. *The Prediction Book of Amulets and Talismans*. New York: Sterling Publishing, 1986.

Medici, Marina. *Good Magic*. New York: Simon and Schuster, 1988.

Chapter 7

Avery, Jeanne. *Astrology and Your Health*. New York: Simon and Schuster, 1991.

Bills, Rex E. *The Rulership Book*. Richmond, VA: Macoy Publishing and Masonic Supply Co., Inc., 1971.

Carse, Mary. *Herbs of the Earth*. Hinesburg, VT: Upper Access Publishers, 1989.

Cunningham, Scott. *Cunningham's Encyclopedia of Magical Herbs*. St. Paul, MN: Llewellyn Publications, 1999.

Dreyer, Ronnie Gale. *Healing Signs*. New York: Doubleday, 2000.

Hoffman, David. *The New Holistic Herbal*. Rockport, MA: Element Books, 1983.

Lust, John. *The Herb Book*. New York: Bantam Books, 1974.

Magnus, Albertus. *The Book of Secrets*. 1550. Reprint, York Beach, ME: Weiser, 1999.

Moore, Michael. *Medicinal Plants of the Pacific West*. Santa Fe, NM: Red Crane Books, 1993.

Nauman, Eileen. *Medical Astrology*. Cottonwood, AZ: Blue Turtle Publishing, 1982.

Shaw, Ira N. *The Practical Herbalist and Astrologer*. The Republic of Singapore, 1970.

Starck, Marcia. *Healing with Astrology*. Freedom, CA: The Crossing Press, 1997.

Tierra, Lesley. *The Herbs of Life*. Freedom, CA: The Crossing Press, 1992.

Tierra, Michael. *The Spirit of Herbs: A Guide to the Herbal Tarot*. Stamford, CT: U.S. Game Systems, Inc., 1993.

Tobyn, Graeme. *Culpeper's Medicine*. Rockport, MA: Element Books, 1997.

Chapter 8

Avery, Jeanne. *Astrology and Your Health*. New York: Simon and Schuster, 1991.

Bills, Rex E. *The Rulership Book*. Richmond, VA: Macoy Publishing and Masonic Supply Co., Inc., 1971.

Dreyer, Ronnie Gale. *Healing Signs*. New York: Doubleday, 2000.

Haas, Elson. *Staying Healthy with the Seasons.* Fairfax, CA: Celestial Arts, 1981.

Jansky, Robert Carl. *Astrology, Nutrition and Health.* Rockport, MA: Para Research, 1977.

Nauman, Eileen. *Medical Astrology.* Cottonwood, AZ: Blue Turtle Publishing, 1982.

Pitchford, Paul. *Healing with Whole Foods.* Berkeley, CA: North Atlantic Books, 1993.

Shaw, Ira N. *The Practical Herbalist and Astrologer.* The Republic of Singapore, 1970.

Tierra, Lesley. *The Herbs of Life.* Freedom, CA: The Crossing Press, 1992.

Chapter 9

Andrews, Ted. *Animal-Speak.* St. Paul, MN: Llewellyn Publications, 1993.

Cruden, Loren. *The Spirit of Place.* Rochester, VT: Destiny Books, 1995.

Kozloff, Eugene. *Plants and Animals of the Pacific Northwest.* Seattle, WA: University of Washington Press, 1976.

Kruckenberg, Arthur. *The Natural History of Puget Sound Country.* Seattle, WA: University of Washington Press, 1991.

Wernert, Susan. *North American Wildlife.* Pleasantville, NY: Reader's Digest, 1982.

Chapter 10

Andrews, Ted. *Animal-Speak.* St. Paul, MN: Llewellyn Publications, 1993.

Cruden, Loren. *The Spirit of Place.* Rochester, VT: Destiny Books, 1995.

Zim, Herbert. *Birds.* New York: Simon and Schuster, 1949.

Chapter 11

Bills, Rex E. *The Rulership Book.* Richmond, VA: Macoy Publishing and Masonic Supply Co., Inc., 1971.

Cunningham, Scott. *Crystal, Gem and Metal Magic.* St. Paul, MN: Llewellyn Publications, 1988.

Elsbeth, Marguerite. *Crystal Medicine.* St. Paul, MN: Llewellyn Publications, 1997.

Greer, John Michael. *Natural Magic.* St. Paul, MN: Llewellyn Publications, 2000.

Medici, Marina. *Good Magic.* New York: Simon and Schuster, 1988.

Mottana, Annibale, Rodolfo Crespi, and Giuseppe Liborio. *Simon and Schuster's Guide to Rocks and Minerals.* New York: Simon and Schuster, 1977.

Nauman, Eileen. *Medical Astrology.* Cottonwood, AZ: Blue Turtle Publishing, 1982.

Telesco, Patricia. *Magic Made Easy.* New York: HarperCollins, 1999.

Index